Mastering Lumion 3D

Master the art of creating real-time 3D architectural visualizations using Lumion 3D

Ciro Cardoso

BIRMINGHAM - MUMBAI

Mastering Lumion 3D

First published: December 2014

Production reference: 1221214

Published by Packt Publishing Ltd.
Livery Place
35 Livery Street
Birmingham B3 2PB, UK.

ISBN 978-1-78355-203-0

www.packtpub.com

Credits

Author
Ciro Cardoso

Reviewers
CJ Arquitecto
Ahmed Osama El-Bakry
Peter-Daniel Fazakas
Filip Joveski
Gianfranco Maiorano

Commissioning Editor
Kunal Parikh

Acquisition Editor
Richard Brookes-Bland

Content Development Editor
Prachi Bisht

Technical Editor
Edwin Moses

Copy Editors
Janbal Dharmaraj
Karuna Narayanan

Project Coordinator
Shipra Chawhan

Proofreaders
Lauren E. Harkins
Paul Hindle
Linda Morris

Indexers
Monica Ajmera Mehta
Priya Sane

Production Coordinator
Nilesh R. Mohite

Cover Work
Nilesh R. Mohite

About the Author

Ciro Cardoso is a self-taught 3D artist and training author specialized in architectural visualization. He started off painting and drawing traditionally and then got into 3D graphics in 2000.

In 2005, he was running his own small multimedia business working on projects as diverse as graphic designing, CAD services, and architectural visualization projects. More recently, he started using Lumion and game engines for multimillion dollar projects in the United Kingdom, Portugal, the Netherlands, Angola, and Cape Verde. He is quite conversant with software in general, with extensive expertise in Maya, 3ds Max, AutoCAD, SketchUp, V-Ray, Corona, Photoshop, Lumion, Unreal 4, and Bentley MicroStation. He is also the author of *Getting Started with Lumion* and *Lumion 3D Cookbook*, both by Packt Publishing.

He now lives in London, working as an architectural visualizer, and does voluntary work teaching 3D. He can be reached through his website, `http://www.cirocardoso.net`.

Firstly, I would like to express my gratitude towards my family for making me a curious person. A big thanks goes to my wife for her support, love, and patience throughout the process of writing this book, even if that meant staying home during weekends. I believe that without her, this book would not have been possible.

I would like to express my thanks to the Packt Publishing team for the opportunity to author this book, and also for the effort and support to produce this book.

About the Reviewers

CJ Arquitecto is a young Portuguese architect born in Lagos, Portugal, in June 1984.

At the age of 24, in 2008, he finished his degree in Architecture from the University of Porto, also known as the Faculty of Architecture of the University of Porto, designed by architect Siza Vieira. Since 2011, he started using Lumion, while working on urbanism projects in his 3D works designed for Angolan customers. Parallel to his professional career, he defined the importance of photography and design as an intimate relationship. Following this, he did three photography expositions in Portugal and published them on the Web. He has participated in several national and international design contests and won two architectural prizes. Also, he has been developing several architectural projects, mostly in Angola; these include projects that range from residential houses to sports complex centers. He had reviewed books on Lumion 3D in 2013, which has led him to have a part in reviewing this book.

Ahmed Osama El-Bakry was born on August 16, 1990, in Cairo. He got his BSc degree from Ain Shams University Urban Planning and Design Department in July 2012. Now, he works as a teaching assistant at Ain Shams University Urban Planning and Design Department. His cumulative ranking is first among his colleagues. Then, he began his premaster studies for 1 year at the same college. After graduating from there, he recently joined the IUSD Master's program jointly organized by the University of Stuttgart, Germany and Ain Shams University, Egypt.

Bakry began his practical work while he was studying, by participating in urban competitions. He works as an executive engineer for architectural interior projects. He works as a freelancer for several urban and architecture projects, especially in Saudi Arabia. As an undergraduate, he participated in a student exchange program between Ain Shams University; Artesis University College, Antwerp, Belgium; and Ecole Nationale Supérieure d'Architecture de Paris-Belleville in Paris, France in December 2010, concerning urbanism and future developments. He attended several conferences and workshops regarding sustainable urbanism and different and contemporary planning approaches and development cooperation between countries, which are organized by UN-Habitat, GIZ/BMZ in Germany. Eventually, he could deal with several engineering and graphical programs that led him to be committed to have a part in reviewing *Lumion 3D Cookbook, Packt Publishing*. Now, he is a cofounder of Square Studio for engineering consultancy.

Peter-Daniel Fazakas is an architect and designer born in Bucharest, Romania. Growing up in a family of intellectuals, scientists, and artists, he was fascinated, from early childhood, with hand drawing and CAD software. He decided to study architecture at the Ion Mincu University of Architecture and Urbanism in Bucharest, where he later graduated with an M Arch degree.

Working as an architect and art director in Romania, France, Cyprus, and China, he gained experience in architecture, graphic design, 3D rendering, 3D animation, and augmented reality, being fascinated by the new computer software. Currently, he lives in Shanghai and is involved in large-scale architectural projects.

Peter's personal website is `www.peter-fazakas.com`.

Filip Joveski is an architect and a 3D artist. He was first introduced to the 3D world in 2002 in a 3D-modeling class at the university he attended. After getting his degree in architecture, he worked in several firms in different countries and for a number of demanding clients.

He is currently employed in an architectural office in Germany, where he works as the head of the visualization team, creating images, animation, and illustrations, and has many projects behind him. He has designed various types of objects and spaces, including houses, apartments, lofts, restaurants, and unique interior designs from the beginning—sketching the floor plans, sections, 3D modeling, and renderings.

He is proficient with software in general, and has extensive expertise in 3ds Max, ArchiCAD, Maya, AutoCAD, SketchUp, Photoshop, Lumion, and Artlantis. He also expresses his creative side through his paintings and sculptures. He has extraordinary hand-drafting skills. His sense of color, texture, and depth has greatly helped him in the world of 3D modeling and visualization.

Gianfranco Maiorano is a creative and talented architect and an EU-licensed construction engineer based in London, UK, since 2013. He studied and completed his Master's degree in Architecture and Construction Engineering from the University of Bologna, Italy. He has experience in both public and private projects in the UK and Italy, including several competition submissions.

Gianfranco is the Founder and Director of gfm Studio Lab. Established in August, 2014, and based in London, gfm Studio Lab provides services from architecture to design and art for architectural firms and private clients, particularly working in the retail and residential sectors.

Since childhood, Gianfranco has always been very passionate about architecture. Possessing a natural intellectual capacity and curiosity about his chosen field, he is driven by a keen interest in researching contemporary architecture, art, and digital tools, especially in connection with quantum physics and parametric and generative techniques for architecture. He has exceptional technical expertise with regards to a wide range of software from 3D modeling and BIM to visualization and animation.

Gianfranco finds inspirations from artists such as Lucio Fontana, Antony Gormley, and Anish Kapoor, and architects such as Renzo Piano, Ben van Berkel, and Rem Koolhaas. He can be contacted through his website, `www.gianfrancomaiorano.com`.

www.PacktPub.com

Support files, eBooks, discount offers, and more

For support files and downloads related to your book, please visit www.PacktPub.com.

Did you know that Packt offers eBook versions of every book published, with PDF and ePub files available? You can upgrade to the eBook version at www.PacktPub.com and as a print book customer, you are entitled to a discount on the eBook copy. Get in touch with us at service@packtpub.com for more details.

At www.PacktPub.com, you can also read a collection of free technical articles, sign up for a range of free newsletters and receive exclusive discounts and offers on Packt books and eBooks.

https://www2.packtpub.com/books/subscription/packtlib

Do you need instant solutions to your IT questions? PacktLib is Packt's online digital book library. Here, you can search, access, and read Packt's entire library of books.

Why subscribe?

- Fully searchable across every book published by Packt
- Copy and paste, print, and bookmark content
- On demand and accessible via a web browser

Free access for Packt account holders

If you have an account with Packt at www.PacktPub.com, you can use this to access PacktLib today and view 9 entirely free books. Simply use your login credentials for immediate access.

Table of Contents

Preface

Welcome to *Mastering Lumion 3D*. Let me start by thanking you, the reader, for picking this book as a tool to help you throughout the process of using Lumion real-time technology.

Lumion can be an intuitive tool, but that doesn't mean we can automatically produce a better architectural visualization. The reason why I wrote this book was because, like you, the first time I picked up Lumion, I felt that there was something missing on my projects.

Mastering Lumion 3D covers the process of picking a 3D model, preparing it, and then start building layers on top of layers of detail, by using textures and optimized 3D models. However, we don't stop here, because several chapters are dedicated exclusively explaining how to use Lumion's effects and other special features to take your project to an expert level.

I wrote this book in a way that will hopefully cover all the questions you may have when starting the first steps with Lumion. On the other hand, if you are an intermediate or advanced user, you can find some unique techniques that will make you look to Lumion in another perspective. The journey to write this book was filled not only with my experience, but also from what I learned while working with other great professionals.

You may find it strange that there isn't any example to follow or project files to be used. The reason is because to fully understand and master Lumion, you have to apply all of these techniques on your own projects. Initially, this can be something daunting, but the book is prepared in such a way that you can gradually build your confidence and skills using Lumion.

And my final advice is not to be afraid to try and fail. Failing is an important part of the process to learn and deeply understand Lumion.

What this book covers

Chapter 1, Getting Ready for Lumion 3D, focuses on preparing a 3D model to be used in Lumion 3D. A special section is used to explain why materials are a key aspect to ensure a smooth and fluid workflow when importing 3D models into Lumion. Common problems and how to solve them will ensure you start with the right foot.

Chapter 2, Creating a Project in Lumion, puts the 3D model in standby while you prepare a scene in Lumion. This involves creating a project and tweaking the terrain to accommodate the 3D model. Layers and workflow optimization are covered to help you get useful and practical professional habits.

Chapter 3, Importing 3D Models, explains how to import an external 3D model and place it inside Lumion. A time-saving feature is explained to enable the reload of new geometry, avoiding importing the same 3D model multiple times.

Chapter 4, Applying and Creating Materials, focuses entirely on how to improve the 3D model's look using Lumion's realistic materials. There are at least three possibilities that are covered giving you the insight to choose the one that best suits the project.

Chapter 5, Creating Your 3D World, is one of the high points in the book because it is entirely dedicated to explain how to use Lumion's native 3D models and completely control them in order to start populating and creating a 3D environment.

Chapter 6, Lighting in Lumion, is a small yet powerful chapter to improve and optimize lighting in Lumion. Exterior lighting is usually covered by Lumion's Sun and Sky system. However, for interior scenes, lights need to be used. Global illumination is explained to create perfect interior scenes.

Chapter 7, Creating Realistic Visualizations, starts explaining how to use Lumion's effects in the Photo mode to produce believable visualizations by mimicking what is present in the real world.

Chapter 8, Non-photorealistic Visualizations with Lumion, explores an almost unknown side of Lumion's effects. This chapter explains how to produce conceptual and technical illustrations.

Chapter 9, Animation Techniques, brings life to a project by exploring the Lumion's animation system. Step-by-step examples are provided to master this difficult stage.

Chapter 10, Creating Walk-through Visualizations, is the final step where final techniques are explained to enhance the quality of an animation and a movie by using not only sound, but also realistic effects.

What you need for this book

Lumion Version 4 is used for all the examples in this book, but you can follow the explanations using the free version or a previous Lumion version. Although Adobe Photoshop is used in some examples, you can use GIMP as an alternative.

Who this book is for

This book is designed for all levels of Lumion users, from beginners to advanced users. You will find useful insights and professional techniques to improve and develop your skills in order to fully control and master Lumion.

However, this book doesn't cover the process of transforming 2D information (CAD plan) into a 3D model.

Conventions

In this book, you will find a number of text styles that distinguish between different kinds of information. Here are some examples of these styles and an explanation of their meaning.

Code words in text, database table names, folder names, filenames, file extensions, pathnames, dummy URLs, user input, and Twitter handles are shown as follows: "Something like `MyProject_version2` sounds great at the moment we save the project "

New terms and **important words** are shown in bold. Words that you see on the screen, for example, in menus or dialog boxes, appear in the text like this: "For now, we will stick with the **New** tab, because all the other tabs are sort of useless if we don't have any project of our own."

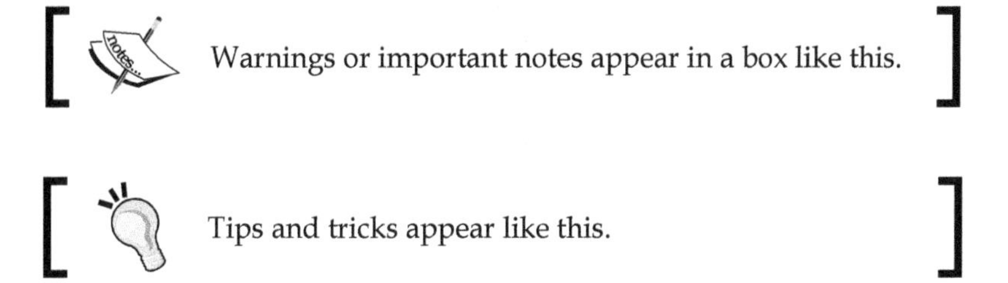

Warnings or important notes appear in a box like this.

Tips and tricks appear like this.

Reader feedback

Feedback from our readers is always welcome. Let us know what you think about this book—what you liked or disliked. Reader feedback is important for us as it helps us develop titles that you will really get the most out of.

To send us general feedback, simply e-mail `feedback@packtpub.com`, and mention the book's title in the subject of your message.

If there is a topic that you have expertise in and you are interested in either writing or contributing to a book, see our author guide at `www.packtpub.com/authors`.

Customer support

Now that you are the proud owner of a Packt book, we have a number of things to help you to get the most from your purchase.

Errata

Although we have taken every care to ensure the accuracy of our content, mistakes do happen. If you find a mistake in one of our books—maybe a mistake in the text or the code—we would be grateful if you could report this to us. By doing so, you can save other readers from frustration and help us improve subsequent versions of this book. If you find any errata, please report them by visiting `http://www.packtpub.com/submit-errata`, selecting your book, clicking on the **Errata Submission Form** link, and entering the details of your errata. Once your errata are verified, your submission will be accepted and the errata will be uploaded to our website or added to any list of existing errata under the Errata section of that title.

To view the previously submitted errata, go to `https://www.packtpub.com/books/content/support` and enter the name of the book in the search field. The required information will appear under the **Errata** section.

Piracy

Piracy of copyrighted material on the Internet is an ongoing problem across all media. At Packt, we take the protection of our copyright and licenses very seriously. If you come across any illegal copies of our works in any form on the Internet, please provide us with the location address or website name immediately so that we can pursue a remedy.

Please contact us at `copyright@packtpub.com` with a link to the suspected pirated material.

We appreciate your help in protecting our authors and our ability to bring you valuable content.

Questions

If you have a problem with any aspect of this book, you can contact us at `questions@packtpub.com`, and we will do our best to address the problem.

1
Getting Ready for Lumion 3D

Lumion 3D's main goal is to provide the best solution to produce believable 3D renders in the simplest way possible. Lumion had a modest start with the first version, but from the beginning, it was easy to see Lumion's potential. The final output is simply amazing when compared to the time it takes to create a movie and still image.

Lumion always aimed to bring the best real-time technology and at the same time provide intuitive and friendly software that empower anyone to transform a simple 3D model into a highly professional still image or beautiful architectural movie. The real-time technology used in Lumion 3D allows us to focus on the artistic side of the project instead of the technicalities and parameters.

Consequently, it doesn't matter what your professional background is; you can use Lumion 3D for your projects, and this book is aimed at helping both beginners and advanced users. However, you might wonder how a book can be useful and practical for two totally different types of users. For someone who is just starting out with Lumion, this book covers in depth the tools, techniques, workflow, and other elements that will enable you to become a Lumion master and produce an output similar to this:

On the other hand, if you are an advanced user, this book can help you explore in more depth how to use Lumion in ways you didn't think possible, helping you to see Lumion from a totally different perspective.

In this chapter, we will cover the following topics:

- Controlling the camera
- Lumion's hotkeys
- Using the **Settings** window
- Modeling for Lumion
- Additional models
- Importance of materials
- Solving common problems
- Exporting 3D models
- Using the COLLADA format
- Exporting animations

Starting to work with Lumion

Now, to get ready for Lumion 3D, what we need is a detailed 3D model. Lumion doesn't have any modeling tools; this means we have to pick a modeling package such as SketchUp, 3ds Max, Modo, or Blender, just to mention a few, and use a **computer-aided design** (**CAD**) plan as a reference to model the building. Modeling with one of these packages is out of the book's scope, but if you are modeling for the first time, you might want to explore SketchUp. SketchUp has a free version; it is a very easy application to learn. There are plenty of tutorials to help you start working with SketchUp, and Lumion imports SketchUp files directly, without the need to use any special format.

Assuming that we have a 3D model, our next step is to import this model into Lumion and start adding more content by adjusting the weather's elements, sculpting the terrain and then adding some camera effects, and finally, exporting this as an image or a movie. In simple terms, this is more or less the workflow to work with Lumion.

Nevertheless, before starting this process, we still need to be sure that the 3D model is ready to be imported inside Lumion. When you look at the topics mentioned in the beginning of this chapter, they might look simple, but we should fight the temptation to jump to the next chapter. This chapter is the cornerstone of the project we are going to develop in Lumion, and the topics mentioned can serve as a checklist that we can run quickly before importing our 3D model, making sure that we don't need to jump back and forth solving issues.

Let's start with a quick overview of some fundamental concepts that will help you work with Lumion and check whether your 3D model is working properly.

A quick overview

After launching Lumion for the first time, it will run a benchmark to check our system or workstation and see if there is any hardware component that we can upgrade in order to run Lumion more smoothly. The next screenshot shows an example of the final result and the components we might want to upgrade:

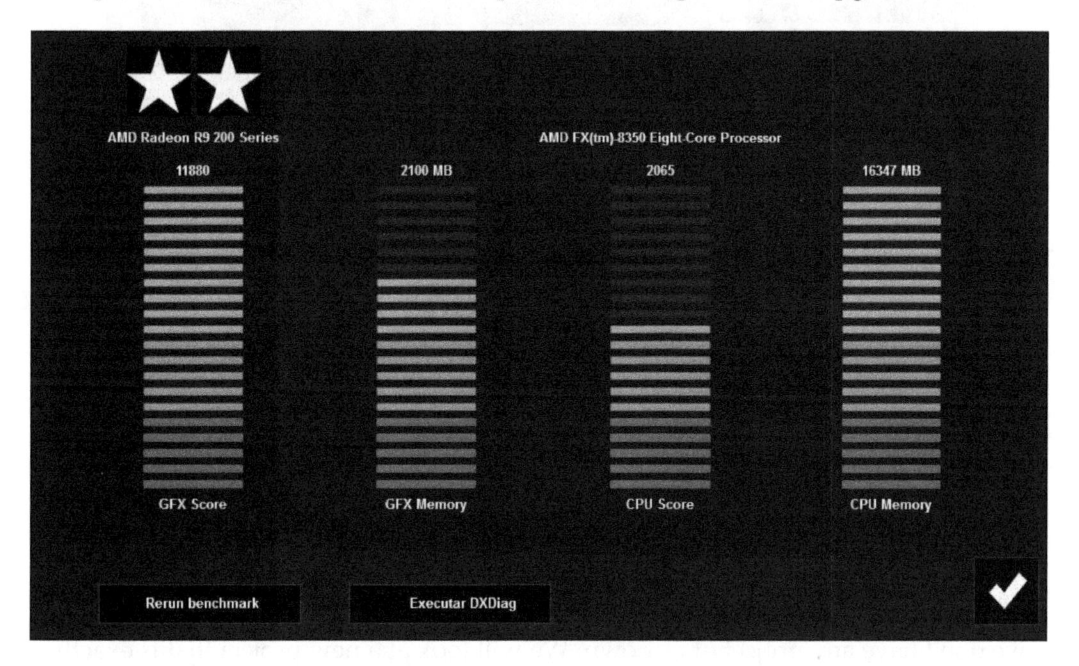

Although **CPU Memory** and **CPU Score** are essential, the most important piece of hardware is the graphics card. Which graphics card we use makes all the difference, and Lumion's official website has some useful information that can help us evaluate the vital role of this piece of hardware.

> To find out what hardware will be best suited to work with Lumion 3D, check out the following link:
>
> `http://lumion3d.com/faq/#hardware`

When the benchmark finishes execution, the next interface that appears is what we can call the main menu, although there isn't any official name. We call this area the main menu because here we find the most important settings to start working with Lumion. As you can see in the following screenshot, there are several tabs, and if we click on each one, we would find different areas that help us work with Lumion:

For now, we will stick with the **New** tab, because all the other tabs are sort of useless if we don't have any project of our own. We will look at a new project that is exactly what we can start in the **New** tab. For this, we can use one of the nine scenes shown in the preceding screenshot. However, which one should we select? All the nine scenes can be accomplished by tweaking the menus we find inside the **Build** mode (the **Build** mode is where we can build the project), and therefore, we can say that these nine scenes work as a shortcut or a preset to get a specific look and mood, although later, we can entirely change the look of the environment. Unfortunately, for now, we cannot save an environment created as a template, but nothing stops you from saving a scene and using it as a template. The only difference is that it will not appear in the **New** tab.

A good starting point is to use the **Grass** scene. The **Grass** scene is highlighted in the previous screenshot and is a good starting point because it is a simple scene with a flat terrain and good light. After selecting this scene, Lumion loads the scene and opens the **Build** mode.

Camera navigation in Lumion

Now that we are inside the **Build** mode, how can we control the camera? The **Build** mode has a very simple interface. Initially, we might feel lost with the lack of information in the interface. On the right-hand side, there is a set of buttons, and if we hover the mouse over the one with a question mark, some information appears that will help us. For now, the information we need is the one located in the top-right corner; this tells us how to navigate or control the camera in Lumion, as you can see in the following screenshot:

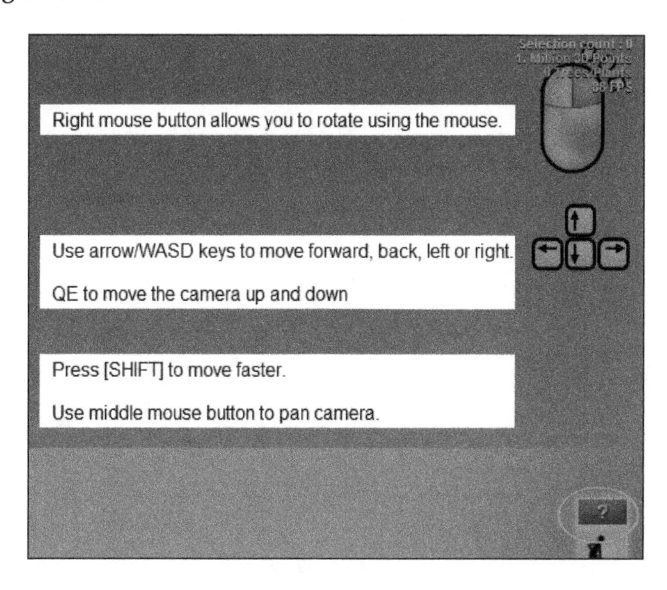

Here is a list of the keys and combinations to fully master the Lumion navigation system:

- *WSAD* / arrow keys: These are used to move the camera forward, backward, to the left, or to the right, respectively
- *Q* and *E*: These are used to move the camera up and down, respectively
- Spacebar + *WSAD*/arrow keys: These are used to slow down the camera
- *Shift* + *WSAD*/arrow keys: These are used to move the camera fast
- *Shift* + Spacebar + *WSAD* / arrow keys: These are used to move the camera very fast
- Use the right mouse button and move the mouse to look around
- Use the middle mouse button and move the mouse to pan the camera
- Mouse wheel up/down: This is used to zoom in and out the camera
- *Ctrl* + *H*: This is used to reset the camera pitch to horizontal viewpoint
- *O* + the right mouse button: This is used to orbit the camera

Now that we know what to use to control the camera, another question arises: how do we control the 3D models inside Lumion?

Controlling 3D models

Every time we place a 3D model inside Lumion, it is normal to accept some controls to tweak and adjust some basic parameters such as move, scale, and rotation. Now, it is a good time to introduce a concept that Lumion uses to control the 3D models in the scene.

Handling the 3D models using Lumion

Lumion makes a distinction between the 3D models we import and the native 3D models. This means we need to use two different Lumion menus to control each 3D model, as explained in the following screenshot:

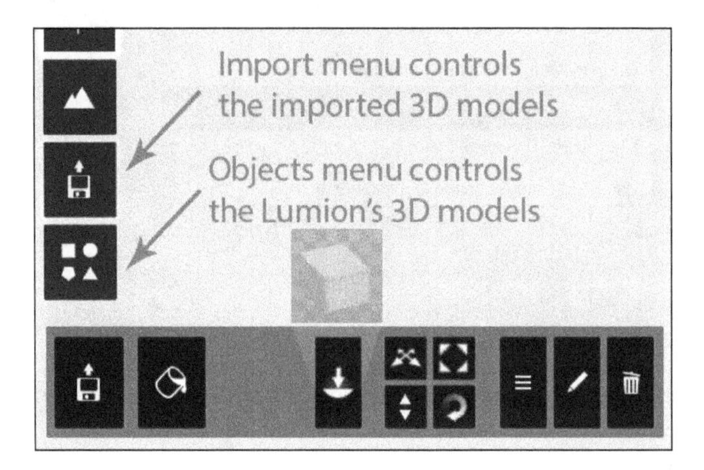

The **Import** menu is where we can find the tools to import external 3D models, and the **Objects** menu is where we can find all the built-in 3D models of Lumion. There are two different menus, two different types of 3D models, and two different ways to select and control. This means that to control an imported 3D model, we need to have the **Import** menu selected; otherwise, we cannot find any tools to adjust the model. The same principle applies, for example, when we need to move a tree, and for this, we need to have the **Objects** menu selected. So, how can we import a 3D model?

Importing an external 3D model

Importing a 3D model is really easy and straightforward. What we need to do is click on the **Import** menu, which can be found on the left-hand side, and then click on the **Add a new model** button, as shown on the following screenshot:

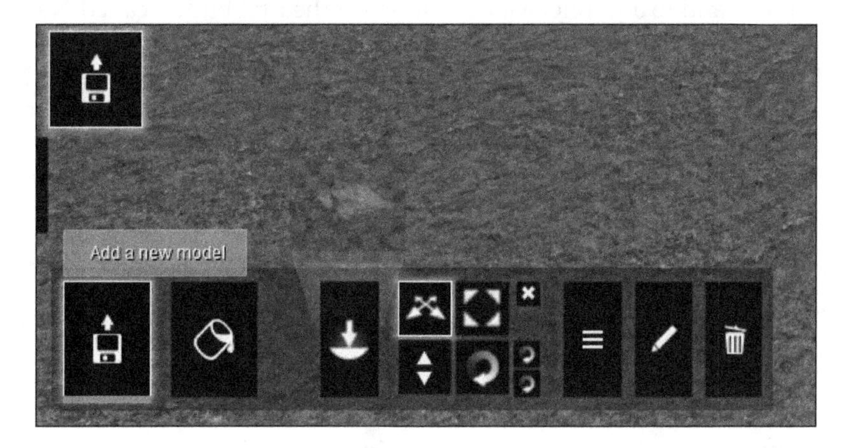

This opens a Windows Explorer window where you can locate the folder that contains the 3D model and select it. After doing this, we need to give a name to the new 3D model and click on the **Add to library** button.

Now, we are back to the **Build** mode, and we are controlling a yellow boundary box that represents the 3D model we just imported. With the left mouse button, we can click to place the 3D model. This is how we import an external 3D model. If you have problems at this stage, have a look at the *Common problems and solutions* section at the end of this chapter.

Using Lumion's 3D models

Lumion has an extra distinction inside the **Objects** menu, and now, we are talking exclusively about Lumion's native 3D models. If you open the **Objects** menu, this is what you will find:

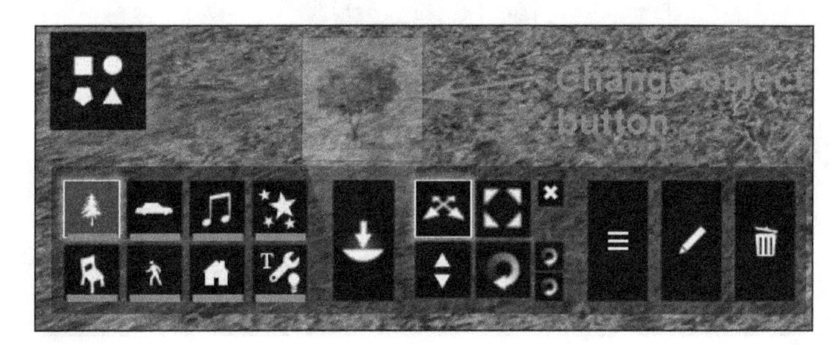

The buttons highlighted show the eight categories of 3D models and other elements such as lights, smoke, and buildings. When we hover the mouse over the buttons, a small label appears identifying the category.

Let's try to add a 3D model to an empty scene. Something that will look really good in the scene is a tree, and to add one, we need to select the first button called **Nature**. So now, we have the **Nature** category activated; this means that we can control any 3D model that falls under this category. To add a 3D model and open the Nature Library, we need to click on the **Change object** button, as shown in the previous screenshot. Select a tree and now know we got back to the **Build** mode and controlled a yellow boundary box that represents the tree. Click with the left mouse button to place the tree somewhere in the scene, and click again next to the first tree to place a second tree.

However, now, we want to add a nice sports car. How can we do this? We will use the same principle we used for the tree, so we need to select the **Transport** button and click on the **Change object** button to open the **Transport** library. Inside this library, select the tab called **Sports Cars** and add a nice sports car to your scene.

At this point, you should have at least two trees and one car in your Grass scene, but how can we control the 3D models placed inside Lumion?

Hotkeys to control the 3D models

When we open the **Objects** menu or the **Import** menu on the left-hand side, a toolbar appears at the bottom of the screen, as you can see in the following screenshot:

If you followed the previous steps, your scene should look something like the one shown in the previous screenshot: two trees, one car, the **Objects** toolbar, and the **Place** object button activated. That is why we still control the yellow boundary box. We can deactivate the **Place** object button by selecting another tool, and for this, we can use the following keys:

- *M*: This is used to move the 3D model
- *L*: This is used to scale the 3D model
- *R*: This is used to rotate the 3D model

The previous screenshot helps you identify where you can find these tools, including a button that is really important; this allows you to delete 3D models. Let's move the car, and for this, press the *M* key or select the **Move object** tool from the toolbar. Since we have the **Transport** category activated and we selected the move tool, we can control any object from this category. To control a 3D model, we need to start by clicking on the small white dot that appears on the car, as you can see in the following screenshot:

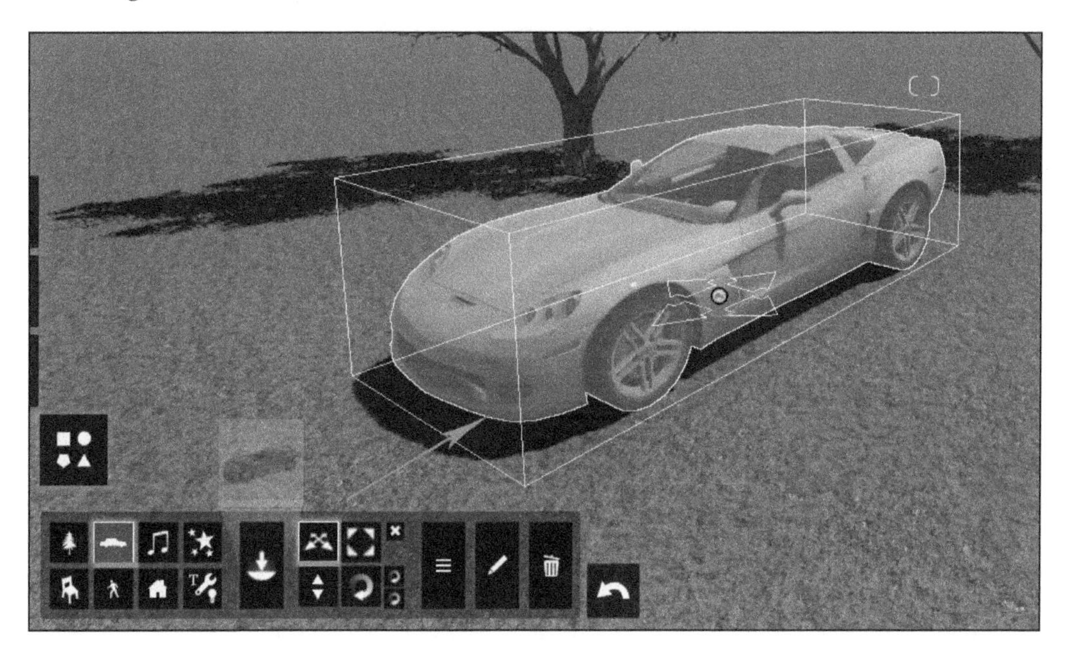

With the left mouse button, click and drag the car to move the car to a different place, and a white line will appear showing the distance (in meters). The same principle applies to the other tools. To delete a 3D model, we just need to select the **Trash object** button and click on the small white dot to delete it.

However, this fantastic scene could look much better if one of the trees was smaller than the other. It is really easy; we just need to press the *L* key and select and scale the tree. However, this is not working, why? Well, right from the beginning, we have a problem because even if you press the *L* key, the move tool is still activated. To solve this, we need to press and hold the *L* key and scale the tree and then click on the **Size object** button. However, even after doing this, we cannot select and scale the tree. The reason is because we need to select the **Nature** category first before doing anything else. This is a key aspect to work with Lumion; we always need to select the category first before applying any transformation to the 3D model.

Now that we have our amazing scene ready, there is something really important we need to do: save the project.

Saving in Lumion

To save any project, we need to select the **Files** menu, which we can find on the right-hand side, as you can see in the next screenshot:

When we open the **Files** menu, the **Save** scene tab is automatically opened. Here, we can save the project by giving it a name and description (optional). After that, we have to click on the **Save** button (if you are in a hurry, press *F5* to quickly save it) to save the first version of our project, as shown in the following screenshot:

When you click on the **Save** button, Lumion will be able to tell that **Version 1** was saved. However, let's say that we totally forgot to save the project, and instead, we opened another project. Is everything lost? No, because Lumion has an autosave system to prevent any loss of work. So, if by mistake, we forget to save the project and we open another scene, Lumion creates an autosave file with the last version. In order to access this file, click on the **Files** button and select the **Load** scene tab on the left-hand side of the **Save** scene tab, as you can see here:

As a result of the Lumion's autosave feature, we can now select the autosaved file to restore the work we did in the previous project, but keep in mind that the autosaved file doesn't last forever and can be overwritten.

Before we finish this quick overview, let's have a look at an additional aspect that can help control and tweak Lumion's speed. For this, we need to open the **Settings** menu.

The Settings menu – how to use it

The **Settings** menu is where we can find some parameters and settings that help us tweak the way Lumion works. We can dramatically increase how fast Lumion works just by decreasing the quality of the editor, terrain, and trees. This will only affect the way Lumion presents the 3D models and environment in the **Build** mode.

There are two ways to open the **Settings** menu. If we are in the **Build** mode, on the right-hand side next to the **Files** button, we would find the **Settings** button, as you can see in the following screenshot:

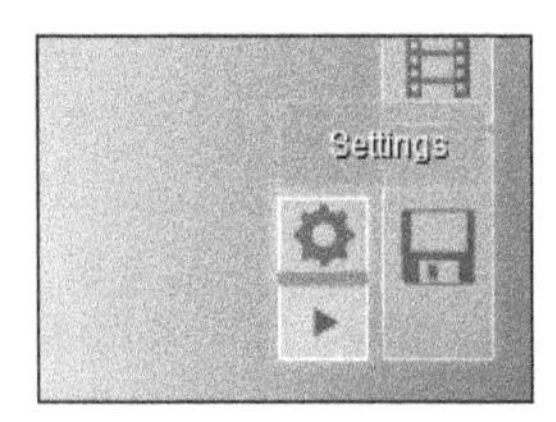

The second option is to click on the **Files** button and select the first tab called **Home** and then click on the **Settings** button. One way or another, we should get this menu:

As you can see, each setting has a number to help you follow along:

- Button **1** limits all the texture sizes to 512 x 512 pixels and saves a bit of memory for huge scenes or low-end graphics cards.
- Use the **Toggle Tablet Input** button if you want to use a graphic table to work with Lumion. It is useful for sculpting the terrain.
- Button **3** lets you invert the way the mouse works when we use it to look up and down.
- Button **4** is another setting to improve Lumion's speed by removing or adding a level of detail to the terrain. The shortcut for this setting is *F7*.
- If button **5** is pressed, all trees and plants in the **Build** mode are rendered with full quality and detail. The shortcut for this setting is *F9*.
- Button **6** mutes all the sounds in the **Build** mode.
- The **Editor Quality** button lets you define the quality of the 3D models, shadows, and materials on the **Build** mode, but this will not affect the output when the scene is rendered. The shortcuts for this setting are:
    - *F1* for low quality
    - *F2* for medium quality
    - *F3* for high quality
    - *F4* for very high quality
- The **Editor Resolution** button lets you control Lumion's resolution, and this setting has a big impact on the real-time performance. By reducing the resolution, you can get quicker updates on the **Build** mode.
- Finally, with button **9** you can define if you want to work with the metric or imperial system. By default, Lumion works with meters, so if your building was modeled using inches, this is the first place to check before importing the 3D model.

Here are a few more shortcuts to help you work with Lumion:

- *F5*: This is used as a quick save option
- **Home** and *F11*: Open the **Home** window and press the *F11* key to toggle between a fullscreen and normal window

Now that we finished with the quick overview, let's jump to another important section that will help us understand how to model using Lumion.

Modeling for Lumion

It is out of the scope of this book to teach you how to model using one of the many 3D modeling packages. However, modeling doesn't have to be difficult or only accessible to those who can afford expensive licenses, because we have SketchUp.

SketchUp is perfect for anyone because it doesn't require any technical background; it is easy to learn and use and is available for free. So, even if you don't have any experience, SketchUp can help you start making your own 3D models to be used in Lumion.

> To download SketchUp, go to the following URL:
>
> `http://www.sketchup.com/products/sketchup-make`
>
> To learn SketchUp, go to the following URL:
>
> `http://www.sketchup.com/learn/videos?playlist=58`

An additional reason to use SketchUp is because Lumion can import any SketchUp file directly, without having to use any special format. We will see this later, but for example, if we are modeling the building using 3ds Max or Maya, we have to export the file as a COLLADA or FBX file.

Now that we have everything we need, let's see some techniques and aspects that we need to keep in mind when modeling for Lumion.

Modeling for visualization

Modeling is a process that will differ from one person to another. The techniques, favorite tools, plugins, and also our experience will dictate how we approach a project from start to finish.

However, what does modeling for visualization mean? Modeling for visualization means that when we approach the project, we ask ourselves: am I going to see this detail? It is true that the greater the detail, the richer and more detailed the results will be. However, it is pointless to transcend certain limits because some of these details will not be caught by the camera angle, and we are wasting time on details that will never be seen.

As an example, the hinges on a door will look great on a close-up render, but at the same time, they would be useless if you are using a bird's-eye view render. So, it is better to start out with rough outlines of shapes that can be tweaked and fine-tuned as the modeling process advances. However, detail is important, as we will see in the following topic.

Improving the scene by adding detail

Lumion does an amazing job at giving the light, materials, and content we need to completely transform our ordinary 3D model into a professional architectural visualization. However, so far, Lumion cannot perform any miracles. It cannot pick a 3D model and make it amazingly gorgeous if there is a lack of detail.

It is this detail that will make our 3D model more believable, provide more visual information from light to dark, create contrast, and deliver an enhanced result. Simple things can make all the difference. So, how can we add this kind of detail?

After modeling the main structure of the building, we need to stop and ask ourselves: what detail can I add to make this living room more believable? Perhaps some electric plugs and switches, wood floor skirting, window frames, and the list goes on. These are small things, but if our project is about a living room, it makes more sense to add these small details. And there is something extra we could always do to further improve the look of our 3D model. Remember that the more detail and geometry we add, the more CPU and GPU power Lumion needs to render the scene. Always try to create a balance between geometry and performance.

Beveling edges

There are almost no sharp edges in real life, and even most man-made objects have a slight roundness. The problem with sharp edges is that you will obtain something flat and lifeless, and it will be harder to achieve a good level of realism.

Beveling edges is one of the most important aspects to improve the level of realism in any 3D model. Why? Beveling edges helps bring out the detail and really sells the realism of our model by allowing the edges to properly catch the highlights from the Lumion real-time lighting solution.

After going through this process, it is time to add some 3D models to the project, in particular, if you don't have Lumion's full version.

Using additional models

Lumion has several flavors that meet the needs of almost everyone. For commercial purposes, we have Lumion and Lumion Pro. Perhaps, the most noticeable difference is the amount of 3D models that are available with Lumion Pro. However, just because we have a Lumion version with less 3D models, that doesn't mean our project has to be empty and lack diversity.

Where can we find good 3D models? The following is a list of some places where you can find free and paid models:

- CreativeCrash: This is available at `http://www.creativecrash.com/marketplace/3d-models`
- 3D Cafe
- Archive 3D: This can be downloaded from `www.archive3d.net`
- Mr. Cad: This can be obtained at `www.mr-cad.com`
- 3Delicious: This is available at `www.3delicious.net`
- TurboSquid: This can be found at `www.turbosquid.com`
- Resources Blogscopia: This can be obtained at `www.resources.blogscopia.com`
- SketchUp Warehouse: This can be downloaded from `http://sketchup.google.com/3dwarehouse/?hl=e`

Now, we have everything we need to start working with Lumion. Our 3D model is ready with detail, including the beveled edges, and we have additional 3D models that can be imported as separate files in Lumion. However, what about the materials? How does Lumion work with materials?

Importance of materials

Lumion has more than 500 ready-to-use materials that are imported in a 3D model, and this takes away a heavy burden from us. Some of the materials available are grass, concrete, bricks, metals, wood, tiles, wallpaper, and some special materials such as the glass and invisible materials.

This doesn't mean we cannot use materials we created while modeling the building. In reality, the materials we used while modeling the 3D model are crucial in order to use the 3D model later in Lumion. Most of the 3D modeling packages will use a default material while we are modeling; for example, SketchUp uses the default material, and this means that by the end of the modeling process, the entire 3D model has the same material, as you can see in the following screenshot:

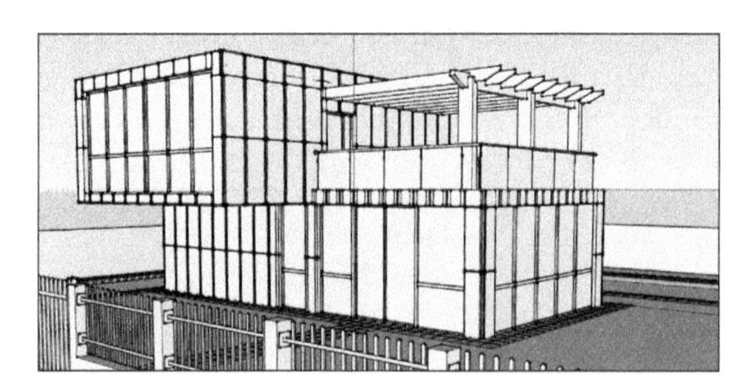

When we import a 3D model into Lumion, we need to use the **Edit Materials** button that can be found inside the **Import** menu, as shown here:

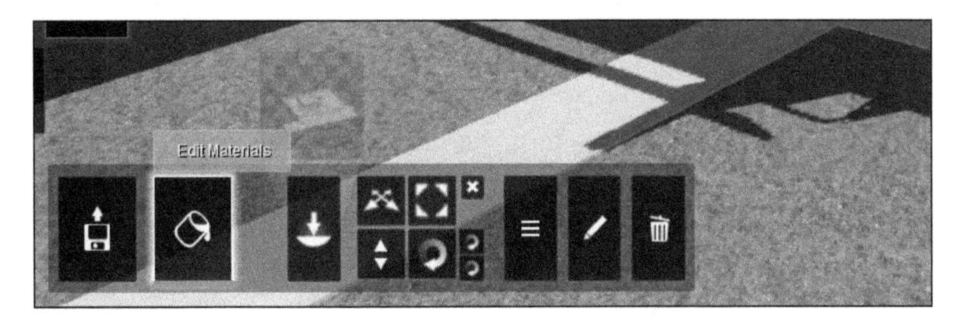

The process to add a material is simple. We need to click on the **Edit Materials** button and then select the 3D model we want to change or add the materials to. When we hover the mouse over an imported 3D model, Lumion highlights the 3D model with a green color. Then, we need to click on the **Add Material** button that appears on the left-hand side and select a material from the 3D model.

We did this with the 3D model shown earlier, and this is what happened:

As you can see in the previous screenshot, we selected the 3D model and added a material, but it is clear that something went wrong. Why?

Materials affecting the geometry in Lumion

Lumion has its own materials as mentioned earlier, but at the same time, it relies on the materials that are imported with the 3D model. As we only used one material for all the 3D models in the example, when the 3D model was imported, Lumion only saw one material, and this is all we could add.

The solution to this *problem* is to assign different materials to groups of geometry that will share the same material inside Lumion while we are modeling. Have a look at the following image:

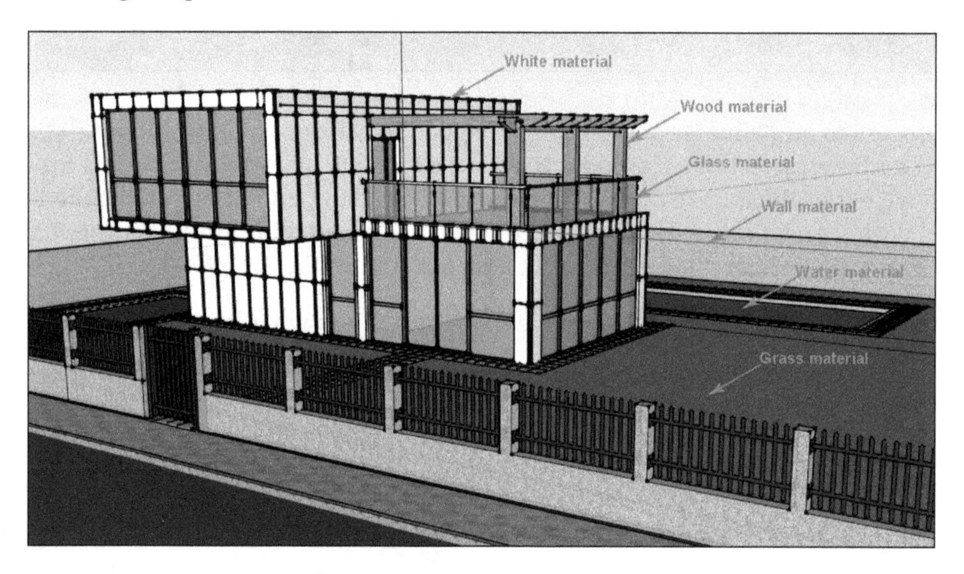

We took the time to add individual materials to the main areas in our 3D model. When we import this 3D model, Lumion will see at least eight different materials. That is why materials are so important, because if they are not present in the 3D model, Lumion will only recognize one material. It is normal that for the first few times, you will have to go back and forth to add materials to the geometry that was left with the default material. That is why, it is a good habit to group the geometry that will share the same material.

However, how can we export the 3D model to start working with Lumion?

Exporting the 3D model

Now, we are ready to export the 3D model in a format that Lumion can import. Lumion supports the following 3D file formats:

- **Autodesk RealDWG**: `*.dxf`

- **Autodesk RealDWG**: `*.dwg`
- **COLLADA**: `*.dae`
- **FBX**: `*.fbx`
- **3ds Max**: `*.max`
- **3ds**: `*.3ds`
- **Obj**: `*.obj`
- **SketchUp**: `*.skp`

If you don't see your favorite application listed, it doesn't mean that Lumion is out of the equation. In most of the applications, it is possible to export the 3D model using the FBX file format. For example, Bentley Micro station lets you export the 3D model as a SketchUp file. This means that in some applications, we have to use SketchUp as the middle man to create a bridge between our favorite 3D modeling package and Lumion.

If you are using Revit, have a look at `http://lumion3d.com/revit-to-lumion-bridge/`, because the Lumion team developed a plugin for Revit.

You can visit `http://lumion3d.com/archicad-to-lumion-bridge/` if you are using ArchiCAD.

Although we can use all the file formats mentioned in the previous list, the option we have is to use either SketchUp or a COLLADA file.

Using the COLLADA file format

First of all, what is COLLADA? COLLADA is a file format used to create a bridge between the different 3D tools, making easy-to-share 3D geometry, shaders, and effects between different applications.

The reason behind using the COLLADA file format instead of FBX, OBJ, MAX, and other formats is that it is a better option because it includes all the textures used, the geometry is better, and there is a low possibility of error. However, COLLADA is not available in all the applications, and in some cases, such as when we are using an older version of 3ds Max or Maya, we need to install a COLLADA plugin called OpenCOLLADA.

Download OpenCOLLADA from `https://code.google.com/p/opencollada/downloads/list`.

Exporting animations

There is a possibility to export simple animations from 3ds Max, but the animations we can import into Lumion are limited to move, rotate, and scale axes. In order to import these animations in Lumion we need to set the frame rate to 25 fps and export the animation as an FBX file.

However, even after doing all this for the 3D model, we might find some issues that can be easily solved. Let's see what the most common problems are and how we can avoid them.

Common problems and solutions

We finished creating the 3D model. The materials are assigned, and we exported the file using the best solution available. Now, the file is ready to be imported in Lumion. On the left-hand side, we will select the **Import** menu and then click on the **Add a new model** button.

After naming the file and placing the 3D model in the scene, we cannot see anything the 3D model, and although we will repeat all the steps, we will still face the same situation: we simply cannot see the 3D model. Why?

I cannot see my 3D model

One reason this happens is because we modeled the building far away from the origin axis. To understand this, check out the next screenshot:

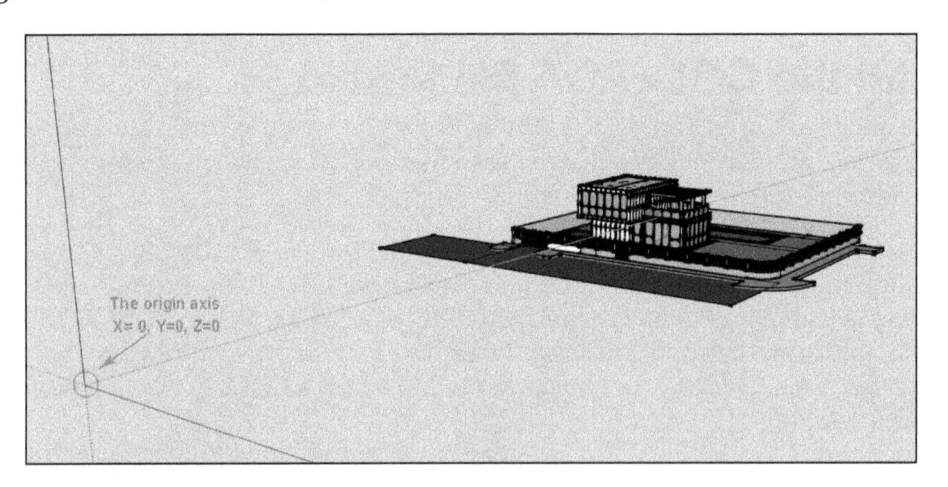

As you can see, the building is distant from the origin axis and might be one of the reasons why we cannot see the 3D model inside Lumion.

Solution

When we import the 3D model into Lumion, Lumion uses the origin axis as the point to place the 3D model. So, if the building is not close to this point, it is normal to see that when we place the 3D model in Lumion, the building is not at the point where we placed it. However, if we rotate the camera, we can see it. The solution to this issue is to move the 3D model close to the origin axis.

I still cannot see my 3D model

Well, there is another reason why we might not see the 3D model. Look at the next image:

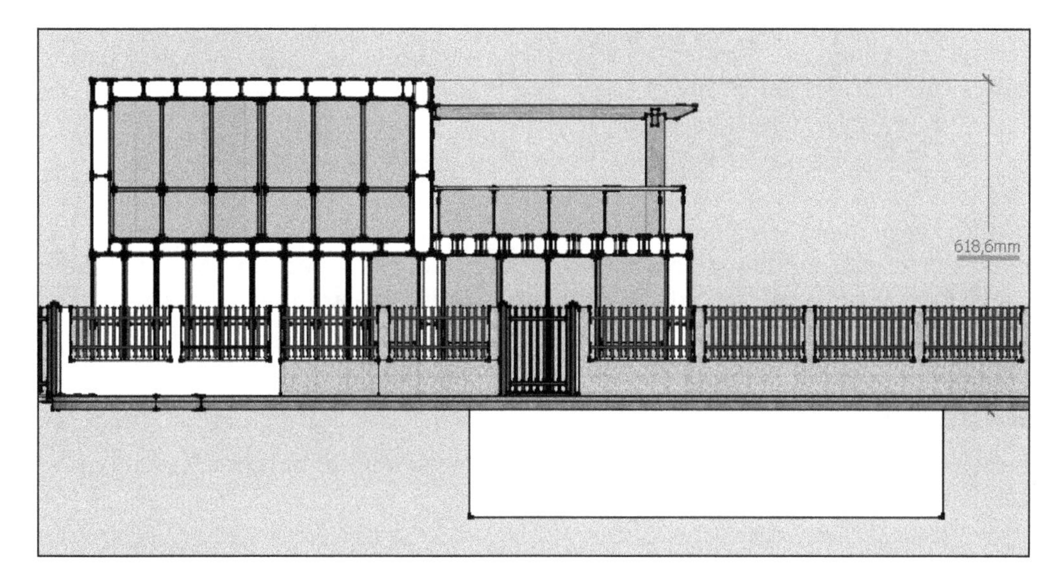

It might be difficult to read the information on the image, but the height of this building is just 6,186 mm or 0.618 meters. So, unless this is a house for ants, there is something wrong with the scale of the building, and when we import the 3D model into Lumion, it is natural that we cannot see the building because it is so small.

Solution

Check the scale of the 3D model and scale it to a real-world size. However, there is another problem that might occur when importing the 3D model into Lumion.

Missing faces

Sometimes, when we are importing the 3D model, something like this might happen:

It is the case of the missing faces; this happens because when the building was modeled in the 3D modeling package, these faces were reversed. So, instead of the normal pointing toward the outside, they are pointing toward the interior, thus making the face invisible.

Solution

The solution depends on the 3D modeling package you used, but the idea is to find these faces and reverse them.

Summary

Here, we are at the end of this chapter, which will certainly prove helpful as you to start working in Lumion with the right foot. We had a quick overview of how Lumion works, how to control the camera, the 3D models, and how to save a project. After that, we checked out some important concepts to help us in modeling, keeping visualization in mind. Then, we explored why materials are so important and how they contribute to a smooth workflow. We also saw how to export the 3D model, and you learned about some common problems and their solutions.

In the next chapter, we will start laying the foundation to create a project in Lumion by creating a scene using one of the nine presets and sculpting the terrain to accommodate the building.

2

Creating a Project in Lumion

The first chapter was a swift overview of some fundamental concepts to begin working with Lumion and now it is time to start getting our hands dirty by creating a scene in Lumion. By now, we are so eager to start that we probably want to import the 3D model that we built with so much care and populate the scene with every single Lumion 3D model available. We can do that and this is one way we can learn software. However, a great difference between an ordinary Lumion project and a professional one is the preparation and planning we do prior to adding any content or even importing the 3D model.

However, even before importing a 3D model, we need to prepare the terrain to place the 3D model in a good light. Since we are talking about preparation and planning, we can also create some layers as well.

In this chapter, you will learn the following topics:

- Creating a scene
- Using the nine presets
- Using a proxy or a low geometry 3D model to test the terrain
- Sculpting the terrain
- Creating and using a height map
- Configuring the Editor quality
- Why use layers?

The main goal of this chapter is to help you start the process of preparing a scene and import the 3D model we prepared in *Chapter 1, Getting Ready for Lumion 3D*. A few things that we will explore are the **Landscape** menu and the tools accessible to start sculpting and adjusting the terrain with the help of a proxy model. A proxy model can be a low geometry 3D model that works as a visual representation of the more detailed 3D model. The reason why we use this proxy model while making terrain changes is because it helps the viewport's performance and makes it easier to tweak the terrain without overwhelming Lumion with details at this stage, which is not necessary. Did you know that you can use a terrain that was modeled with an external package or that you can use height map and 3D terrains to replicate real-world locations?

Since we also need good light to see the 3D model, we will cover how to use the **Weather** menu and how to reproduce different times of the day, including a night-time scene. In conclusion, to keep our scene organized, we will explore the out-of-sight **Layer** menu, which will help us to optimize the workflow and improve our efficiency. Let's start by creating a new scene in Lumion.

Creating a scene in Lumion

A project encloses everything that we use to create the final image or video so that we can say that a scene is the heart of our project because it is the basis to import a 3D model and start adding content until we reach the final stage where we get the output, the result of hours of hard work. Let's see the different ways we can use to create a scene in Lumion.

Using the nine scenes

You will notice that each and every time we launch Lumion, the opening menu that appears is the **Files** menu with the **New** tab opened. The **New** tab is where we can find nine scenes or presets to start a scene, as shown in the subsequent screenshot:

What is the difference between them? Is there any benefit of using the **Hills** scene over the **Grass** scene for example? After reading and testing this chapter, we will understand that the differences between each scene are merely the type of terrain and the weather used, thus there isn't anything *special*.

Are there some benefits of using each scene? This is a personal choice and the reason is because it really depends on the type of the project and the type of a user you are. Initially, we may feel more comfortable using the template scenes just to play safe and as a faster way or a shortcut to achieve a certain look without too much effort.

Nevertheless, with time and after a few projects, we will understand that we actually spend the same amount of time, or even more, in adjusting the terrain and the weather of a Lumion template than making everything from scratch. Just to give an example, the difference between the **Grass** scene and the **Night** scene is merely the sun height.

Now that we know what the Lumion scenes are, let's open one. To do this, open the **New** tab and select a scene by clicking on it with the mouse button and Lumion will load this scene. Don't be afraid to mess around once you open a scene because these scenes work as a template and any changes in the scene will not affect the original template. Therefore, this means we need to save the scene from time to time; otherwise, everything we do could be lost. We say *could* because Lumion has an autosave system.

Saving the scene

We have covered this point in the first chapter. So, if you took the time to read the **Quick Overview** section, pick a shovel and jump to the **Changing the Terrain** section to start digging the terrain.

To save the scene, we need to turn our attention to the right-hand side of the screen and locate the **Files** button that looks like this:

The **Files** button is represented by a floppy disk icon and when we click on this button, the tab that is open is precisely the **Save scene** tab and as you can see in the following screenshot, there are a few things that we need to fill before saving the scene:

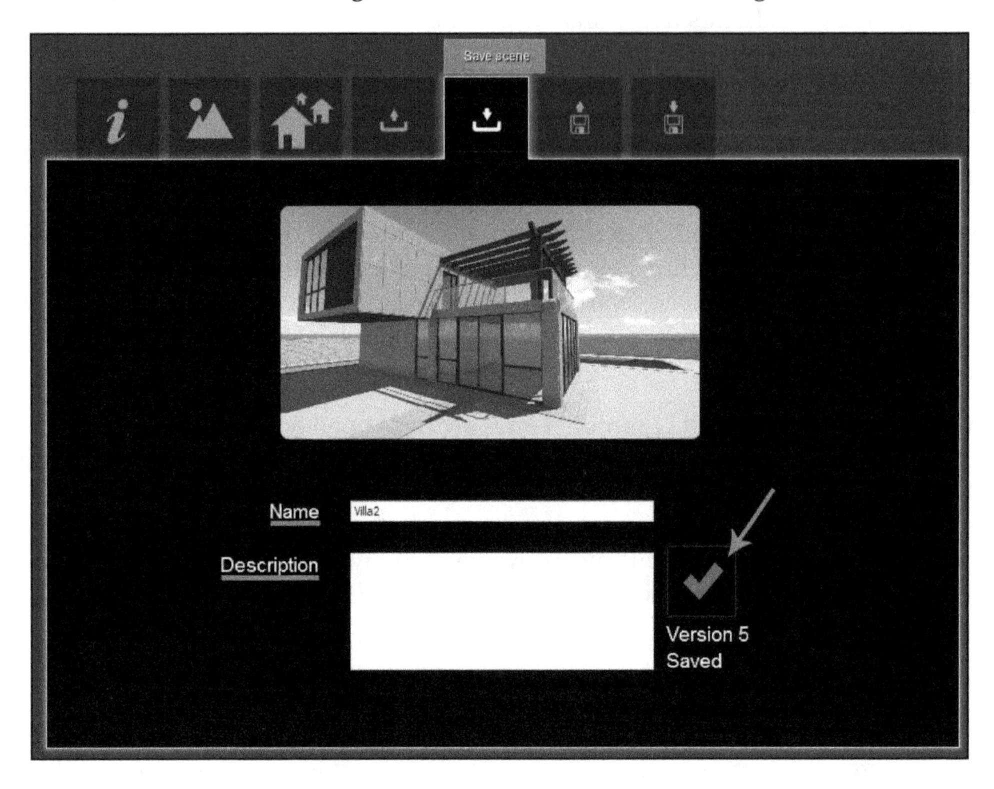

Firstly, we need to give a name to our scene, which is something pretty obvious to do. We fill the **Name** box and if you wish to add a small description to the scene, you can do that on the **Description** box. Adding a description may prove valuable, in particular, if we are saving several versions of the scene. Then, you may enquire why the screenshot in this page is different from what you have on your screen.

How the save system works

The reason why the previous screenshot is slightly different from what you have is because the scene was already saved and in this particular case, five times. The first time we save the scene, Lumion creates a version 0 and every time the scene is saved after that, Lumion increments the version number. Great, we may say, because if something goes wrong, we can open an older version and start from there. Unfortunately, this is not the way Lumion works, so don't let this version number deceive you to think that somewhere we have the previous version saved because in reality, when we save the scene a second time, we are in truth overwriting the scene.

It is always good to play safe than sorry. Hard working hours can be lost with just a simple click and it is always a good habit to save some versions of the progression of the scene. So, if we are going to make any major change, sometimes to see what the best solution is, we need to take extra care and save another version of the scene. Something like `MyProject_version2` sounds great at the moment we save the project, but it is a good idea to add a small description to the scene describing the changes we perform or what the purpose of that version is. After saving the scene, if you put the mouse over the thumbnail, it also tells you the date and the time when the file was saved.

Autosave – the life saver

We also mentioned that the autosave system can be a life-saver. When we open the **Files** menu, another option available is the **Load scene** tab and it may happen that, by mistake, we may select another project or close Lumion without saving and it is strange. However, Lumion doesn't tell us to save the project. Yet, Lumion does a favor to save a copy of the scene as an autosave file, as shown in the following screenshot:

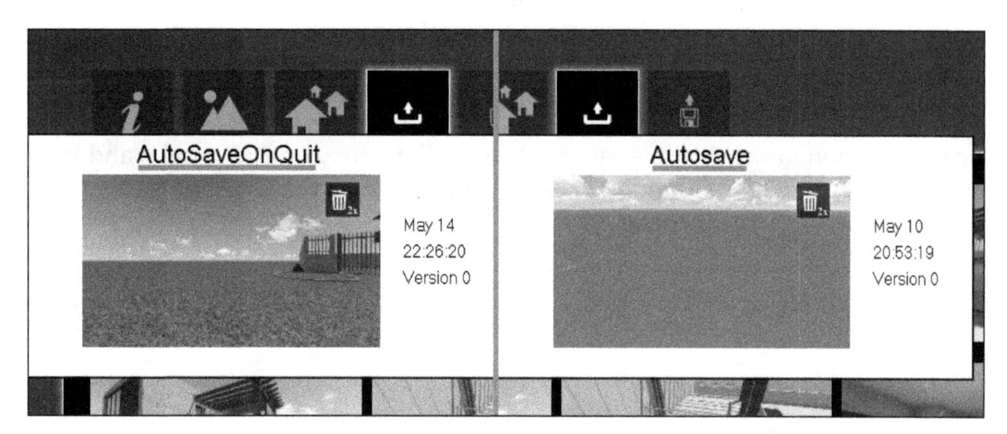

As shown in the screenshot, we can find two types of autosave files, one when we exit Lumion, which is called `AutoSaveOnQuit` and the second one, is when we open another project or create a new scene without saving, which is named `Autosave`.

Now that we have a scene open and saved, the next step is sculpting the terrain, but before doing that, it is useful to have a look at the concept of using a proxy.

Importing a proxy or a low geometry 3D model

What is a proxy? In simple terms, a proxy is a substitute for something. When working with applications such as 3ds Max, we can use proxies in our scene. The benefit of using a proxy is removing geometry from the scene and improving the viewport and the render speed. When the rendering starts, the render engine reads the proxy and knows that it is necessary to load the geometry. Although in the viewport, a proxy can be just a rectangle, but when we do the rendering, we don't see the cube, but the entire geometry.

Now that we know what a proxy is, let's explain why a similar concept can be used in Lumion and what the benefits are. Lumion is a powerful application and although there isn't any official number, we can import geometry with millions of polygons. Then, we need to add another big amount of polygons from the additional content, such as trees, plants, people, animals, cars, and water. For a scene, like the one we are using for this book, this is not a big issue, but when we start working with urban models, the initial adjustments that we need to perform, such as sculpting the terrain, adding content, and other tasks can start to make Lumion's viewport slow and difficult to manage, particularly when our workstation doesn't meet all the requirements.

A big explanation to say this: we can create a similar proxy of a 3D model and import it in order to improve the Lumion's speed. A proxy can be really simple, as we can see in the following screenshot:

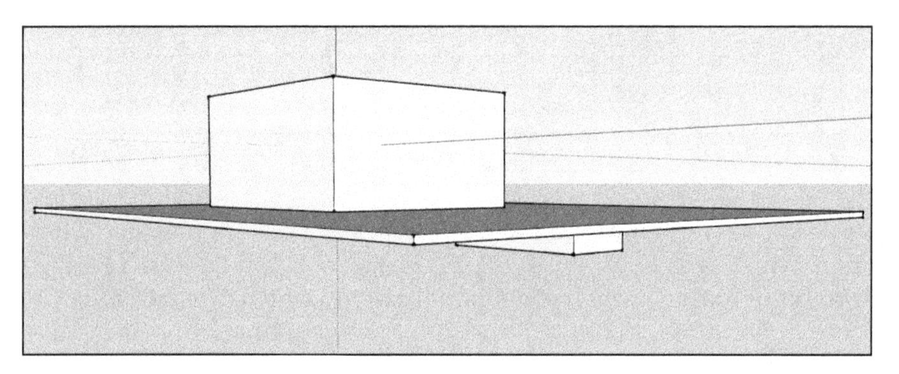

The proxy used in the screenshot uses outlines in the fence, the swimming pool, and the main building. Still, this is just a suggestion and not something that we need to create to work with Lumion, particularly when our workstation is powerful and can handle millions of polygons. Let's pick the shovel and start digging the terrain.

Sculpting the terrain

Finally, the section for which we were waiting so eagerly, adding hills and digging valleys. Preparing the terrain to get the 3D model should be our next logical step. Why? Let's say that we skip this stage and add not only the 3D model, but also additional interior and exterior 3D models. Then, if we start to sculpt the terrain, it is more than certain that our scene will be messed up because the 3D models use the terrain as the base and if that base is changed, we may need to tweak again the 3D models present in the scene.

For some, the idea of sculpting the terrain looks like a difficult task, but actually is easy, and the time it takes, depends on the approach we choose. And it may look somehow confusing having some options to change the terrain, but these are ways to accomplish different results. The options available to create the terrain are:

- Lumion's tools
- Modeling a 3D terrain
- Importing a height map
- Creating a 3D terrain with an external application

Unless we need something really specific, the Lumion native tools are good and enough to produce good results. However, we are going to cover each solution and this will help us understand when and where they can be used and applied. Let's start with the native Lumion's tools found in the **Landscape** menu.

Lumion's sculpting tools

Lumion provides a complete set of tools that help us to sculpt and modify the terrain. There are brushes to sculpt the terrain; we also have some predefined options to create mountains, bodies of water, and on top of this, a wide variety of textures and landscape types. All these features and tools are grouped in the **Landscape** menu. The **Landscape** menu can be found on the left-hand side under the **Weather** menu, as shown in the following screenshot:

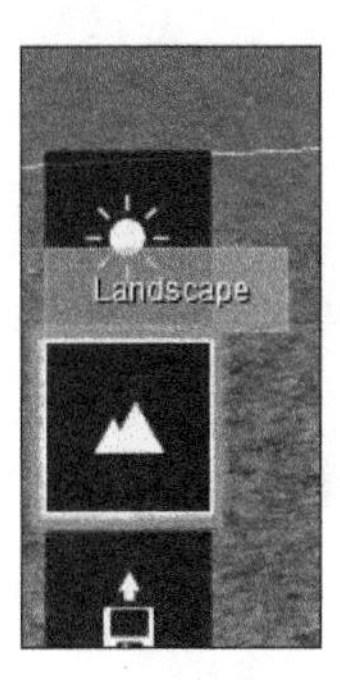

Let's select the **Landscape** menu and a different toolbar appears at the bottom of the screen with the **Height** submenu open by default. The **Height** submenu is one of the six different submenus that give us access to a wide variety of tools to control not only the terrain but also elements that are part of the landscape. The next screenshot shows what we can find if we click on each button:

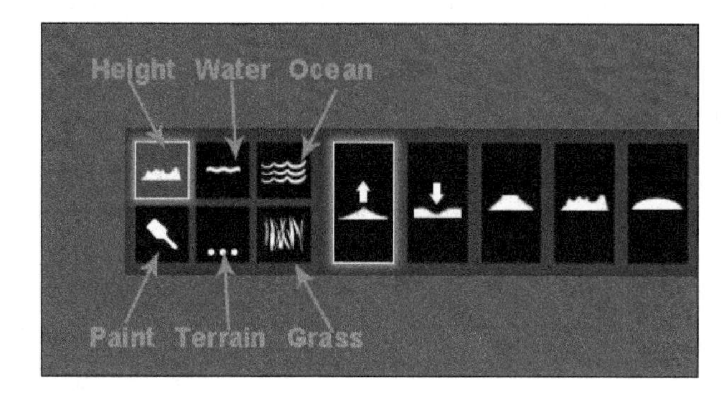

We are going to cover some of these submenus in this chapter. So, if you want to know more on how to use the **Grass** submenu, just jump to *Chapter 5, Creating Your 3D World*. For now, let's start with the **Height** submenu as the next topic.

Shaping the terrain with the Height submenu

Let's unlock the power of the **Height** submenu by seeing what each brush can do to the terrain. There are five distinct brushes and if you put the mouse over the button, a small label appears giving the name for each brush. The best way to understand how this submenu works is by opening a new scene and start messing the terrain with each brush, as shown in the next screenshot:

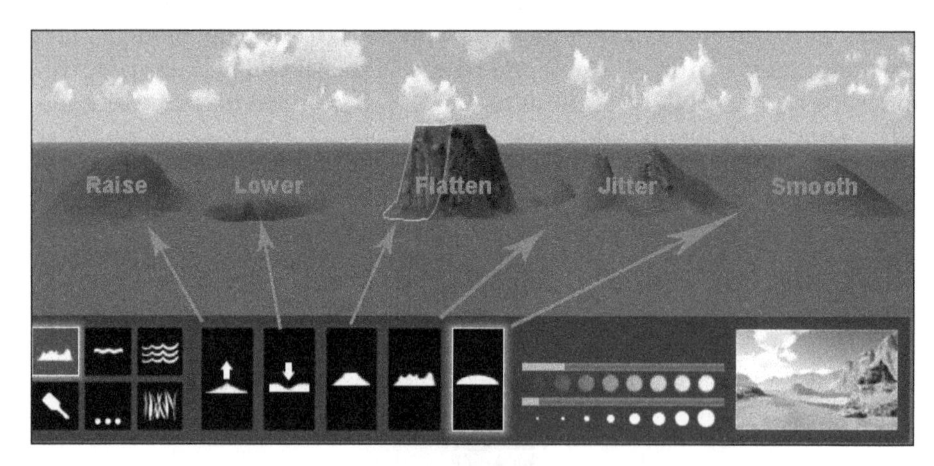

Great, now we know what each brush does, but we can take the control we have over the terrain to the next stage by tweaking the brush size and speed. These two settings can be found next to five brushes and the next screenshot shows the names of each bar:

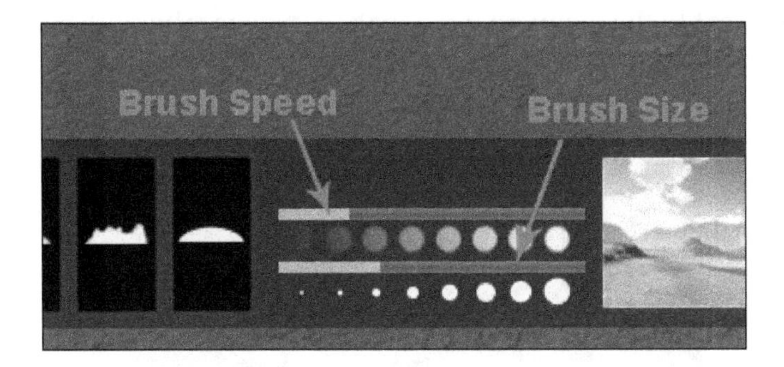

It is obviously the **Brush Size** setting that controls the terrain, but we can be confused by what the brush speed does. The easiest way to explain this setting is by testing it, so let's start by selecting the Raise brush and set the **Brush Size** setting to the highest value, which is **5**. To control the value of the brush size, we need to click on the bar with the left mouse button and drag from left to right in order to increase the value.

The next step is setting the brush speed to the lowest value, `1`. Now, click once with the left mouse button on the terrain. Did you see any change on the terrain? Probably not, so now, we need to change the brush speed to the highest value, `5`, and click again on the terrain with the left mouse button. Now, we saw a small bump being raised in the terrain. Do you understand how the brush speed works? The brush speed controls the relation between the time we press the left mouse button and the speed or the amount of change that is applied to the terrain. This creates an opportunity to use different brush sizes to add different layers of details to the terrain. It requires patience and skill, but the final result can help to sell the scene as realistic.

We may think that it is great to have a small bump in the terrain, but we really would love to have our terrain the way it was before this testing.

The great Undo button

The **Undo** button is not that great when we start to use it. There is a problem with the **Undo** button and this is a word of caution when we are doing changes on the terrain or in other areas; the **Undo** button only goes back one action. The **Undo** button appears next to the menu after we make a change, although this doesn't happen in all instances, as you can see in the following screenshot:

If you feel a little bit adventurous and now you want a flat terrain again, have a look at the *Working with the Terrain* section found in this chapter.

Using a graphic tablet to sculpt

Now, it's time to apply this knowledge and shape the terrain for the 3D model. If you have a graphic tablet, there is an option you may consider for exploring. To make this option active, click on the **Settings** button that can be found on the right-hand side. In the **Settings** menu, select the **Toggle Table Input** button, as shown in the following screenshot:

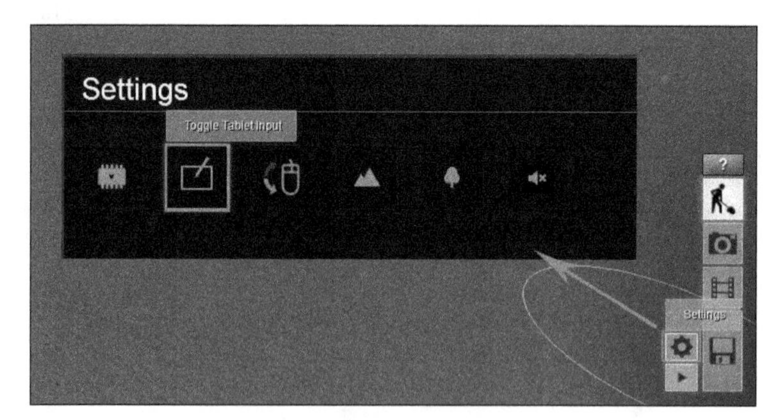

With the tablet input, it is possible to use the pen pressure to sculpt the terrain and have more control over the final result. It is not something essential, but can help us speed up the process.

Sculpting techniques

Each project is different, so it will be difficult to stipulate a standard way to use the five brushes available. Still, we could approach this subject in two different ways.

Technique number 1

Technique number 1 should be used if our main goal is to add some variation to the terrain without being too worried about any specific detail or area. We can start by selecting the Jitter brush and set the brush speed to `3`. For example, adjust the **Brush size** according to your scene and 3D model. When we click on the terrain with the left mouse button, we'll add a subtle variation to the terrain and we can keep clicking on it to increase that variation or pick the Smooth brush to smoothen the result in areas wherever required. This is a quick and dirty way to add variation to the terrain without too much effort.

Technique number 2

For technique number 2, we need to save some camera positions in key points around the 3D model. It is also useful to save a camera placed on the top of the 3D model, as exemplified in the next screenshot:

To save camera positions, we need to use a combination of keys:

- *Ctrl* + *0/1/2/...9*: This saves up to 10 camera positions.
- *Shift* + *0/1/2/...9*: This loads the previously saved camera positions and these saved slots are accessible in the Photo mode.

As you can see, each camera was placed around the 3D model and we can easily load the camera positions using the key combinations mentioned previously.

This technique uses the brushes to start shaping the terrain around the 3D model and we can jump from one camera to another to check if the results we are getting is what we need. The top view camera can help us to add details in large scale and then using the other camera positions to tweak the terrain according to our needs.

Terrain for a swimming pool

Inserting a swimming pool in our project can be an issue, particularly when the swimming pool is placed on the ground. Lumion doesn't have any square brushes and even with the smallest brush it is difficult to open a hole in the ground for the swimming pool without affecting the terrain around it. We can solve this by creating a plane around the swimming pool, or in most situations the entire area where the building is located that represents the ground. So, when you adjust the terrain to accommodate the swimming pool, all imperfections are hidden because of the plane we used. However, how does this help us? This helps because we can add the Landscape material to the plane in the ground to have grass or any other landscape material.

So, there isn't any specific way to shape the terrain around the 3D model and the final result only depends on our skills using the brushes. There is a quick way to flatter the terrain and add mountains with the **Terrain** menu.

Working with the Terrain submenu

The Terrain submenu is where we can find some useful tools to add some detail that is not practical with the **Height** submenu. Have a look at the following screenshot:

The first tool is **Make Flat** and we can look at this tool as a way to *clean* the terrain from any changes made. Then, if we are interested in adding a nice background to the scene, we can use **Make Mountains** to create a circle of mountains. If we place the 3D model in the middle, wherever we look, we can see mountains.

The next tool is **Make large mountain**, which could be your favorite tool in Lumion because it creates a nice, big mountain.

While moving the camera around, we may notice that some of the mountains are disappearing, but don't worry, because there is nothing wrong with our scene. The reason why this is happening is because Lumion uses this feature to remove detail from the background and improve the viewport speed. We can turn off this option by clicking on the Settings button and selecting the **Slow high quality terrain in the editor** button, as shown in the following screenshot:

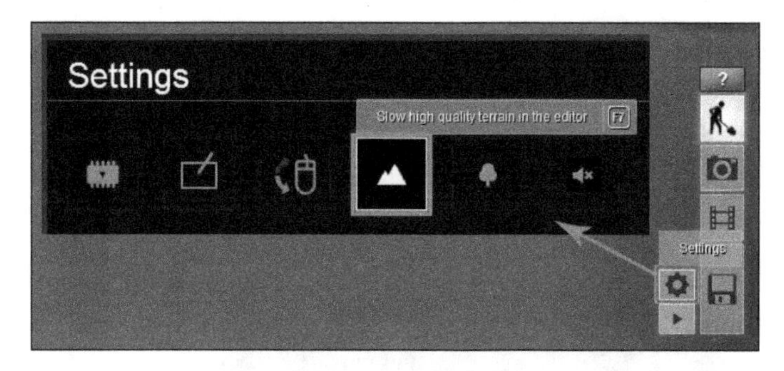

You can also press the *F7* key to toggle between on and off.

While shaping the terrain, we might have possibly noticed that when we raise or lower the terrain above a certain point, a rock texture appears blended with the grass. The same rock texture appears when working with mountains and this may be something we want or not, but there is an option to turn off or on this texture on the terrain. When we look into the **Terrain** submenu, there is a button called Toggle Rock. The next screenshot shows where we can find it:

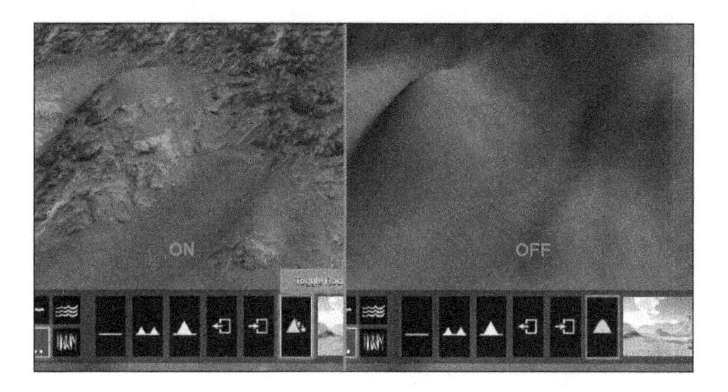

Now, you may be thinking that if we can turn off and on the rock texture, it is possible to change the textures? Yes we can, but that is something we will cover in *Chapter 4, Applying and Creating Materials*.

For now, we will cover the mysterious **Load terrain map** and **Save terrain map** and see what they can do for us.

Using terrain or height maps

Let's start by explaining what a terrain map is. A terrain map is a representation of the physical characteristics of the land. This usually involves specification of the elevation, slope, and orientation of terrain features. We can save some time by using a terrain map for the scene and this proves to be particularly useful when we need a real location to place the 3D model.

It is the **Terrain** submenu that gives us the opportunity to import and save these maps using two buttons, as shown in the following screenshot:

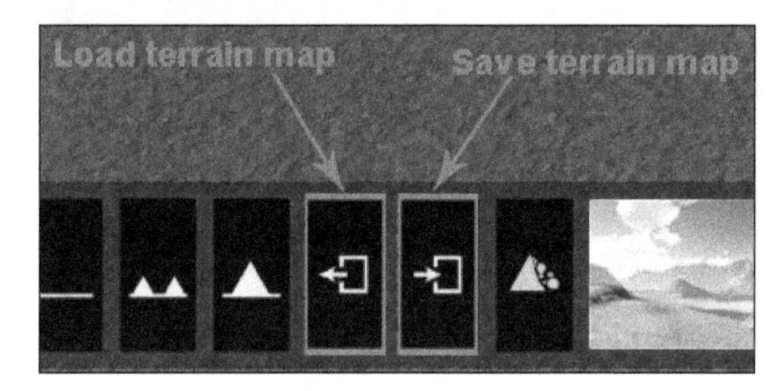

Let's click on the **Load terrain map** button, and Lumion will tell us the image files that are supported. The supported image files are as follows:

- `.bmp`: Windows bitmap
- `.jpg`: Joint Photographic Experts Group
- `.dds`: DirectDraw Surface
- `.png`: Portable Network Graphics

We can say that the terrain map is the result of a height map. Let's exemplify this with the following screenshot:

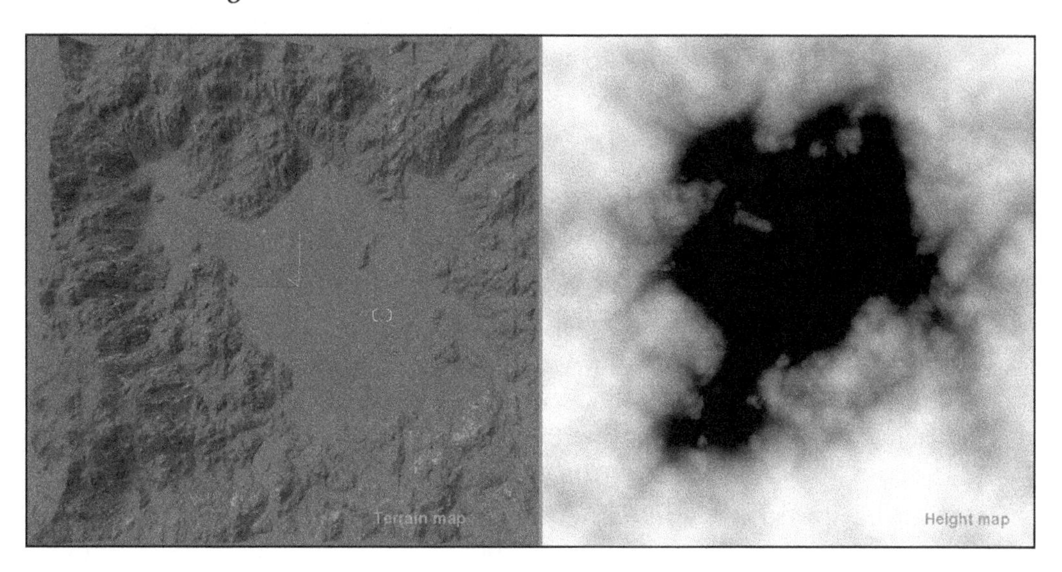

The image on the left is the result of the Make Mountains button and the image on the right is the height map that was used to create it. By importing an image like the one shown previously, we can create a beautiful terrain full of detail. It is easy to understand that the black color represents a flat surface while the scales of gray and finally the white color represent the different altitudes. However, how can we create an image like that and how does it work?

Creating a height map

We have at least two options to create a height map. You can use any of the techniques by following the given instructions:

- Using Adobe Photoshop and GIMP

  The first method is using Adobe Photoshop or GIMP to create this height map, which can be a very tedious task and it is more difficult to get good detail. In order to create a height map, we need to download some texture tools.

> Download NVIDIA texture tools for Adobe Photoshop from the following URL:
>
> `https://developer.nvidia.com/nvidia-texture-tools-adobe-photoshop`
>
> Download the GIMP DDS plugin from the following URL:
>
> `https://code.google.com/p/gimp-dds/`

First of all, the editable parts of the terrain in Lumion occupies 2048 x 2048 m2 area, and even if we create a texture with just 512 x 512 m, this texture will be stretched to the full extent of 2048 x 2048 m. So, the first step is to create a texture with 2048 x 2048 m. Then, just edit the area we want.

Then, there is another thing we need to keep in mind and that is the colors used to create the height map. The colors are as follows:

- **Black**: This is equal to a terrain height of 0 m.
- **White**: This is equal to a terrain height of 200 m.
- **Grayscale**: Each shade of gray step from the 256 available. This is equal to 0.78 meters.

When working with an 8-bit image, the range we have is from 0 m to 200 m, but we can increase these values by changing the mode from 8 bits to 16 and 32 bits. When using an image with 16 bits, we will increase the height to 400 m and when using 32 bits, we increase it to 600 m.

Also, if we are using Adobe Photoshop, some filters such as the Clouds can create a wide variety of surface distortions that are great as a base. The final step is saving the height map as a 32-bit DDS in the 32f format using Nvidia's DDS plugin.

This is one option we will choose in some projects, but there are some better alternatives too.

- Using an external application

  Creating and editing high-quality height maps can be a complicated and demanding process that typically requires the assistance of specialized software. Which application can we use? There are some free and commercial applications that are worth exploring:

  - **L3DT** (free/commercial): **Large 3D Terrain** (**L3DT**) is a Windows application for generating terrain maps and textures and it is intended to help game developers and digital artists create vast high-quality 3D worlds. For more information, visit `http://www.bundysoft.com/L3DT/`.

- **World Machine** (free edition/commercial): Powerful and flexible, World Machine combines procedural terrain creation, simulations of nature, and interactive editing to produce realistic-looking terrains quickly and easily. Go to `http://www.world-machine.com/` for more information on this.
- **Terragen** (free edition/commercial): Terragen is very good at generating a ground texture and allows us to create and manipulate highly realistic terrains, both height field and procedural. For more information, visit `http://www.planetside.co.uk/`.

Now, what if I told you that you can create a height map of any location on the planet? Let's see how we can do this.

Creating height maps for real locations

The USGS is a scientific agency of the United States government and they provide a useful application called **Global Data Explorer**, which can be used to locate real-world locations and export height maps. How can we do that?

We can find Global Data Explorer at `http://gdex.cr.usgs.gov/gdex/`.

The first step is to create an account because we need to log in to download the file created. Then, we can define an area by country, entering coordinates and drawing a polygon or a rectangle, as shown in the following screenshot:

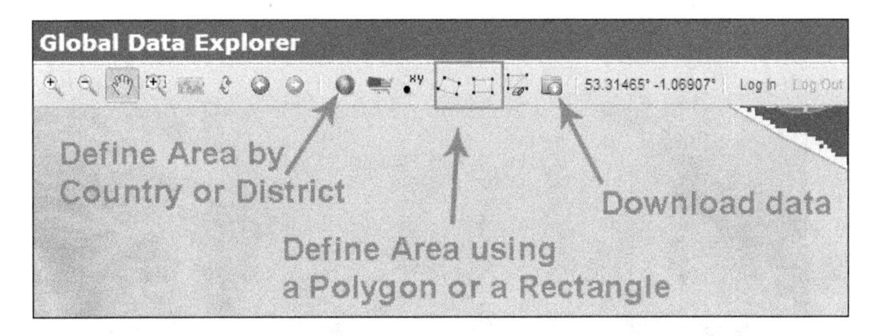

After defining the area, we need to click on the Download data button, as shown in the screenshot, to download the file. To save the file in a format that can be used by Lumion, we need to select **ASTER Global DEM V2** data and export the image as JPEG, as shown in the following screenshot:

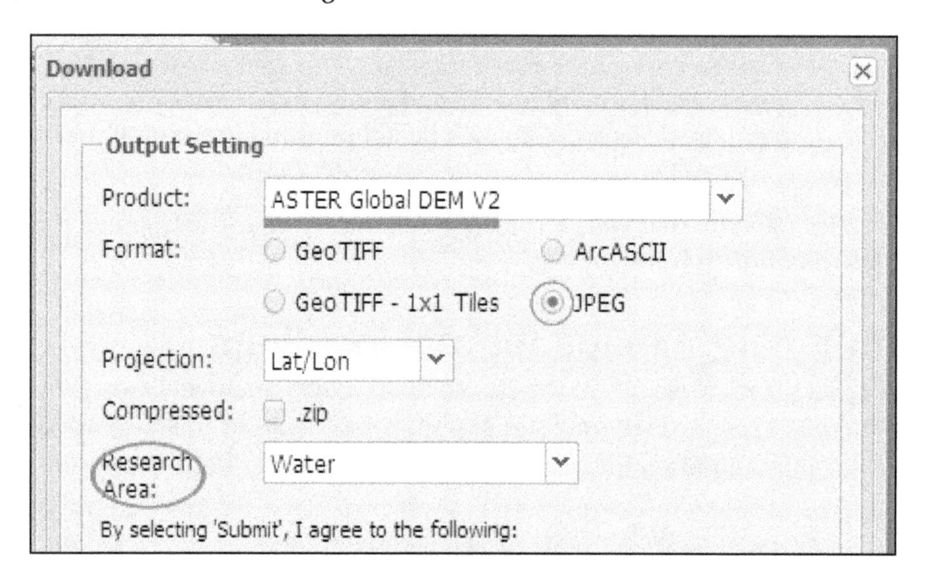

Also, we need to select a research area to download the file and then click on the **Submit** button. After all this process, click on the Load terrain map button to load the file and enjoy the beauty of using height maps to create your terrain. The following image is an example of a height map exported and imported in Lumion:

After loading the image, we may need to use the Smooth brush to smooth some areas in the terrain. We can also use the other brushes to tweak the terrain. However, we still have another option.

Modeling a 3D terrain

An additional option is modeling a 3D terrain to use in Lumion. The way we will approach this solution really depends on our skills and the landscape information available. With some projects, a landscape plan can be provided and usually these plans not only provide information regarding the type of plants required, but also the elevation data that can be used to model the terrain. Modeling the terrain can be part of the solution used for the scene because we can add more detail to areas that will be close to the camera and use a height map for the more generic areas.

However, how can we use this 3D modeling inside Lumion? Is there any way we can blend the 3D model with the existing terrain? Yes, we can.

The Landscape material

The **Landscape** material is a fantastic material that is easily assigned to a 3D terrain and then can be blended with the rest of the terrain. It is like the 3D model that we imported as a part of the terrain and this means that we can change the textures or even paint textures on the 3D model imported.

After importing the 3D terrain, we will click on the **Edit Materials** button and select the 3D terrain. Then, we will click on the **Add material** button and select the **Landscape** material from the **Custom** tab, as shown in the following screenshot:

We mentioned earlier about the opportunity to paint textures on the terrain, but that is something we will cover in *Chapter 4, Applying and Creating Materials*.

Working with height maps can slow down Lumion's performance, particularly when we are working with big areas. How can we improve Lumion's performance? How can we optimize our scene to cope with the content presented? Let's see the answer to these and other questions.

Workflow optimization (best practices)

There are a few things that we can do in order to improve the way Lumion works. This is something directly connected to the workstation we have or, in other words, if our workstation or system is powerful enough, perhaps we will never feel the need to follow some of the suggestions mentioned here.

Configuring Editor Quality

Editor Quality is something we mentioned briefly in *Chapter 1, Getting Ready for Lumion 3D*. So, if you had the opportunity to read the *Quick overview* section, you may want to jump to the next section called *Using Lumion's layers*.

To configure the quality we see while working on the **Build**, **Photo**, and **Movie** mode, we need to open the **Settings** menu. As mentioned in this chapter, the Settings button is found on the right-hand side. When we click on the button, the **Settings** menu appears, and for this section, we will focus our attention on just a few settings, as shown in the following screenshot:

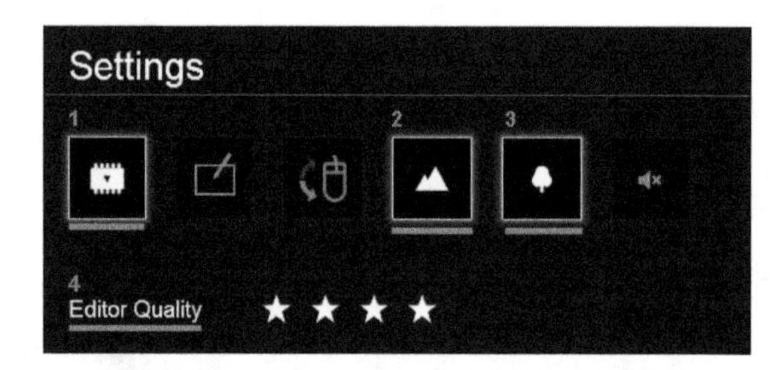

Remember that we can use our own textures inside Lumion and that they are imported with the 3D model, but the size of the texture influences the time Lumion takes to render the image. The buttons of **Settings** are as follows:

- The first button (**1**) limits all texture sizes to 512 x 512 pixels and saves a bit of memory for huge scenes or low-end graphics cards.
- The second button (**2**), in the previous screenshot, was already covered in this chapter, but let's revisit it. When we click on this button, we will improve Lumion's speed by removing or adding levels of detail to the terrain. The shortcut for this setting is *F7*.

- The third button (**3**) is one that affects trees and when we activate this setting, all the trees in the **Build** mode are rendered with full quality and detail. The other side of the coin is that even if the tree is far away from the camera, Lumion will still render the tree with full quality. Even if we have a powerful workstation, it is not a bad thing to have this feature turned off. The shortcut for this setting is *F9*.

Then, we have the **Editor Quality** setting that lets you define the quality of the 3D models, shadows, and materials on the **Build** mode. We can use this menu here to select the level of quality, but it is a better idea to use the following shortcuts:

- *F1* (for low quality): With this, we have the lowest quality possible, which is not that bad. We don't have any shadows in the scene; materials such as water and glass are not rendered properly on the viewport.
- *F2* (for medium quality): Here we begin to have some rough shadows and more detail on the 3D models.
- *F3* (for high quality): The shadow quality begins to improve and the same happens with the materials in particular water and glass.
- *F4* (for very high quality): With this setting, we have the highest quality possible.

However, remember that all of these settings will not influence the image or movie rendered by Lumion. There is another way to improve the workflow and Lumion's viewport speed.

Using Lumion's layers

Layers are an essential feature found in almost all 3D applications. The reason why layers are so useful in Lumion is because we can organize our scene, animate them with some special layer effects, and use them to improve the speed of Lumion's viewport. If we look to the top-right corner of the **Build** mode, we will see something like this:

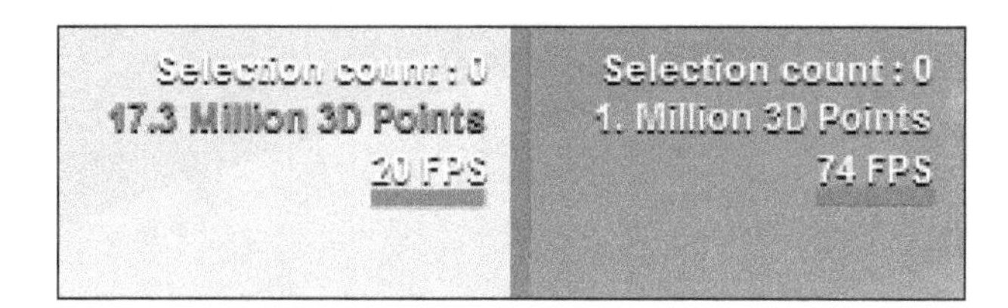

What is the difference between each image and how does that affect us?

Why use layers?

The number highlighted in the previous image represents the frames per second that is rendered by Lumion. In the image of the left side, the layers with trees, plants, and additional content were turned on and the frames per second was 20, which is not too bad.

However, when they were turned off, on the right-hand side, we see the frames per second going from 20 to 74. With frames per second, the higher the value, the faster the Lumion's viewport will be, and the control we have over the scene increases drastically. So, we can see that it pays to make good use of layers, but we may be wondering: where is this menu after all?

Where is the Layers menu?

The **Layers** menu is a peculiar menu because it will only be available if we are working with the **Import** or the **Objects** menu. Click on the **Import** or the **Objects** menu and the change is very subtle, but on the top-left corner a small rectangle with a number appears and if we put the mouse over the rectangle, the famous **Layers** menu appears, as shown in the following screenshot:

When importing a 3D model or adding an object from Lumion's library, by default we will be using **Layer 1**, as shown in the previous screenshot. Now is the best time to learn how to use this menu taking into account that in the next chapters we will start adding content to the scene.

How layers work in Lumion

As mentioned, by default when we import a 3D model or add an object, the layer used by default is **Layer 1**, but we can change the layer's name, add a new layer and hide layers. How? Let's have a look at our screenshot:

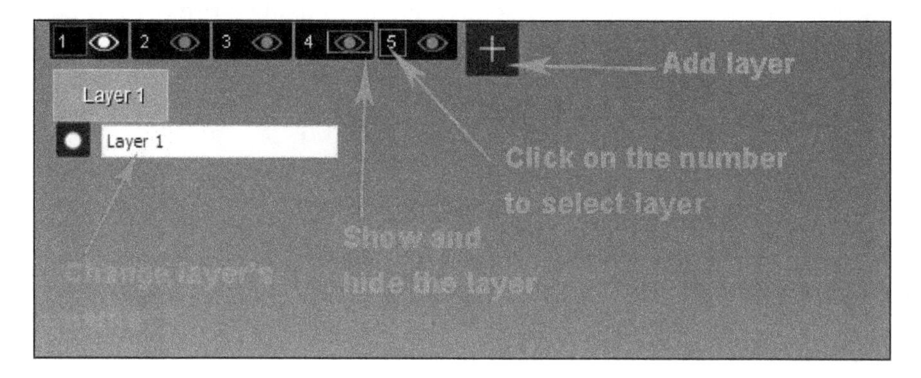

We can add up to 20 layers, so there isn't any excuse for not using this fantastic feature. We need to select a layer first and then add the 3D model in the order that the model placed inside the layer is selected. However, let's say we totally forgot and we need to move some 3D models to the correct layer. How can we do that? Firstly, we will have to select the 3D model and the easiest way is by holding the *Ctrl* key and clicking and dragging with the left mouse button to draw a selection rectangle around the 3D model. Then, we will select the correct layer and click on the Move selection to the layer button, as shown in the following image:

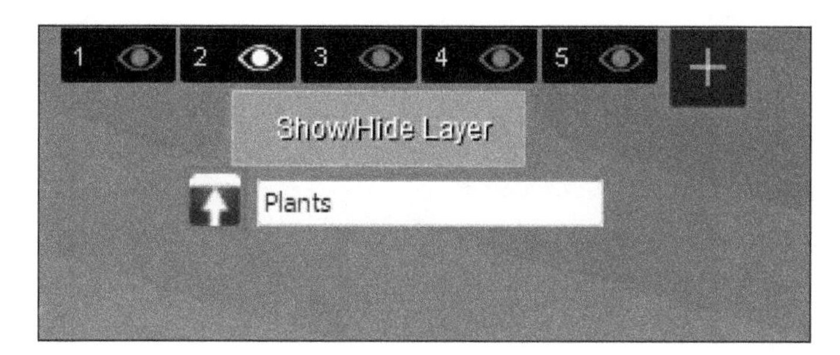

Summary

This was a big chapter, but hopefully provided a good foundation to create your first scene in Lumion. Not only have we seen how to create a scene, but also the advantage of using the nine scenes available that work like a template. After creating our first scene, we looked at some of the advantages of using a proxy to test and set up the terrain. And for the terrain, we covered several options; each one with their good points and how they fit in each type of the project. A height map, when well applied, can create a fantastic and believable result.

Our final sections helped us to understand how we can take the best from the quality settings available and how layers are a key aspect to help having a smooth workflow.

In the next chapter, we will take our scene to the next level by starting to add content and populate the scene. Here, we will find how vast Lumion's library is and how to add 3D models. However, it doesn't stop there because we will also see how to import and control our own 3D models.

3

Importing 3D Models

By this time, we should have a scene prepared, and hopefully, it should have a terrain sculpted to accommodate our main 3D model. The main goal of this chapter is to provide a robust foundation to import external 3D models and also have some notion of what is available on Lumion's fantastic library to populate the scene. It is true that this subject initially looks simple and rudimentary, but there are so many things involved that we should consider this chapter as one of the cornerstones of the project.

We have now arrived at a stage in the project where we will start to explore Lumion's potentiality. The previous two chapters have certainly helped us understand the need of a good foundation to achieve a smooth workflow. This means that we can start and finish a project without facing too many issues and by constantly solving problems.

In this chapter, we will cover the following topics:

- Importing 3D models
- Adding Lumion content
- Placing and reallocating 3D models
- Hotkeys
- Accurate placing
- Updating a 3D model with new geometry
- Replacing 3D models
- Common problems (troubleshooting)
- Locking a 3D model

The main topics mentioned here give us a reasonable overview of what is involved in importing 3D models. Although we did our best to check and rectify problems with the 3D model, we might need to reimport or even replace the 3D model. These and other tips and tricks will ensure the best result possible to progress to the next stage.

The importance of planning

We might think that this topic should be something related to importing a 3D model, but it pays off to stop for a few minutes and create some layers. Let's be honest! Most of us tend to be a little disorganized not only in adding a decent name to an object, but also using layers to organize the scene.

In the *Using Lumion's layers* section in *Chapter 2, Creating a Project in Lumion*, we covered topics such as the layer's menu, and you learned how to create up to 20 layers to organize the scene.

One of the benefits stated is that we can improve Lumion's viewport speed by hiding objects that, for the instant, are not needed. So, what layers can we create? The answer to this question is related to the project we are developing; nevertheless, think how you can separate the objects in the scene. Do you think a layer just for trees will be helpful? What about special effects such as fire and fog? What about importing a layer for the 3D models or creating a layer for the imported 3D models? These are some points that we can keep in mind while creating layers.

Checking Lumion's content

However, being organized also means thinking ahead and seeing in what ways Lumion's features can help us save time in the modeling process and provide more time to tweak and add detail to the scene. For example, do you know what is available in Lumion's library? Let's find out by opening the **Object** menu that can be found on the left-hand side in the **Build** mode, as shown in the following screenshot:

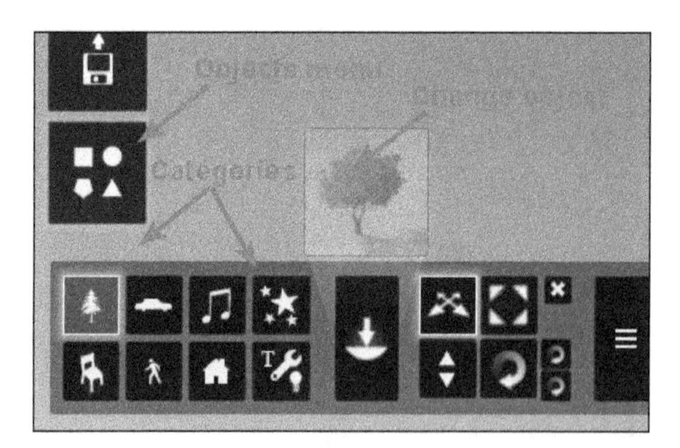

This menu gives us access to eight categories, which are as follows:

- **Nature library**: Inside this library, we can find several species of trees from Africa, Europe, and tropical regions. Then, we have several types of grass, plants, flowers, cacti, and rocks.
- **Transport library**: Here, we can find boats, buses, cars, sports cars, construction vehicles, trucks, vans, SUVs, planes, air balloons, bicycles, caravans, motorbikes, and even a wheelchair. We also have trains and emergency vehicles.
- **Sound library**: As you can see, it is not only 3D models that are available but also a sound library. These sounds can be used to create a nice environment for the movies that we will create later. There are sounds from different locations such as coffee shops, car parks, casinos, construction sites, farms, ferries, harbors, high schools, museums, and so on. We also have nature (beach, jungle, forest, park, rain, and so on), things, and people. This is a valuable asset when well applied, but we will cover this subject in *Chapter 10, Creating Walk-through Visualizations*.
- **Effects library**: Here, we can find some special effects such as fire, fountains, smoke, fog, and leaves. Some of these special effects are covered in the *Chapter 7, Creating Realistic Visualizations*.
- **Indoor library**: This is the library where we will find everything we need to improve an interior scene. We have the assorted objects (from basketballs, beds, guitars, to shopping carts), decoration items (which include objects from books to canvases and pictures), electronics and appliances, food and drink, kitchen tools, interior lighting, taps, chairs and sofas, cabinets, tables, and utilities. These interior elements can be used for a commercial project, such as a restaurant, in an urban environment.
- **People and animals library**: Here, we have people (men, women, and children), one amazing cat, birds, farm animals, fish, 2D people, and animals. Keep in mind that in this library, we have five types of objects: idle, walking, static, 2D cutout, and silhouettes. We will cover some of these objects in *Chapter 9, Animation Techniques*.
- **Outdoor library**: Here, we have elements such as bollards, fences, traffic cones, and concrete walls to populate exterior scenes. We have flags, barbecues, basketballs, baseballs, and tennis courts. Then, we have buildings, construction elements, railway tracks, exterior lighting, benches, deckchairs, garden tables, traffic signs, containers, postboxes, and waste storage.
- **Lights and special objects library**: This is another library that focuses on lighting elements and some utilities to improve the lighting in the interior and exterior scenes. We will cover more about this library in *Chapter 6, Lighting in Lumion*.

Lumion undoubtedly has a very wide ranging library, which covers almost everything that one needs. But why are we reading the description of Lumion's content here in this section?

At this stage, we should have a 3D model ready, but it is not unusual to realize that we need extra content for the 3D model imported. Knowing what Lumion has will help us avoid unnecessary modeling, and this will save our precious time that can be spent in tweaking and adding effects to enhance the project.

However, we will not remember every object available in Lumion, so one solution is to take screenshots of every single tab and save them as a file that can be easily consulted when we prepare the project.

To open one of these libraries, we need to select one of the categories and click on the **Change object** button to open the library.

But enough talk now. Let's see how we can import an external 3D model and 3D models from Lumion's library.

Importing 3D models

In most projects, we start by importing the 3D model that we have modeled using an external application. By now, we should have the 3D model waiting to be imported, and if you need help with this topic, take a look at the *Exporting the 3D model* section in *Chapter 1, Getting Ready for Lumion 3D*. Here, we can find what formats are supported by Lumion and an explanation on why we should export the 3D model as a COLLADA file. Let's start by importing our first 3D model in Lumion.

External 3D model

Let's assume that Lumion is running, and a scene was created to start working. With Lumion, we have some modes that are used for specific tasks; in this case, to import a 3D model, we need to be in the **Build** mode. On the right-hand side, there is a column of buttons, and the second button is the one that should be activated.

Now, let's turn our attention to the left-hand side, and here, we can find some buttons to open the four menus available. For now, only the third menu called **Import** is needed, as you can see in the following screenshot:

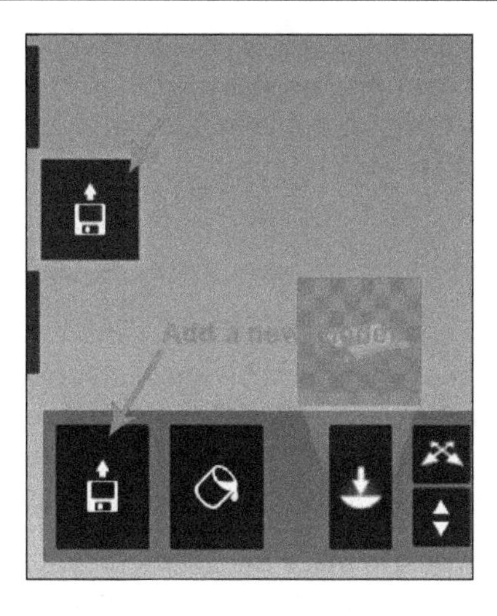

After selecting this menu, different tools appear at the bottom of the screen, but the most interesting one is the **Add a new model** button. Click on this button, and an explorer window appears. This window gives us the opportunity to navigate and find the folder where we saved the 3D model.

It might be possible that we cannot see the 3D model, and probably, we need to change the file extension in order to see the file. On the right-hand side, there is a small button called **Object file *.dae, *fbx, *skp**. If you click on this button, a small pop up with additional file formats appears, as shown in the following screenshot:

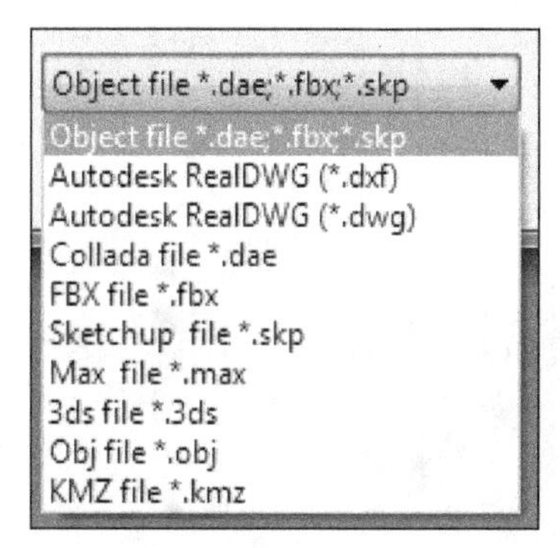

Select the file and click on the **Open** button. Lumion notifies us of the name that will be assigned to the 3D model; it also informs us that we can change this name if necessary. Additionally, we also have the opportunity to import animations if there are any available.

Although we can import animations, this is not as linear as it sounds, because we have a mediocre control over imported animations. In most cases, the basic animations that we import are conceivable inside Lumion. Another downside of importing animations is that we get an infinite loop, and this might raise some issues while creating a movie.

To know more about how to control these animations, take a look at *Chapter 9, Animation Techniques*.

The last step is to click on the Add to library button to import the 3D model to the Import library. We are now back to the **Build** mode that controls a yellow wireframe box, and a big white arrow informs us that if we click with the left mouse button, the 3D model will be placed in that exact location.

Click with the left mouse button to place the 3D model, but notice how we still control the Place object tool. This means that we can carry on placing the same 3D model over and over, but eventually, we need to stop and control the 3D model. The best way to do this using the Move object tool is by pressing the *M* key. If we need to place the 3D model again, do we have to import it again? No, because all the 3D models imported, even from other scenes, are saved in the Import library. This library can be accessed by clicking on the Change object button, as shown in the following screenshot:

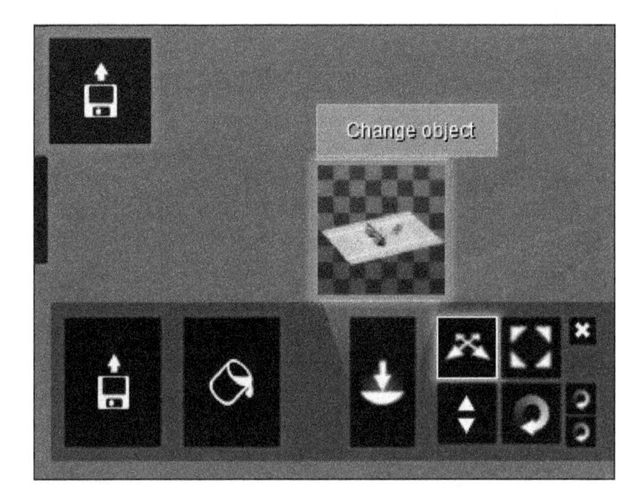

This opens a new window where we will find the 3D models imported, and now, we have the opportunity to select a 3D model or delete it. When you hover the mouse over the thumbnail that represents the 3D model, a small button called **Delete** appears. You need to double-click on it in order to delete the 3D model.

So, now that we placed our first 3D model, let's have a quick look at how we can perform the same action with Lumion's native models.

Adding Lumion's objects to the scene

To *import* a Lumion 3D model, we need to use another menu called **Objects**. I am sure you still remember the *Checking Lumion's content* section, where we saw that after opening this menu, we have access to eight categories of 3D models and objects to populate the scene.

On the left-hand side, open the **Objects** menu, and by default, the Nature category is selected. Let's stick to this category for now and select the Place object button, as shown in the following screenshot:

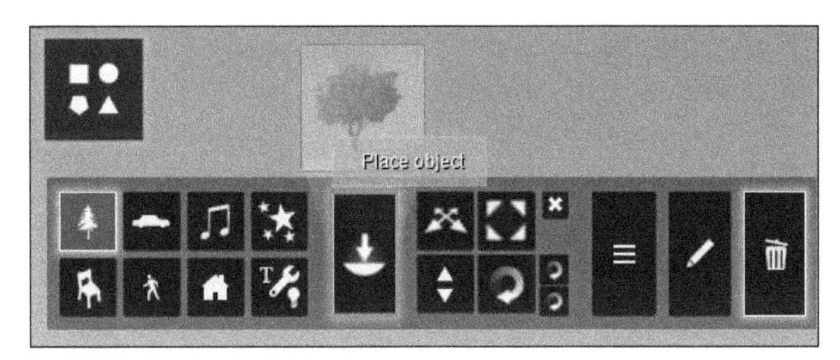

As you can see in the previous screenshot, a tree is already loaded, and when we click on the button again, the yellow wireframe box appears. This yellow box is very useful because, without too much effort, we get feedback on how big the object is. Also, since the box is only a wireframe, we can see where the 3D model will be placed. If you need to change the 3D model, there is a thumbnail called Change object above the Place object button; this thumbnail gives you access to the different libraries available for that category.

Placing the 3D models

There is another Lumion feature that can help us place the 3D model and inform us if there is something wrong with the location. Let's have a look at the following screenshot:

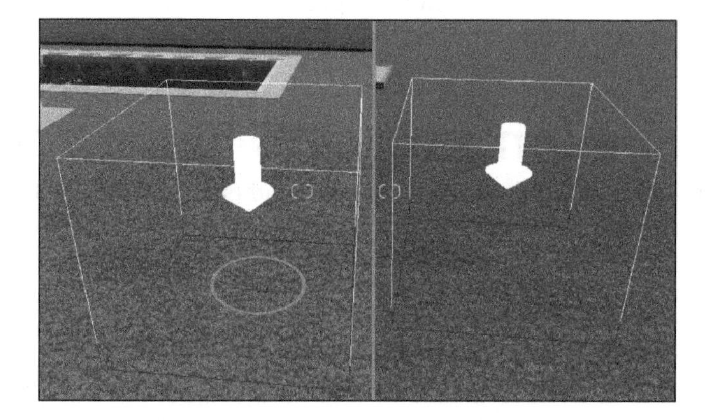

The difference between the images is that on the left-hand side, there is a small dimension that appears below the arrow. The feedback that we get tells us that if we place the 3D model at this location, the 3D model will not touch the ground, and in the case shown in the screenshot, the 3D model will be placed 0.2 meters above the ground. Why?

Well, in this example, we have a swimming pool, and to avoid any problems with the ground around the swimming pool, a plane will be used to cover the ground. This introduces the concept that Lumion recognizes surfaces, and these surfaces can receive any type of 3D model. To place a 3D model, click with the left mouse button.

Now, we know how to place and import a 3D model, but what if, by mistake, we import the wrong 3D model? Or if we place a 3D model and it needs to be updated with a new version? Can we keep the same materials? Can we perform accurate placing?

Rearranging 3D models

After placing a 3D model, we have full control over the position, rotation, scale, and even some additional properties, according to the 3D model used. When we place or import a 3D model and we choose one of the tools available, for example, the Move object tool, a small white appears in the center of the 3D model, as shown here:

From now on, when it is mentioned that we need to select the 3D model to perform a specific task, it means that we need to click on this small dot to tweak and change the 3D model. If you have a closer look, it is possible to see each dot as an icon that represents the type of 3D model. So, if we select the Move object tool and cannot find this small dot, it means we don't have the correct category selected. This concept is explained under the *How Lumion works with 3D model* section in *Chapter 1, Getting Ready for Lumion 3D*.

What tools do we have available to control and rearrange the 3D model that is imported?

Using Lumion's tools

Let's open the **Import** menu again and have a look at the toolbar at the bottom of the screen, as shown here:

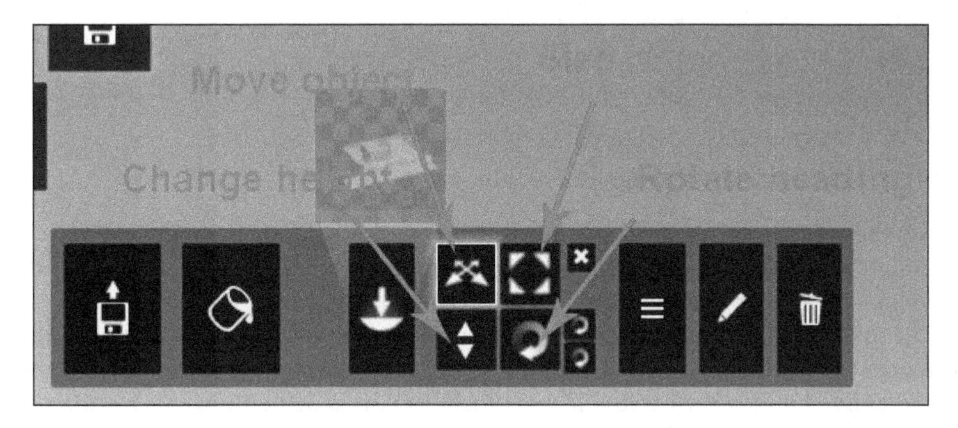

It is easy to understand the level of control we have over the 3D model imported. The basic operations such as move, rotate, and scale are covered with the tools shown in the screenshot. In any 3D-modeling package, when we use the rotate tool, there is a gizmo that represents the *x*, *y*, and *z* axes, and although, in Lumion, we don't have this gizmo, it is possible to perform the same task using the three rotation options.

The process is really simple. This is what you need to do:

1. First, select the tool.
2. Then, select the 3D model with the left mouse button.
3. Finally, hold the left mouse button and drag to tweak the 3D model.

When the 3D model is selected, Lumion gives us this information by highlighting the 3D model, and using visual aids, it tells us the direction in which we are rotating the 3D model. When moving, it gives us the offset distance from the initial point, and when changing the height, it tells us the distance from the ground.

By now, you might think that it is not very productive to click on a button to activate a tool for every task. This is true, and the reason why we should use hotkeys is to access these tools.

Making good use of hotkeys

It might not look like a big issue, but using hotkeys can improve the speed of our work with 3D models. Changing quickly from one tool to another helps us focus on the task and avoid some extra clicks. The hotkeys to control the 3D model are:

- *M*: This is used to move the 3D model
- *L*: This is used to scale the 3D model
- *R*: This is used to rotate the 3D model's heading
- *P*: This is used to rotate the 3D model's pitch
- *B*: This is used to rotate the 3D model's bank
- *H*: This is used to change the height

Let's try these hotkeys? What if our first action is rotating the 3D model? Well, according to the preceding list, we need to press the *R* key and select the 3D model, and we now realize that this hotkey is not working. What happens is that when we use the hotkeys to change from one tool to another, we need to press and hold the key in order to perform the adjustment. If we don't press and hold the key, Lumion automatically changes back to the Move object tool. It is difficult to say whether this is a bug or a way in which Lumion ensures that, by default, the Move object tool is always selected.

Although it is possible to place and relocate a 3D model, in some situations, we need to be very specific, and the control we have with the mouse is not enough. Is it possible in Lumion to control 3D models accurately?

Placing any 3D model accurately

So far, we have been using the mouse to place a 3D model in a relative way, and nine out of ten times, this is not a problem. In any case, we are more focused on producing beautiful still images or movies than producing 100 percent accurate representations. This is true in small projects, but when we need to work on a massive project with a team, we have to introduce a little more accuracy. Why? Usually, each member works on a specific area, and if everyone uses the correct coordinates, we can pick the work of each one and combine them to create a big master plan.

How can we work with these coordinates? Let's have a look at the following diagram:

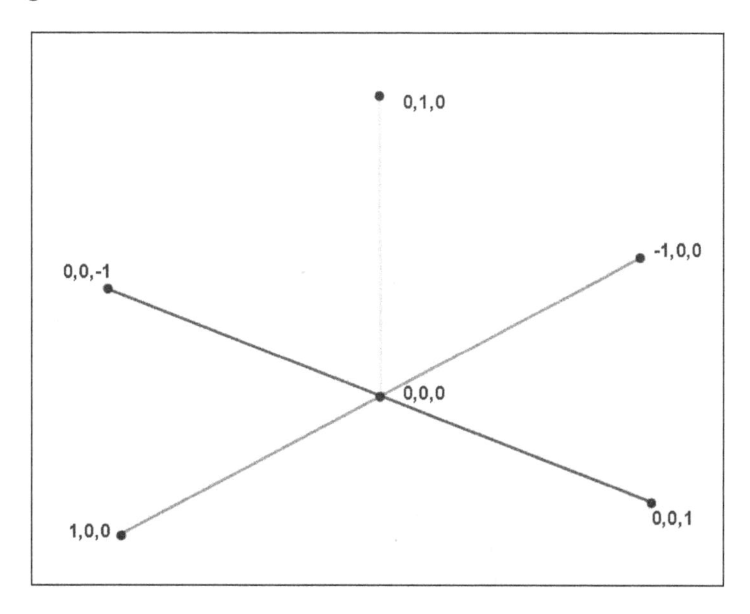

The previous diagram shows how the coordinate system works in Lumion. The center of the universe in Lumion is the point in which $x = 0$, $y = 0$, and $z = 0$. How do we know which axis we are looking at? It is almost universal that the x axis is red, the y axis is green, and the z axis is blue. Usually, the z axis is the up axis; this means that to go up or down, we use the z axis, but this is not true in Lumion. In Lumion, the up axis is the y axis.

However, the best way to learn is by seeing this feature in action. Let's try with the model we imported into Lumion and see how we can use the **Edit properties** menu to place a 3D model accurately. The **Import** menu needs to be selected, and in the toolbar, there is a button called **Edit properties**, as shown in the following screenshot:

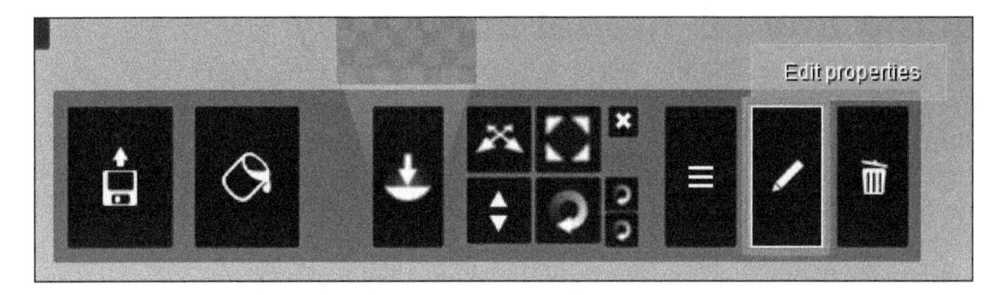

[This is not constrained to an imported 3D model, because the same principle is used for any 3D model.]

Now, we need to select the 3D model, and a window similar to the one shown here appears:

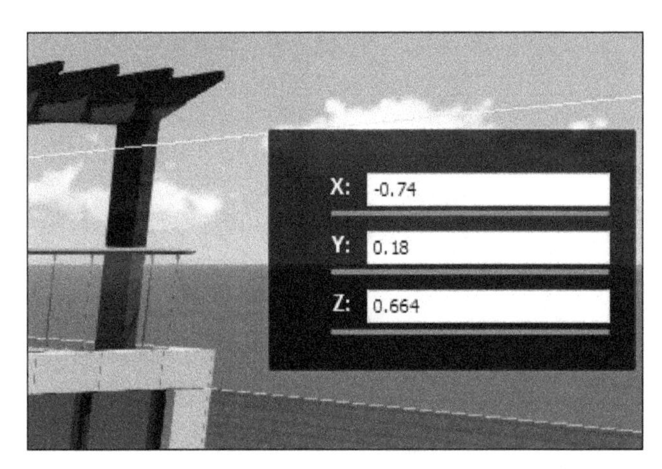

The information we see, is telling us that the 3D model is slightly offset from the origin axis. For example, if we have a 3D model that needs to be placed one meter above the ground, which axis are we going to use? For this, we need to use the *y* axis. If the 3D model needs to be more to the left or to the right, we can use the *x* axis or the *z* axis, respectively.

Rearranging an imported 3D model is not as difficult as you think, and the amount of control we have gives us the opportunity to perform very accurate adjustments. However, let's say you received an e-mail from the client telling you that there is a new CAD plan that is consequently going to affect the 3D model. Do you have to delete the 3D model and import it again? Perhaps, you already added some materials and 3D models. Are you going to lose all this work?

Updating a 3D model with new geometry

Fortunately, we don't have to lose more time. Being a user-friendly application, Lumion helps with this problem by providing a clever way to update the 3D model. The first thing you need to do is change the 3D model with the modeling package you used to create the 3D model.

The next thing is exporting the 3D model again with the same name. This means you have to overwrite the initial file used; this gives you the responsibility of creating a backup file, just in case something goes wrong.

Since we are talking about an imported 3D model, it makes sense that the next step is to open the **Import** menu and find the Edit Materials button. When we click on this button, Lumion needs to know which imported 3D model we need to change, so select a surface from the 3D model and see how Lumion highlights the 3D model.

Although there is a new window on the left-hand side, full of fantastic materials, we need to turn our attention to the bottom-right corner where we will find a set of buttons. The button we need is the one called **Reload model and reapply materials**, as shown in the following screenshot:

Lumion will think for a while and then show the updated 3D model in the same position and with the same materials. However, this might not work in your case due to the nature of the changes you made. For example, if for some reason we changed the name of the material (although for us, it is the same material with a different name), to Lumion, this is a new material.

Sometimes, we have to work at an earlier stage of the project, such as the concept-designing stage. In this stage, there are a lot of changes, and some things that were removed at an earlier stage can be back in another revision. As a safety net, it is a good habit to save the old files, along with a text file, with a small description for each file. Later on, when a detail is back again, we don't need to open every single file to check where the detail is. There is a second option to replace a 3D model.

Replacing 3D models

There is a second way to replace a 3D model in Lumion, and this is especially useful when we don't want to overwrite the file with the changes, but instead, use a new file. When we need to use a new file with the updates, we cannot use the feature mentioned in the previous section. What we need is a way to pick a new file and at the same time avoid losing all the changes made, which can include materials. How can we tackle this issue?

In the previous section, we saw how to reload the same file with the changes, and if we follow the steps mentioned, let's stop before pressing the **Reload model and re apply materials** button. Instead, press and hold the *Ctrl* key and notice how a new button called Reload model appears and reapply materials new file, as shown in the following screenshot:

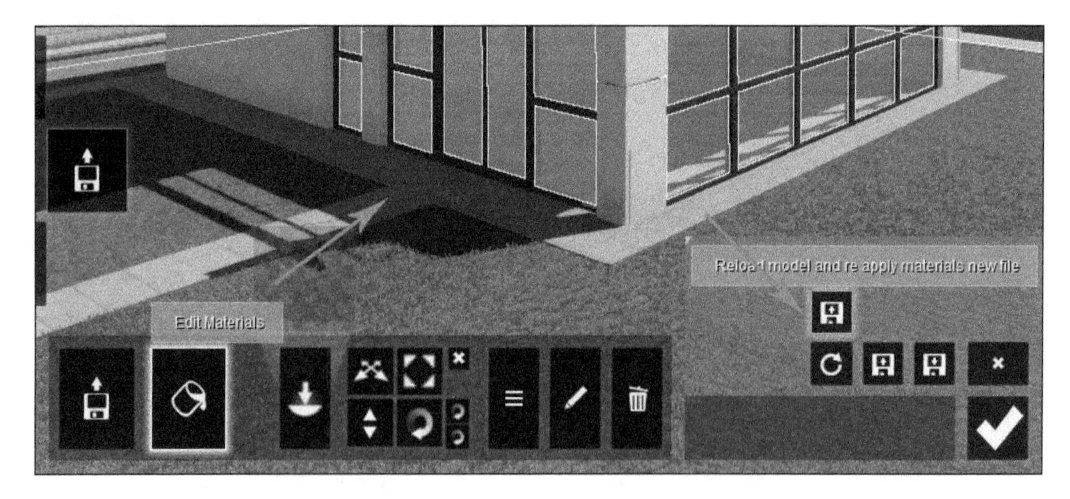

After clicking on this button, we have the opportunity to navigate to the folder where the new file is located. Select the file and click on the **Open** button to replace the 3D model in Lumion with a new file.

Keep in mind that this will not work flawlessly, and the reason is because there are changes that Lumion cannot track. For example, let's pretend we have a window called `window_small_01`, and in the modeling package, we change the scale, orientation, and position of this object. In Lumion, this object has a material called `Wood_01`, so when we reload the model, Lumion recognizes `window_small_01`; updates the changes made to the scale, rotation, and position values; and assigns the same material called `Wood_01`.

So far so good, but let's say that for some reason we changed the name of the object to `Window_Small_01`. Now, when we reload the 3D model, Lumion sees a new object and will not assign the `Wood_01` material. For us, it is the same object; the only thing changed was the name, but for Lumion, this window is a new object.

These two Lumion features are really useful not only to deal with 3D model changes but also to verify and correct some problems.

Common problems (troubleshooting)

The following are some issues that might occur while importing a 3D model. There are also solutions to help you.

Problem	Explanation	Solution
Reload a 3D model, and a message appears informing you that there is an error in importing the model.	When Lumion doesn't have access to the drive with the original file, it gives this import error.	You need to replace the file, and while doing this, you need to set the new path for the file.
When you navigate around the 3D model, some surfaces might start to look strange.	This can happen occasionally when the scene is so complex that it cannot be processed by the graphic card, because it runs out of memory.	Rebooting the PC can help clean the memory of the graphic card. However, this also has to do with the number of polygons/3D points in the scene.
When you import a 3D model, Lumion crashes.	A complex model with a lot of detail can make Lumion slow while importing the 3D model.	Unless the camera views need loads of detail, you should try to simplify the model for other areas where there isn't a need for high-detail 3D models.

Problem	Explanation	Solution
When you export a 3D model from Revit, the materials inside Lumion don't match.	Some Revit materials are created using procedural textures or advanced shaders and can't be easy converted to real-time materials, so Lumion tries to find the best representation based on base texture maps.	The solution would be to stick to simple and basic materials.
When you import a SketchUp file, Lumion crashes.	An invalid texture duplication can make Lumion crash.	Check the materials for any double-ups on textures and remove any characters such as #, @, and & from the material and texture names.
While importing a file, objects shift out of place.	When the file is exported, the internal relative position is not translated properly to world coordinates.	Try to explode the 3D model, because this will convert everything to world space coordinates.
When you import a 3D model with several objects inside, some don't appear in Lumion.	Sometimes, while modeling, we import a 3D model in the modeling package we are using and export everything to Lumion. It might happen that the 3D model we imported doesn't appear in Lumion.	Try to explode the 3D models before exporting the 3D model.

If you have an issue that doesn't match with the ones mentioned here, or if the possible solution doesn't work, you can try to export the 3D model using another file format or using SketchUp as the middle man.

Now that we have the 3D model imported and the issues solved, it is time to perform one last action before moving to the next chapter.

Locking a 3D model

Why should we lock a 3D model? Locking a 3D model is a safety net for any undesired changes regarding the position, scale, and orientation. When a scene starts to get complex with the 3D models imported, it is easy to change a 3D model by mistake. So, it is a good habit to lock the 3D models, in particular, when the basic things are defined.

Does this mean that any time we need to change something in the model we need to unlock and lock it again? Not necessarily. We still can replace and reload the 3D model, and there is no problem when assigning materials. This also applies to Lumion's native models. How can we lock a 3D model?

Let's open the **Import** menu and on the toolbar we have to select first the Context menu and then select the 3D model, as shown in the following screenshot:

As we can see in the previous screenshot, when we select the 3D model, two options appear, and in this scenario, we need to select the **Transformation** option. When the **Transformation** menu is selected, more options appear. We need to select the **Lock position**, which, in turn, opens a third menu where we can lock and unlock the 3D model.

Now, the 3D model is locked, and we cannot move, scale, and change the orientation, but as mentioned, other adjustments are possible.

Summary

Hopefully, I didn't bother you with this chapter, as this is somehow more technical than the previous two chapters. However, it is important that you understand the earlier chapters, as they provided the necessary technical background to create a stable and good foundation. When we know that we did everything we could to create a good model with a solid foundation, our mind can focus on creating a beautiful architectural visualization.

In this chapter, you learned not only how to be more organized, but also how to import an external 3D model and content from Lumion's library. Since we cannot place the 3D model perfectly the first time, we saw what tools are available to do this. We also saw the corresponding hotkeys to swiftly move from one tool to another.

The fact that we can reload or replace an imported 3D model is, without doubt, priceless, especially when we have to solve common problems either while importing or reloading a 3D model.

With this, we can jump to the next chapter where we can see how to add some beauty to our scene with fantastic materials. Lumion's materials are fully optimized to provide the most believable results possible. We will not only see how to use them, but also see what is the best way to create, import, or own materials. In addition to this, you will learn some techniques to save and paste materials and also learn how to solve common issues.

4
Applying and Creating Materials

We are progressing fairly quickly toward a beautiful architectural visualization using Lumion. Now that we have imported an external 3D model or, in more complex scenes, several 3D models, we have three options in order to advance to the next stage:

- The first option is to use the imported materials, and this means we had to spend some time to create these materials in the modeling package we used.
- The second option is to use Lumion's remarkable and optimized materials.
- The third option is to create materials using Lumion's Standard material.

Which one we are going to use depends on several factors such as deadlines, resources, and skills. However, this chapter is designed to help you in all situations and the topics mentioned in the following list provide a good idea of what will be covered here. We will see what is available in Lumion in terms of materials and how we can use them. Later in the chapter, we will see how we can create our own textures.

In this chapter, we will cover the following topics:

- Available materials in Lumion
- Adding materials
- Special materials
- Importing materials
- Tweaking imported materials
- The Glass special features
- Creating materials in Lumion
- Using the Standard material

- Creating bump maps
- Working with materials
- Organizing materials
- Saving materials
- Copying and pasting materials
- How to solve flickering

However, before we start, let's explore what materials and textures are.

Material or texture

In simple terms, a texture is an image that is mapped on to a 3D object and a material simulates a physical material.

However, we can say that the line between these two expressions is blurred. Why? Frequently, textures such as bump maps are used to influence lighting. A **bump map** is a texture that is used to modify the to affect how the light reacts to the surface, rather than modifying the color as a regular image texture would do.

A texture also can be used to provide details to a surface. For example, by applying a brick-tiled texture to a surface, we can simulate a brick wall instead of modeling the geometry of each individual brick. The following screenshot shows a good example of this in action:

Sometimes, we tend to confuse a texture with a material. So, what is a material? We mentioned already that a material simulates a physical material. In other terms, a material in 3D is a set of equations that defines how the lights interact with the surface.

These equations describe the important characteristics of the surface at a specific point, such as the diffuse, specular, glossiness, and various other parameters, depending on how complex the material is. To give an example, let's see some of the parameters used to create the brick material we saw previously. These are shown here:

As we can see, there are more steps involved than just assigning a texture to a surface. This concept needs to be kept in mind if we want to create believable materials in Lumion, and a second point that is crucial is to always create a material using references. Don't trust your memory or simply what looks good to your eyes. References are an important aspect to achieve a realistic result.

Now, you may be asking: so, which materials are available in Lumion and what is ready to use?

A quick overview of Lumion's materials

Lumion has more than 500 materials that can be used in our scene. To give you an idea of what is available, have a look at the following overview:

- **Custom**: This material stands for what the name suggests. Inside this tab, we can find some special materials that will be covered later in this chapter.
- **Wood**: This is used for several wood materials that can be used for doors, windows, and other elements made of wood.
- **Wood Floor**: Here, we have more wood materials designed for floors.
- **Bricks**: These are a variety of materials from normal house bricks to stone walls.
- **Tiles**: Here, we can find tiles to our bathroom, patio, or a swimming pool.
- **Ground**: This tab provides materials to simulate a terrain to a ground covered with grass.

- **Concrete**: This consists of a wide variety of concrete textures including blocks of concrete.
- **Carpet**: Although these materials contain carpet textures, we can easily create cloth materials.
- **Misc**: On this one, we will find pavement stone, exterior walls, plaster, and roof tiles.
- **Asphalt**: This consists of some materials to create roads.
- **Metal**: This consists of a wide variety of metal that is painted, new, or rusty.
- **Marble**: This includes several qualities of linoleum and marble.

Each material is prepared to be assigned easily and without too many adjustments. This is another reason why Lumion is such a powerful application because technically, we just need a 3D model and Lumion does a fantastic job, particularly with the materials. Creating materials can be time-consuming because of the amount of tests we need to perform in order to ensure we get the best result possible.

However, this may seem too good to be true and you will want to check these materials or start assigning materials to your 3D model. How can we do that?

Working with materials

At the beginning of this book, we covered this important aspect. So, we can now work with Lumion materials. To refresh your memory, have a look at the *Why materials are important?* section in *Chapter 1, Getting Ready for Lumion 3D*.

To assign materials, we need a 3D model that is already exported with several different materials assigned to its surfaces, and the following screenshot from *Chapter 1, Getting Ready for Lumion 3D* shows us an example:

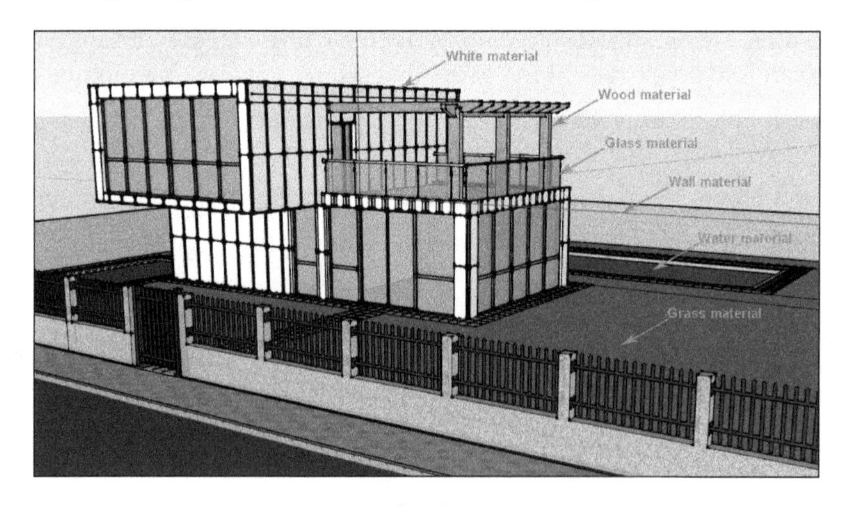

When this model is imported in Lumion, we can add at least nine materials and as you can see, the materials used during the modeling process don't need to be anything special. The **Wood** material, for example, is just a basic texture from SketchUp; the **Water** material is a solid color, and the same happens with the **Glass** material. Later, we may need to perform some rearrangements on the materials imported from the 3D again and reload the Lumion file. How can we do this?

In the previous chapter, we saw that we can reload a 3D model and keep the materials assigned to the surfaces. So, what we have to do is get back to the original file, add an additional material, and export the 3D model again. Then, in Lumion, we will use the Reload model and re-apply the material's button to reload the 3D model. If you need help with this, have a look at the *Update a 3D model with new geometry* section in *Chapter 3, Importing 3D Models.*

Assigning materials to a 3D model

To start assigning materials to a 3D model, turn your attention to the left-hand side, where we can find the four main menus in Lumion. The menu we need is the **Import** menu and after selecting this menu, the next button we need to click is the Edit Materials button. The next step is to select the 3D model with the left mouse button; when we put the mouse over the 3D model, Lumion highlights the 3D model, as shown in the following screenshot:

Now, we can start assigning materials to the 3D model by clicking on the Add Material button and selecting a surface, as shown in the following screenshot:

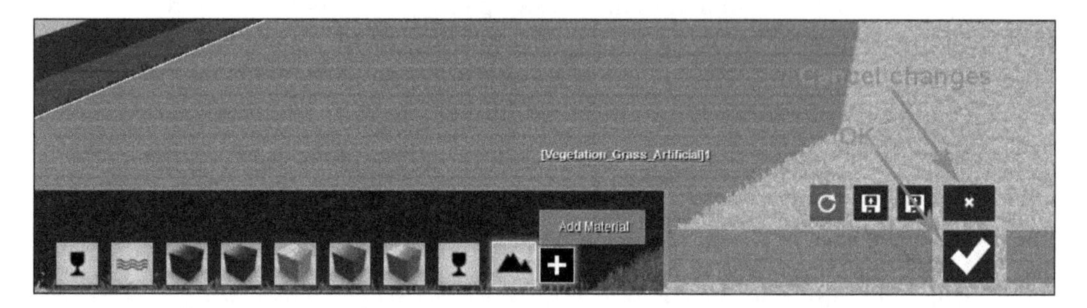

When we put the mouse over the surface, the name of the material used on the modeling package is displayed as shown in the previous screenshot. So, how can we set a name for the material? The screenshot shows that the material used for the grass is called `[Vegetation_Grass_Artifical]1` and this was defined in the modeling package, which in this case was SketchUp.

Once we click on the surface, Lumion opens the materials library where we can discover all the materials organized in twelve tabs, as shown in the following screenshot:

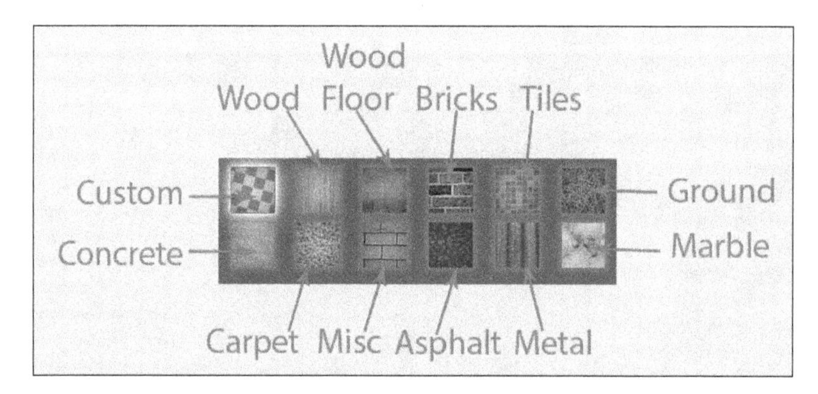

Now, it's your turn to start adding materials. When you are done, check if every material was assigned correctly and save the materials by clicking on the **OK** button.

Naming materials

We still need to explore a few more points to fully master Lumion's materials. Something that really helps is having the habit of taking some time and renaming the materials prior to exporting the 3D model. This is extremely useful later when we have to tweak a material or change it.

Earlier, it was mentioned that when we put the mouse over the surface, the material's name appears. Have a look at the following screenshot:

The material in this window is called `Translucent_Glass_Blue`, but that probably is not the best name. Why?

This scene is fairly simple and we can probably have a number of materials between 15 and 20 materials. In a scene like this, it is not too difficult to recognize where the material is assigned. When we put the mouse over the thumbnail, not only is the material's name displayed, but Lumion highlights the surface(s) that have the material assigned. So, why should we lose time renaming the materials?

This is not a requirement to work with Lumion, but it can substantially improve your workflow when working with big and complex scenes. Imagine developing a scene with a massive building or buildings and trying to find where `Translucent_Glass_Blue` is assigned. Was this assigned to a window or a vase? It is true that Lumion highlights the surface where the materials are assigned, but that is not going to help you if the scene has, for example, 700 m^2.

However, if you make a good habit of naming the materials, you will not have to orbit the model around trying to find the material assigned here. Now, while tweaking, you notice a mistake because there is a material that was assigned to the wrong surface.

Removing a material

While assigning materials, it is natural that at a certain point, we will make a mistake and select the wrong material. If our goal is just to change the material, the most logical way to correct this mistake is by selecting another material. What if we assign a material to a surface, but in reality we want to use the imported material?

Once again, to work with the imported 3D models, we need to click on the **Import** menu and click on the Edit Materials button. However, there is a slight difference between the first time we were starting to add materials and now that some materials are assigned to the 3D model. The difference is that now when we place the mouse over the 3D model, Lumion doesn't highlight the entire 3D model as before. Instead, Lumion highlights the materials we have assigned to a 3D model and when we click with the left mouse button, Lumion directly opens the material, as shown in the following screenshot:

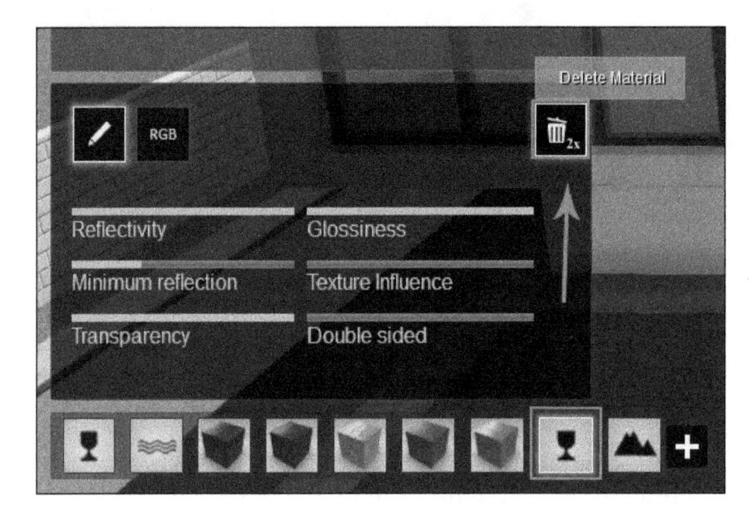

As shown in the previous screenshot, it is on the material properties that we can find the Delete Material button, and we have to click twice to delete the material.

Now that we know the basics of working with Lumion's materials, it is a good idea to expand our knowledge of what is available to change and tweak the materials. These next sections will be purely technical, but the understanding of the concepts mentioned can make a difference between a beautiful render and an OK render.

Modifying and tweaking Lumion's materials

To fully master Lumion's materials, we need to explore some of the parameters available. When we assign a material to a surface, as mentioned before, we are specifying how the surface should react to the light. Why can we easily recognize if an object is made of metal, wood, or glass? It is true that the color plays a big role, but things such as reflection, refraction, and glossiness are key points to achieve a believable material.

We will cover a few points that are useful while assigning materials and in order to create a not-so-boring section, let's see a few materials used for the example mentioned in this book.

The scale and texture positions

Lumion's materials are good looking and can be optimized for the best result possible, but this doesn't mean that we just assign a material and it is done. There are always small adjustments we need to perform such as adjusting the scale of the texture and the position of the texture in relation to the 3D model. The next screenshot shows an example of what we need to do in some situations:

The image on the left shows that the bricks are too big for the wall. To solve this issue, we need to use the **Scale** setting, as highlighted in the screenshot, to create something more realistic and with the correct proportion, as shown in the image on the right of the preceding screenshot. This setting is found under the **Properties** menu, which appears when we add the material to a surface.

With this issue resolved, there is an extra detail that we can use to turn this flat surface into something more interesting to our eyes. How can we do this? Again, let's have a look at the following screenshot:

In the left image, we can easily spot a flat surface with an assigned texture, and this could be OK in a situation when the surface is going to be far away from the camera. Also, this surface gives an idea of the material used. However, the image on the right side shows the same image, but in this case, we used the **Bump** setting to add more depth and realism to the surface. We are not adding more geometry; instead, we are given instructions on how the light should react with the surface and because of the texture used, we can achieve this level of detail. We will see how we can create a similar texture to use with your own materials.

Another example of how we can tweak the texture use on a surface is shown in the following screenshot:

The image on the left of the screenshot shows that the material used doesn't match the squares in the 3D model, as exemplified by the red lines. To solve this issue, we need to open the second menu, called **Placing**, as highlighted in the previous screenshot. In most situations, we should use the **X**, **Y**, and **Z** settings to adjust the position of the texture.

[Remember that if you need to perform small increments on the sliders, you can press and hold the *Shift* key to do so.]

The **Pitch**, **Heading**, and **Bank** settings can also be used to rotate and move the texture. This is somehow ambiguous, but each setting will behave differently depending on whether the texture is on a horizontal or vertical surface.

However, for the example shown in the previous screenshot, we adjusted the **X** and **Z** settings so that the texture matches the 3D model. The red lines show where the tiles should be, and using accurate adjustments, it was possible to match the texture with the geometry, as shown in the image on the right-hand side. This is not necessarily something that is crucial to secure a beautiful material because this is just a small detail. However, when we combine all the small details, this can be a difference between a good and a perfect render.

The other two settings are found on the **Placing** menu and will be covered under the *Common problems (troubleshooting)* section.

Reflection, glossiness, and more

The control we have over the materials is not just about scaling and adjusting the texture. We can tweak the way the material reacts to the light and how it reflects that light. To explain some of these properties, it will be great if you add the `Concrete_018_1024` material found under the **Concrete** tab to a surface in your 3D model. This will help us to stay on the same page and understand how each setting contributes to the look of a material, and most importantly, how you can totally transform a material, creating an even wider range of materials available.

The first step, under the **Properties** menu, is to increase the value in the **Reflectivity** setting to 1 by dragging the slider, as shown in the following screenshot:

Now, the surface of the 3D model is highly reflective, but what is reflection? Perhaps the best way to understand this is by looking at the following diagram:

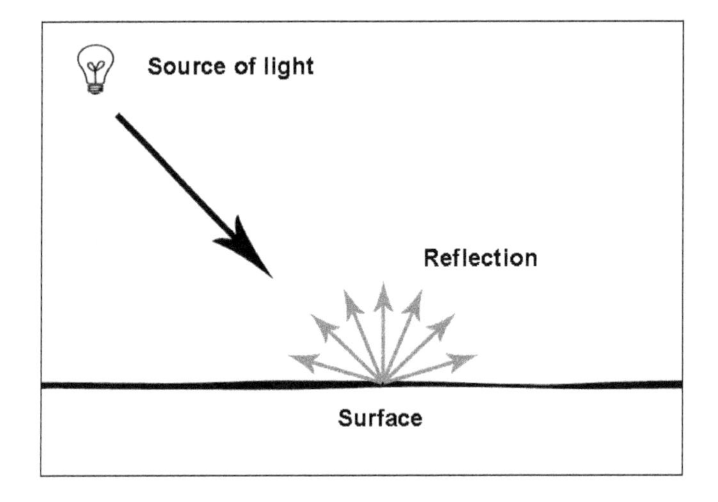

In plain English, when a light ray hits a surface it is reflected, and the angle at which the light ray hits the surface is equal to the angle at which it is reflected. However, this is a little bit more complex and the way the light ray is reflected also depends on the type of the material. In the case of the concrete material which we are using, unless the concrete gets a layer of varnish, it doesn't make sense to have the concrete so reflective. However, at the same time, we should not remove all the reflectivity because even cloth materials have a certain level of reflectivity.

Along with this setting, we have two more settings to control the way the reflection in a material behaves. If we pick the **Reflection Colorize** setting and start to move the slider from one extreme to another, it is easy to understand why the word "colorize" is used to describe the setting. Here, we can control how the material will reflect the environment and the sources of light present in our scene.

And we can go even further on tweaking the reflection by turning our attention to the **Reflection Falloff** setting. We could also use the word Fresnel to describe what this setting does to the reflection.

Fresnel

Fresnel is the amount of reflection visible on a surface, which depends on the viewing angle. It may be difficult to see this effect on the following screenshot:

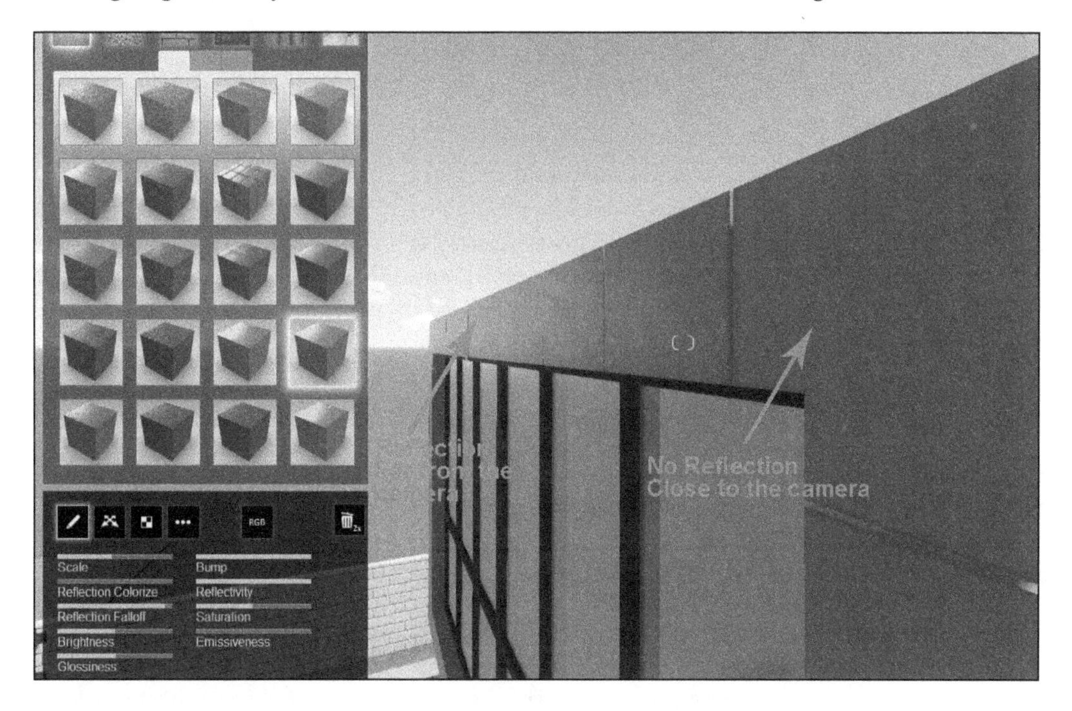

However, try to place the camera at the same angle and start increasing the **Reflection Falloff** setting, and when we look at the surface or when the surface is close to the camera, we will not see much reflected light. When we have the camera angle similar to the one shown in the preceding screenshot, we see many more reflections on the surface. However, we still have a few more settings that need to be covered. The **Brightness** setting is self-explanatory—a high value creates an extreme bright material and a low value an extreme dark material. However, what about the **Glossiness** setting?

Controlling the refection sharpness

When working with Lumion's materials, we have the option to control how sharp the reflections are with the aid of the **Glossiness** slider. Usually, the glossiness texture defines the uniformity of the surface in terms of visible texture and defects and this can create a very shiny surface with sharp reflections or a blurry reflection, as shown in the following screenshot:

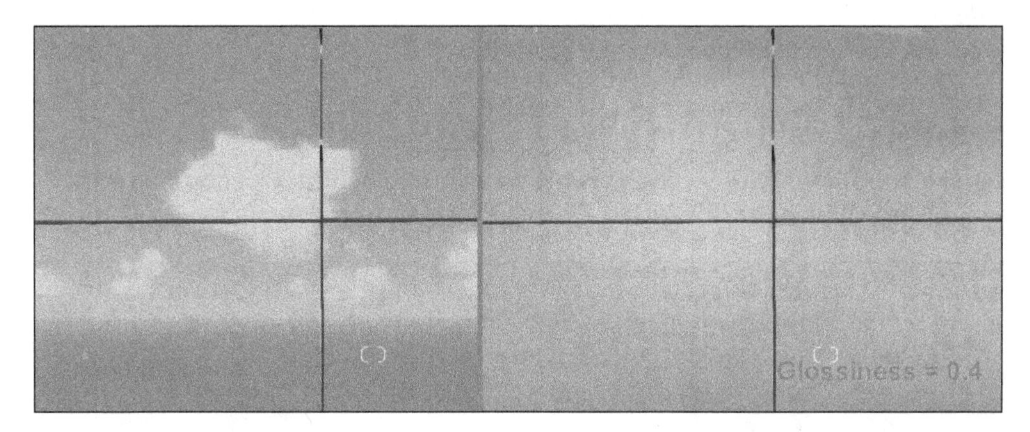

This setting is useful when we want to create a material for a 3D model and show that the object is new, or create a material for a 3D model and show that the object has some age to it. Two more settings that are worth mentioning in this menu are **Saturation** and **Emissiveness**.

Saturation

Saturation is a uniform increase in the intensity of all colors in the material. This can result in oversaturation of certain colors, resulting in loss of details in those areas, leaving them looking too orange and unnatural. On the other hand, when we decrease the saturation, we will transform the texture used into a grayscale texture.

In some situations, a texture may look dull because of the light used or because of other aspects, but a small increment of the **Saturation** setting will help to bring out the colors again. Finally, there is another useful setting when working with lamps and other sorts of lighting objects.

Emissiveness

The best way to understand what this setting does is to have a go and increase the **Emissiveness** slider to the `100` value. The concrete material that we have been using is glowing, but certainly, this is something we don't desire for a concrete material. Is there any useful application?

One practical way is using this setting to simulate the glow effect that appears on a bright bulb. This means that we have to plan beforehand and see if we will use any lamp in the scene and if so, create a material specifically to mimic the bulb glow. Another possibility is having neon signs, and in this case, the entire surface is used to create the same effect. A third possibility is to reproduce the burning wood in a fireplace. Try selecting a wooden material, particularly one where there is a better contrast between dark and light areas, and increase the **Emissiveness** value to `100`. After placing a fire emitter on top of it, we can easily create a fireplace with some burning wood.

By now, we may think that this is all the knowledge we need to have in order to create believable materials. It is true that this is essential to create good materials, but if we want to master Lumion, there is a more obscure menu that we need to cover, as well. However, we will see this under the *The mysterious Advanced Options menu* section.

If you are amazed with the control and quality of the materials available, you will certainly understand how powerful Lumion is after having seen some of the *special* materials available.

An extra touch with the custom materials

The **Custom** menu is the initial menu that appears when we add a new material to the 3D model. We have nine custom materials available that are crucial to every project at this stage. We will probably use the materials shown in the following screenshot:

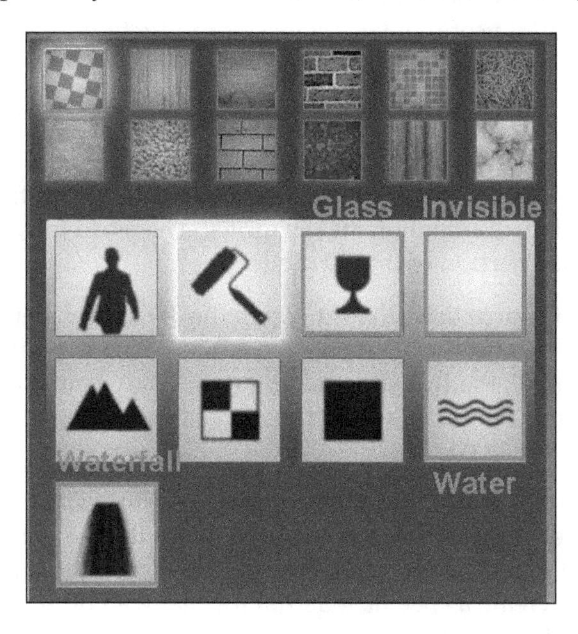

Some of the other materials will be covered in the following section when we start to create our own materials. You also can recognize the Landscape material that was covered in the *The Landscape material* section in *Chapter 2, Creating a Project in Lumion.*

Just a quick reminder for this material: the Landscape material is a great material that can be easily assigned to a 3D terrain that then blends with the rest of the terrain. This material is so powerful that it lets you change the textures or even paint textures on the imported 3D terrain.

Working with the Glass material

One of the initial materials we assigned to a 3D model was the **Glass** material. Glass is an important part of modern architecture, and we can see this in buildings such as the Louvre Pyramid, the Farnsworth House, the Glass Houseboat, and the National Grand Theater of China, just to mention a few.

By now, you would have added this material to some surfaces of your 3D model, and as you can see, the result is good, but it could be a little better. There are several ways to improve this material. We will see one of them later in *Chapter 6, Lighting in Lumion*, where we will use the Reflection cube, and a second (more realistic) way in *Chapter 7, Creating Realistic Visualizations*. It is natural that we would want to improve the look of the glass, but for now, let's focus our attention on adding just the materials. Feel free, however, to jump to these chapters and tweak the Glass material.

Although the following material has little to do with believable and stunning materials, we may find it useful in later stages of production.

Hiding geometry with the Invisible material

The **Invisible** material can be found next to the **Glass** button and when we are assigning this material, the entire surface disappears and this surface will not be used to calculate global illumination and shadows. This is, in fact, really useful when there is a need to *hide* a section of the 3D model.

It is true that the best course of action is to open the 3D model, perform the necessary changes, and then re-import the 3D model in Lumion. However, if we need to remove something small, the **Invisible** material can easily lend a hand, and in *Chapter 5, Creating Your 3D World*, we will see a practical example.

Another situation in which we may find this material useful is when we are creating a camera angle and we intersect it with the geometry. This can be really annoying even if we use a super slow camera to accurately place it. Again, the **Invisible** material can be used to hide some walls, but we still need to go back to the 3D modeling package to create a specific material for that wall or other section and re-import the 3D model in Lumion.

Another possibility is to assign this material temporarily to an exterior or interior wall in order to have a better view and tweak interior objects. However, with experience, you will eventually find other useful and practical applications.

Although this material didn't bring something special to improve the quality of our project, the next two materials definitely will.

Creating swimming pools and other water surfaces

Every time we see a good 3D render of a house, most of the time, there is a common element in all of them. Swimming pools delight everyone no matter where they come from. Creating swimming pools in Lumion is so easy, but at the same time so powerful that you will wonder how this is even possible.

Using the fantastic Water material

The project we will use to show some of the examples have a big swimming pool where we can use the **Water** material. To apply this material, we need to add a plane beforehand, not on the top of the swimming pool, but a few centimeters below to reproduce the water line, and as shown in the following screenshot, the result is really good even with the default settings:

There are few settings we can tweak to improve the look of the water and make it even more believable. By the way, a swimming pool looks superb with the `Tiles_027_1024` material and you can find this material under the **Tiles** library.

In the initial setting, what we can start tweaking is the **Bump factor** setting where a value close to `0` creates a flat surface, but what we need is to increase this value to something close to `1`.

The second setting that is necessary to adjust is the **Tiling** slider, and this is because of the size of the surface and consequently the size of the reflections in the water. If you try to adjust this slider and at the same time look at the reflections, you will see how they change in size, which makes us perceive the water surface as big or small.

When we increase both these values, the water surface also gets more agitated, so this needs to be balanced with the mood we are trying to achieve. However, you may be thinking: what about the rest of the settings? What can we do with them?

Every project has it own requirements and there may be some situations in which we need to tweak the way the water reacts with the light from the sun or other direct source. The **Reflection Power**, **Specular Low**, **Fresnel Power**, **Anisotropic**, and **Specular High** are settings that deal precisely with how the water reacts with light, but most of these settings are only perceived when the camera is placed almost parallel to the water surface. This means that if you try to tweak the water with a camera placed perpendicular to the surface, you will not see any changes there at all.

Two settings that are worth exploring are:

- **Specular Low**: This controls the strength of the reflections on the water surface. For example, to create a crystal clear swimming pool, we can remove the **Specular Low** settings to produce a water surface with no reflections.
- **Caustics Tiling**: This is another setting that needs our attention depending on the size of the swimming pool. The next screenshot shows the difference between a low and high value:

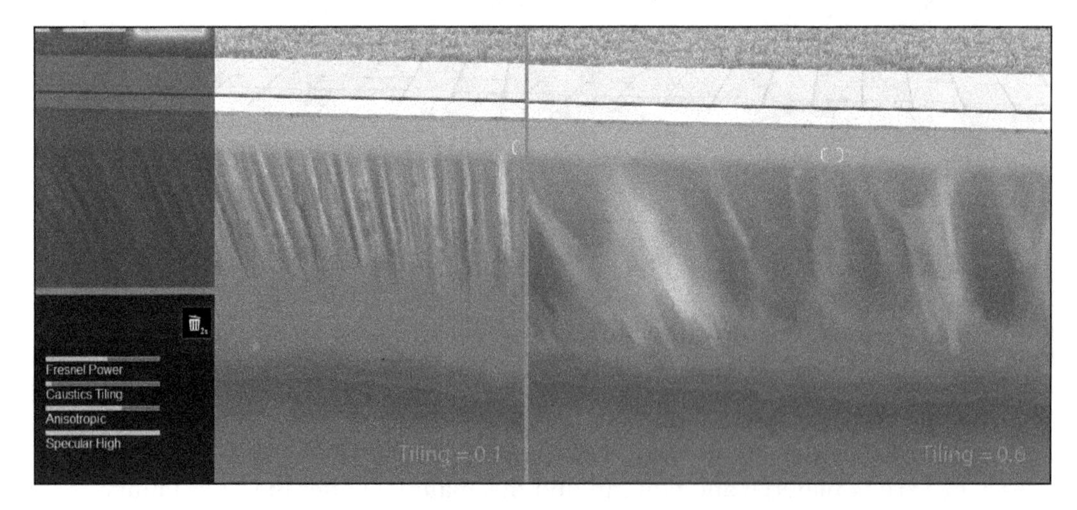

With these settings in mind, we can start tweaking the appearance of the swimming pool. And then, if necessary, we can open the **Color** menu to tweak the color of the water. In this menu, we can also change the saturation, and this will help in giving depth to the swimming pool, as shown in the following screenshot:

These settings are most useful when dealing with swimming pools that are deeper in some areas. And now it is time for another water material that can be used in some particular situations.

Exploring the Waterfall material

As the name suggests, the **Waterfall** material was created with waterfalls in mind, and this material also works perfectly to create other bodies of water. However, the Waterfall material can also be used to mimic water running. There are several applications on an architectural visualization. If we stop to think for a few seconds, there are things such as exterior and interior taps, and we can also reproduce a shower with running water.

For this to work, we need to create some geometry for the running water, something like this:

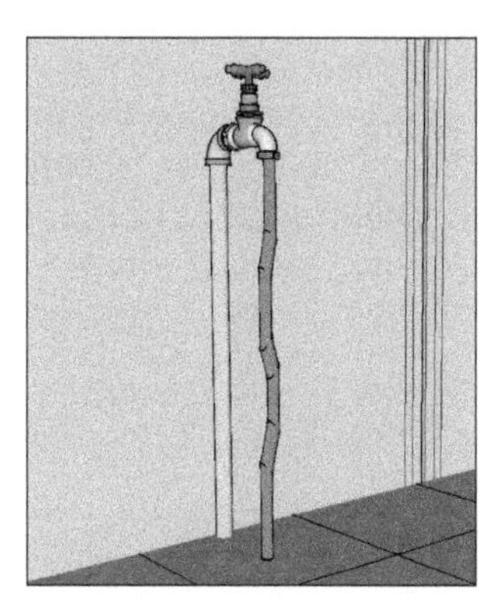

Then, in Lumion, we will have to assign the Waterfall material to the geometry, and the initial result is not great because the water will be running really fast. When assigning this material, we can easily see how the settings are the same as those found in the Water material. And to reduce the water velocity, we have to tweak the **Tiling** setting, as shown in the following screenshot:

However, we have to keep in mind that this is very limited and if we have a camera close to the water it may not look great, but it will do the trick from a certain distance. And of course, we can use this material for waterfalls, if by any chance we have one.

Advantages of using Lumion's materials

By now we have a strong understanding of how we can assign and tweak Lumion's materials, and the benefits of using these materials are quite clear. They are prepared and optimized to produce the best results possible, giving us the opportunity to focus our time on creating more detailed 3D models or increasing the quality of the project with small details and effects.

Certainly, you are aware that it is possible to use the materials imported along with the 3D model, and the next section is going to help us see how we can use the materials that were created in the 3D modeling package.

Using imported materials in Lumion

Using materials is a key aspect to working in Lumion. If we don't have even the simplest material assigned to a surface, when the 3D model is imported in Lumion, we have no way to work with Lumion's materials. This means we have to apply materials to each surface; these materials can be simple colors or we can use a material with a diffuse texture.

What is a diffuse texture? In simple terms, a diffuse texture is the image file with color information that will transform a surface into a brick wall or metal floor. Some examples of diffuse textures are shown in the following screenshot:

How can we use these textures in our project? And also, what are the benefits of using them?

Creating materials in this instance is not a very complex task because we only focus on using a diffuse texture for the surfaces of the 3D model. It is always a good idea to use only simple materials; for example, when working with 3DS Max or Maya, the materials we have to use are the Standard and Lambert, respectively. Materials from other render engines, such as V-ray and Mental Ray, are not supported. If we use these in the 3D model, when this is imported, the 3D model appears with no textures. There is no point in using textures in other slots, such as glossiness, specular, and bump, because Lumion will only read the texture used in the diffuse slot. However, where do we get the textures to use in the material?

Transforming images into textures

Sometimes, Lumion doesn't have what we need in terms of materials. In some projects, it is common for the client to provide a document where he or she chooses the types of materials that need to be used in the building. And in some situations, even the manufacturer is mentioned, giving us the responsibility to create a Lumion project close to the reality.

There are some places on the Internet where we can find good images that can be used, and maybe here we can find what we need:

- Flickr
- Stock.xchg
- iStockphoto
- deviantART
- CGTextures (probably one of the best ones)

Some of these websites are paid, some provide some free textures, and others have a limit of textures to be downloaded daily. So, the best option is to start creating your own library using a camera, and you don't need a very expensive camera to take some photos to be used later. Companies that sell construction materials often provide free samples that can be used to create excellent textures.

Irrespective of whether you are using images from your camera or a website, we still need image-editing software, such as Adobe Photoshop, which is a paid or free software like Gimp.

We need this software not only to correct some imperfections in the image, but also to create seamless textures. What they are and how to create them is what we will see in the next section.

Creating seamless textures

Firstly, we need to understand what a seamless texture is. A **seamless texture** is an image that can be placed side by side with itself without creating a noticeable boundary between the two copies. Seamless textures are relatively easy to make, but making them look less repetitive is something else and this process can, in some situations, be time-consuming. This is one of the reasons why CGTextures is such a great place to look for images, because usually we can download tiled textures, which are the same as seamless textures. Although this book is not a texturing book, in the next section, we will have a quick overview of the basic steps to create a seamless texture both in Photoshop and Gimp, but you need to have at least some basic notions of where the tools are and what they do.

Gimp – how to create a seamless texture

Creating seamless textures in Gimp can be easy in some situations because of the **Make Seamless** filter. This filter works fine with some images where there aren't any specific patterns, and this can be found under the **Filters** menu and on the **Map** category, as shown in the following screenshot:

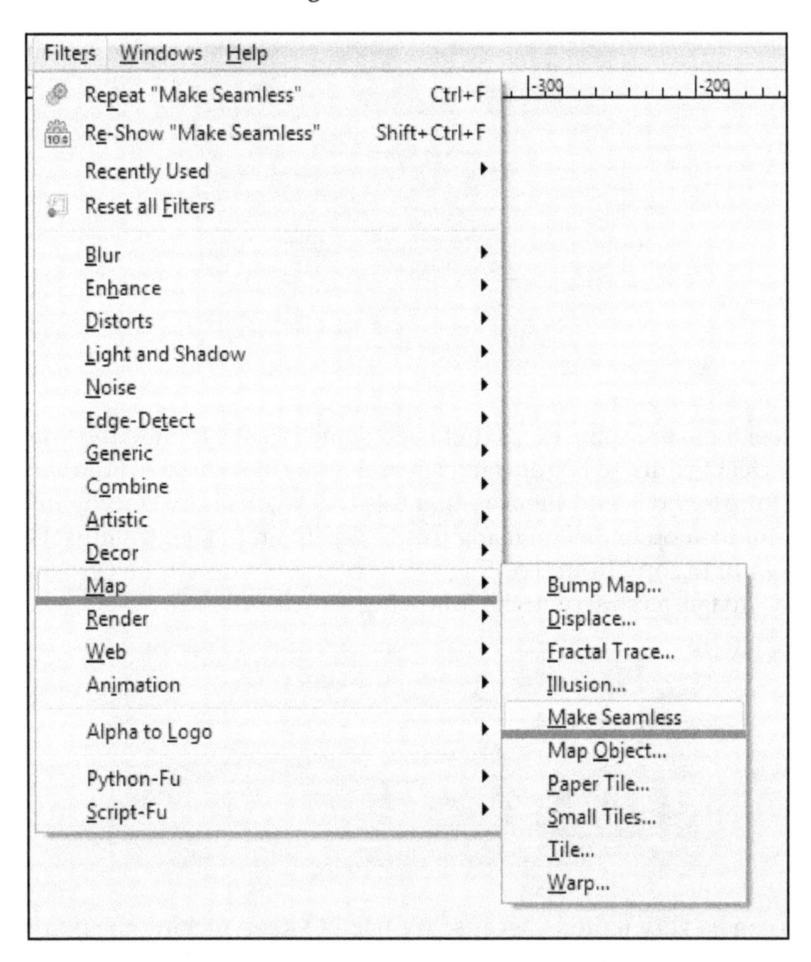

Now, let's see a more difficult way. One thing that is important to keep in mind when creating a seamless texture is to have a photo with not many eye-catching features. The lighting also needs to be even because even a small difference in lighting will be noticeable in a seamless texture.

To start with, we need to transform an image into a square using the **Crop** tool (*Shift* + *C*) and crop the image into something such as 1024 x 1024. Now, let's start creating a seamless texture, also known as a tileable texture, by using the **Offset** tool (*Shift* + *Ctrl* + *O*), as shown in the following screenshot:

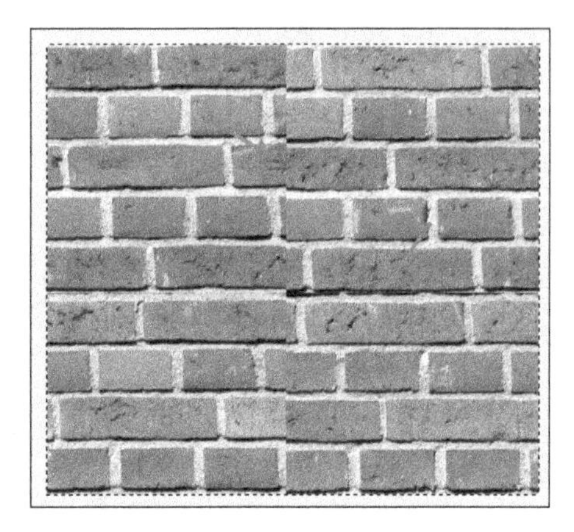

As we can see, there are some areas that need some tweaks to hide the seams and create the perfect texture to be repeated several times in a surface. For this, we have to use the **Clone** tool (*C*), and the way that this tool works is by cloning information from one point to another. When using this tool with an image, we must GIMP the location we want to copy from. For this, we have to hold down the *Ctrl* key and click on the source image, as shown in the following screenshot:

The process can be very tedious because we need to keep picking the point to be copied and copy to another section of the image, but after just a few minutes of work, we will have something like this:

It is the same image, but in this case, we cannot see any seam or edge that would look horrible in the material. Now, we have a seamless texture that can be applied to a surface without any problems. Now, let's see how we can do the same thing, but with Photoshop.

There is a great plugin whose purpose is to generate large textures from a small sample. It can be found here:

`http://gimp-texturize.sourceforge.net/`

Photoshop – how to create a seamless texture

If you have a look at the previous topic, you will find that the process to create a seamless texture in Photoshop is practically the same.

Using the **Crop** tool (*C*), we will create a square texture and then offset the image using the **Offset** tool, as shown in the following screenshot:

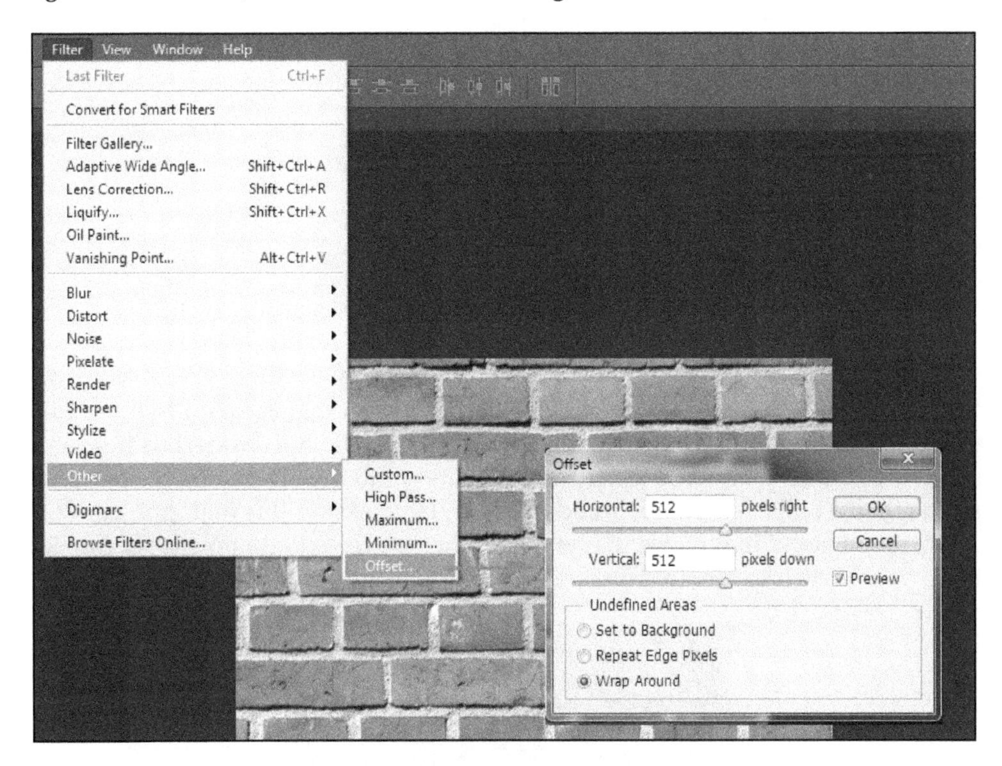

In the **Offset** window, adjust the **Horizontal** and **Vertical** fields to half of what the pixel dimensions of your image are. The image in the example is 1024 x 1024, so we are using the 512 value with the **Wrap Around** setting.

Next, we have to select **Clone Stamp Tool** (*S*), and to use this tool, we have to hold down the *Alt* key, click on a specific point in the image, and then paint the area that needs to be corrected. After a few adjustments, we should have a perfect image to be used in the 3D model.

Using UVs in Lumion

Along with the texture, we can also use the UV's that are created in 3D modeling packages, such as 3DS Max, Maya, Blender and Modo, just to mention a few. UV mapping refers to the way each 3D surface is mapped to a 2D texture. This means that if we have UVs on the surface, we can have accurate control of how the texture is presented on that surface. The following image shows an example of how UVs are used to control the way that the texture affects the surface:

In this case, we have the UVs for a tree, but if we want to use these UVs to control the texture in Lumion, we have to use the **Standard** material that is found in the **Custom** tab. After importing the 3D model, we need to click on the **Edit Materials** button found in the **Import** menu and assign a new material to the 3D model. Then, on the **Custom** tab, we will click on the **Standard** material to assign this material, but don't worry; you are not going to lose the texture. What we have to do now is set the **Scale** slider to `0`, as shown in the next screenshot:

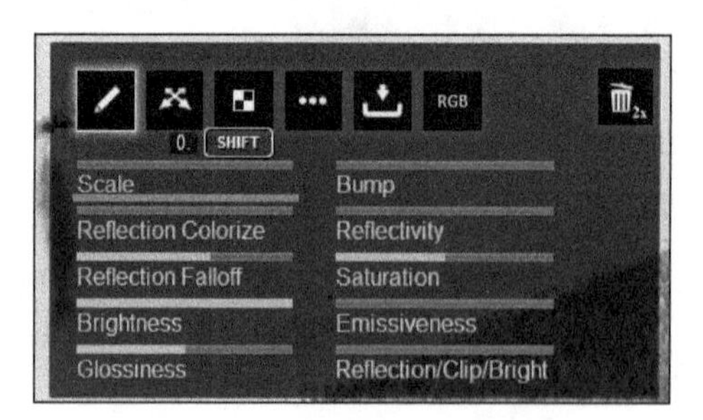

With complex 3D models, it is very beneficial to make use of UVs because usually with one image, we can provide color and texture to large areas in 3D models avoiding the use of several materials.

We also have another benefit from creating our own textures, which is using a texture to control how the reflections behave on a surface with the material.

Controlling the reflection with an alpha channel

When we are creating a texture, there is also the possibility to produce an alpha channel. So, what is an alpha channel? The alpha channel is essentially a mask that can have a degree of opacity and specifies how the pixel's color in an image is merged with another pixel when the two are overlaid. However, what does it mean after all and how can it be useful for us?

An image is created by merging three channels, and each channel represents the **Red**, **Green**, and **Blue** color. This creates the image we can see and use for a material, but we can create an additional channel, called **Alpha**, that can contain additional information, as shown in the following screenshot:

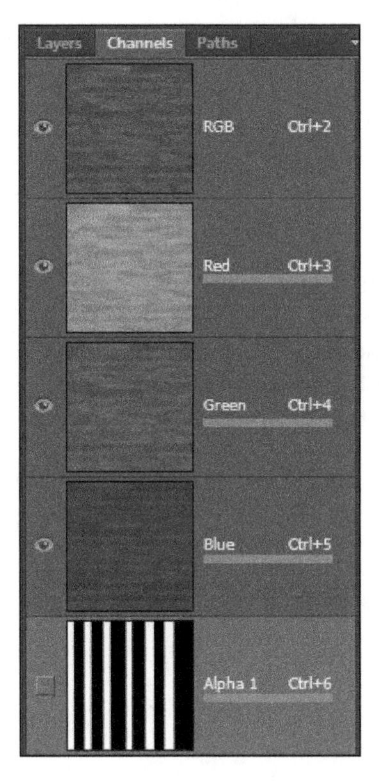

In this case, we have a wooden texture. When we check the **Channels** tab, we can see that there is one channel for **Red**, **Green**, and **Blue**, and the thumbnail on the top shows the result when these three channels are combined.

Also notice that the alpha channel has some information, and in this case, white stripes. Although this information is not visible in the image, Lumion can read it and use it to control the surface's reflection. When we assign the **Standard** material to the surface, initially we cannot perceive any change, but as soon as we start to increase the **Reflectivity** property, the result is obvious, as shown in the following screenshot:

The black area blocks the reflection and the white stripes show the reflection, but in what ways can this be useful in a project?

In the alpha channel, we can use values between the black and white colors, which means that we can use shades of gray. With this in mind, we can control how some surfaces reflect in the environment or in some cases, decrease the reflection in one area without compromising other areas in the 3D model.

An additional way is to improve the result by using a normal map. Later in this chapter, we will cover an easy way to create a normal map, but a normal map is used to create the bump effect. For the texture that was used in the example, we need to create the normal map with the same stripes and increase the **Bump** slider. This will add some depth, increasing the bump effect on the surface.

The following topic is going to cover a feature that can only work with an alpha channel.

Clipping a surface with an alpha channel

Lumion can use an alpha channel to create some interesting tweaks, and in this case, we can clip a surface. In the previous topic, we saw that the black area blocks the reflection and the white area shows the reflections. The same principle is applied, but in this case, the black area removes the geometry and the white area leaves the geometry visible.

However, you may wonder: why is this practical? Let's have a look at the following screenshot:

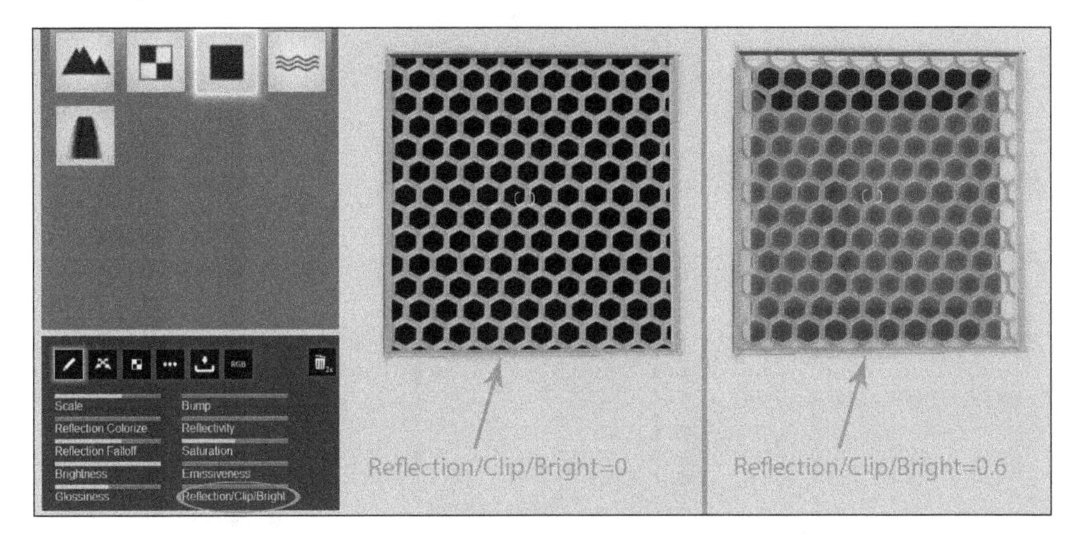

In the previous screenshot, we can see a ventilation grid, and in this case, we have simply applied a grid texture. However, along with this grid texture, we have also saved an alpha channel. In this alpha channel, the metal grid is filled with the white color and the holes are filled with the black color.

When the texture is loaded in the **Standard** material, we need to pick the **Reflection/Clip/Bright** slider, which by default is set to `0`. Then, we have to use a value between 0.5 and 0.9, and Lumion will read the alpha channel in the texture and use that information to remove the geometry. With an alpha channel, we can, in seconds, create the illusion of a very complex geometry. This technique saves time in the 3D modeling process, allowing you to spend more time focusing on other sections of the project.

The Glass special feature

Although we can create our own textures, there are a few materials that cannot be fully represented only by images. We saw previously how believable and great the Water material is, but we also have the Glass material. The Glass material is a special material because we can blend a texture with this material in Lumion. As an example, we are going to use a texture that, although not the best, will make it easier to see the results:

In some projects, we may have to mimic various types of glass, such as hammered and security glass, but with Lumion's Glass material, that is practically impossible to reproduce. However, we can add a texture to the surface and then tweak the Glass material in order to achieve something close to the reality.

Hammered or security glass can be difficult to perceive, and this is the reason why we will use the texture shown in the previous screenshot.

So, after importing or reloading the 3D model in Lumion, the first thing we have to do is assign the Glass material to the surface with the texture. When we do this, the texture is replaced by Lumion's material, but that's not the end of it. Notice that one of the settings available to tweak the material is called **Texture Influence**, so let's bring the slider to the maximum value, which is `1`. At this point, we can start seeing the texture on the glass, and if this is enough for you, just leave it. Otherwise, if you tweak the **Transparency** slider to something like `0.7`, the result is more noticeable, as shown in the following screenshot:

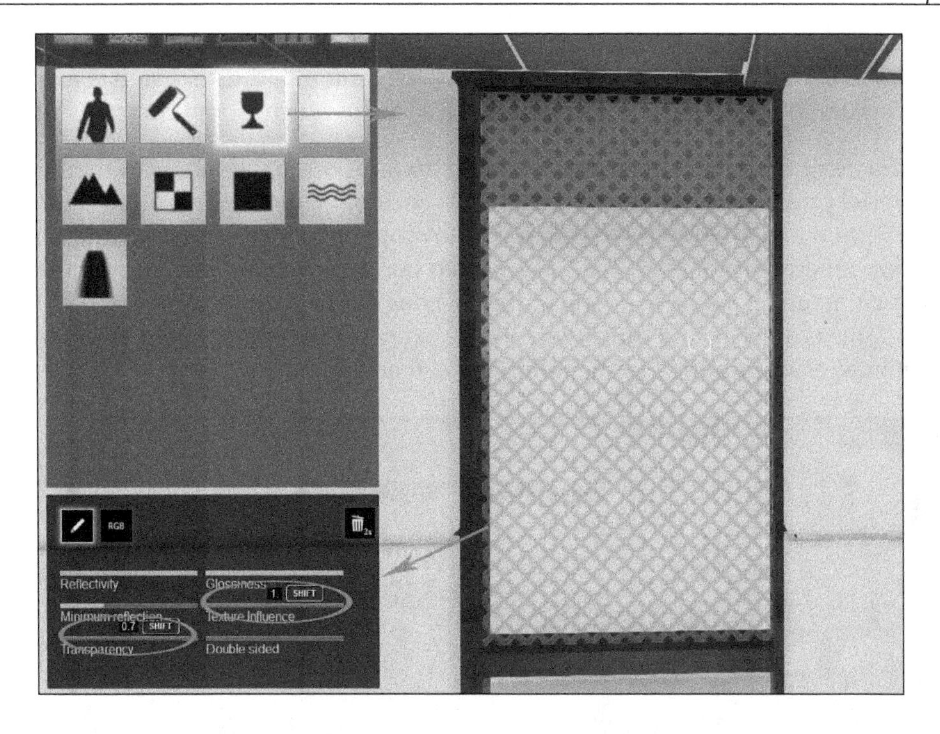

Another useful application of this feature is reproducing the rain drops on a window surface.

Now that we have a full understanding of how to create and use our own textures, it is easy to understand the benefits. We are not limited to the textures available in the Lumion library and we can have better control over how the textures should react to light. However, don't think that just because we are using our textures, we are stuck with one specific result. We can actually combine the best of both worlds by optimizing Lumion's materials and our own textures.

Creating materials in Lumion

Creating a material in Lumion is a mix between what we saw in the previous topics and using the Standard material. The reason why it is a mix is because to use the Standard material, we need at least one texture to use a diffuse texture slot. This topic is slightly different from the previous one because although we created the textures, here we are using Lumion's material to assign textures to a surface.

Before we start covering how the Standard material can be used, let's explore another possibility to create materials in Lumion. Let's assume we have a concrete texture to use in a surface, but for some reason, we are in a rush and don't have much time to tweak the material to get the same concrete look found in other Lumion materials.

Firstly, we have to open the Lumion material library and try to find a material that is similar to the texture we have. After finding the material, the next step is to assign the material to the surface, and this will work as a way to cut some corners. But how?

Well, after assigning the material, all we have to do is open the **Textures** menu in the material properties and here we will find two slots with textures. One is the diffuse texture and when we select it, a window opens to load a new texture. The other slot, called normal map, is also imported because we need this information to add the bump effect, so have a look at the *Creating bump maps* section found in this chapter. This is an easy and quick way to use external textures without too many adjustments, as exemplified in the following screenshot:

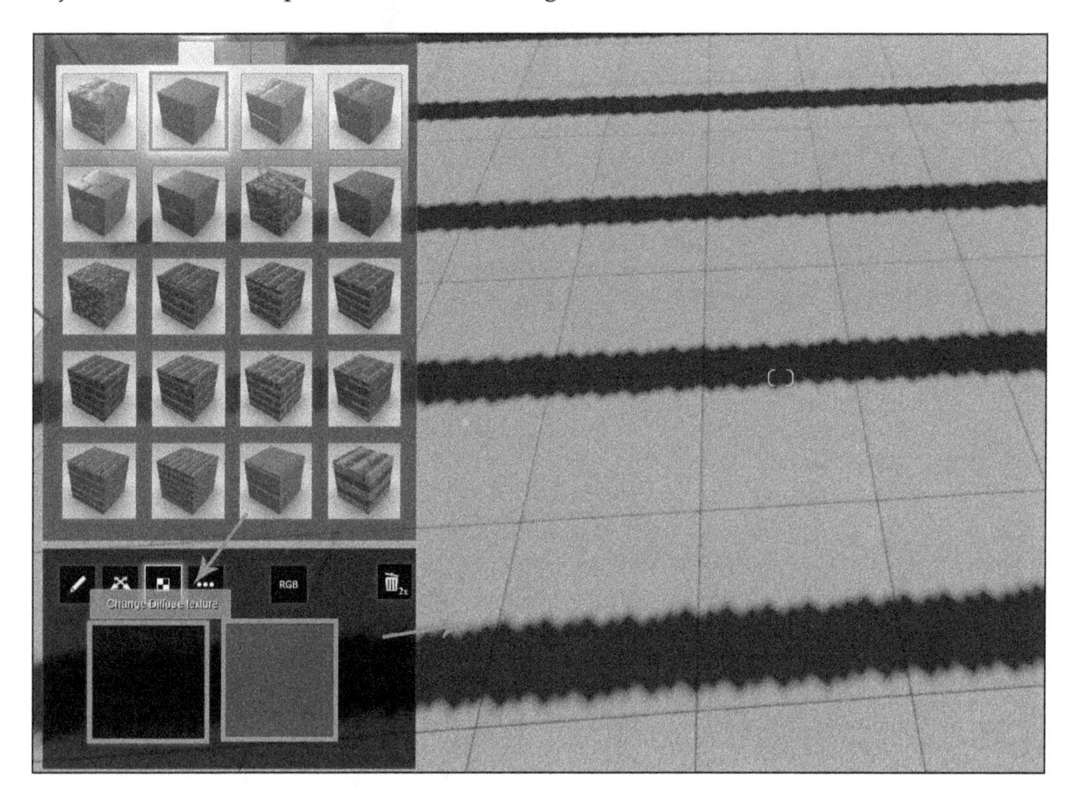

When there is more time, the best habit is to use the Standard material that we are going to explore in the next topic.

The Standard material

The Standard material is Lumion's way of giving you the opportunity to start a material from scratch. Almost every material found in Lumion is produced using this Standard material; this shows how powerful Lumion's material system can be.

The benefit of using this method is the level of control we have over the materials and this, combined with all we saw in the previous topic, will certainly help to produce the best result possible. A detailed 3D model is something important, but a good material and texture is equally crucial to create beautiful renders in Lumion.

One benefit of using the Standard material with an imported material is that the Standard material recognizes and keeps the texture applied to the surface if there is one, as shown in the following screenshot:

The use of the Standard material is simple and the settings were already covered when we explained how to use Lumion's materials. However, there is an extra menu that is important to know if we want to fully master Lumion.

The mysterious Advanced Options menu

The **Advanced Options** menu can be found next to the **Textures** menu. This menu is not essential to create most of the materials, but when we start to work with more reflective surfaces, the **Advanced Options** menu gives us the control we need to adjust how the light reacts with the surface. The control we have is not seen when the camera is perpendicular to the surface, but instead when the camera is looking at the surface from different angles.

Creating a normal map

The need to create a normal map has been mentioned throughout the chapter so that we can add a bump effect to the surface. As mentioned earlier, we will not add geometry, but instead provide information on how the light reacts with the surface. The next screenshot shows the difference between the diffuse and normal maps:

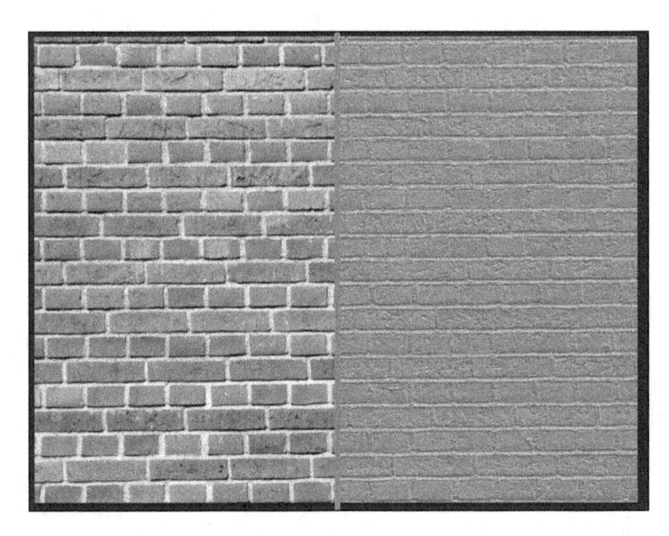

How can we create this normal map? There are several commercial applications in the market, such as CrazyBump and nDo2, that will create a normal map from any diffuse texture. However, there is a free Photoshop script called nDo that is from the same creator of nDo2, which despite having less functions, still produces good results.

To find more about this Photoshop script and how to use it, visit `http://www.philipk.net/ndo.html`.

Before we finish this long chapter, let's have a look at some of the useful features necessary to organize the materials we created with the Standard material.

Organizing materials

After producing some projects with Lumion, we will get to a point where some materials are the same as those we used previously in another project. However, is there any possibility to create our material library in Lumion? It is not possible to create a library inside Lumion, but we can save the material and then later use it for another project. Keep in mind that this will only work with Standard materials and not the native Lumion materials.

When we add a Standard material to the 3D model, notice that there is a new button that is not visible with the other materials:

This menu gives us the following three buttons initially:

- **Copy**: This allows us to copy one material to another inside the scene. When we click on this button, a new one appears called **Paste**.
- **Save material**: Press this button to save a Lumion material file (extension `.lmf`).
- **Load material**: This will load the Lumion material file that you saved previously.

There is another way to save the materials, but this option saves the materials of the entire 3D model.

Saving and loading material sets

While assigning materials to the 3D model, you probably noticed these two buttons:

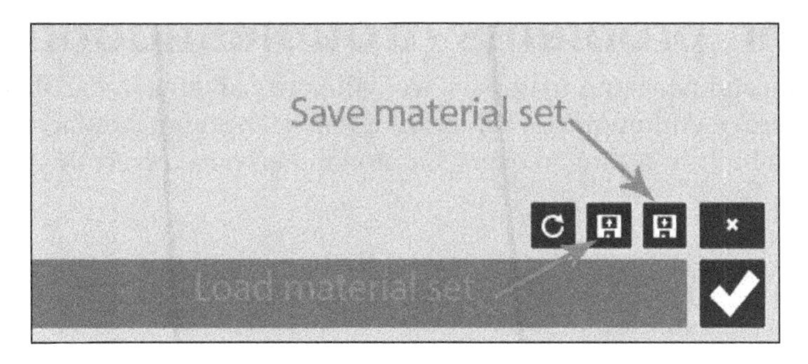

The use of this option is somehow subjective because we can save the entire set of materials used for this 3D model, but when loaded, the material will only be applied to the same surface. The file we save with the materials is called the Material list (extension `.mtt`) and when the same file is loaded, something like this will appear:

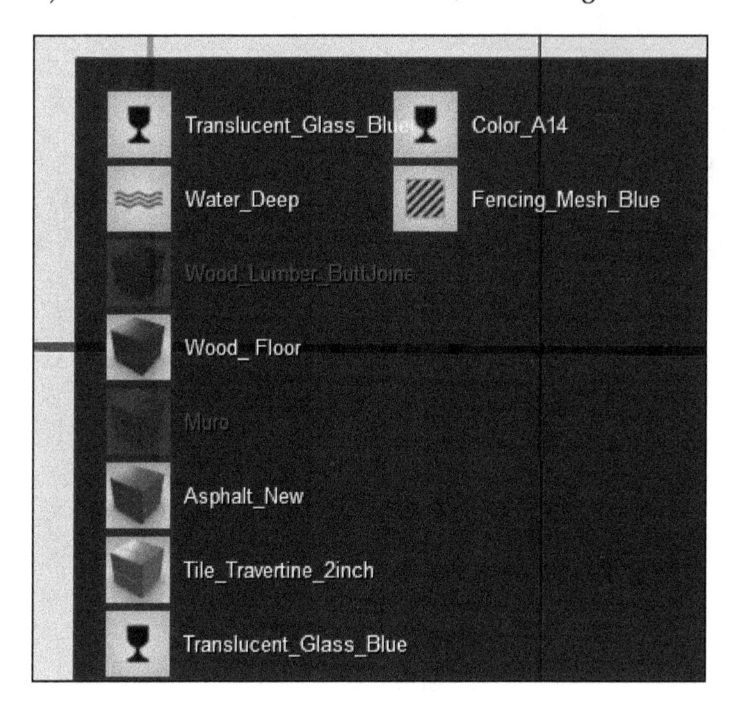

This will give the option to load only certain materials and, as shown in the previous screenshot, we selected two materials to be loaded. This Lumion feature can be used to back up materials, in particular when we are not too sure about the changes.

Common problems (troubleshooting)

While applying and tweaking materials, we will notice an area in the 3D model with a strange flickering. Although this can be avoided by checking two faces on the same place, there is a built-in setting in every Lumion material to correct this problem.

How to solve flickering

When this happens on the material properties, we have to open the **Placing** menu and locate the **Depth Offset** slider, as shown in the following screenshot:

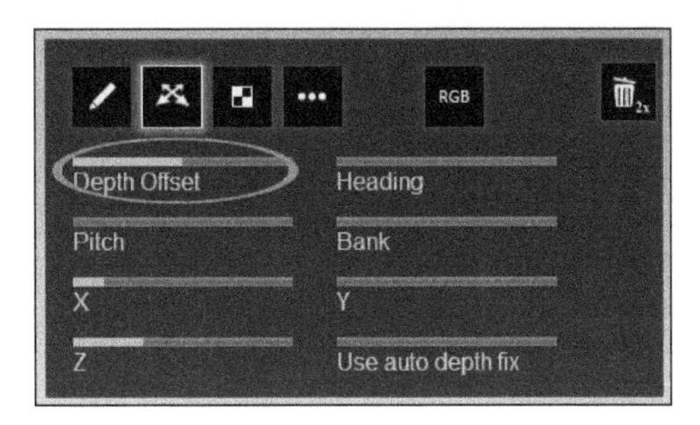

To solve the flickering problem, we have to adjust the **Depth Offset** property, but avoid making extreme adjustments. The best option is to press and hold the *Shift* key to make accurate adjustments until the flickering stops.

This flickering happens because when two surfaces are on the same place, Lumion does not know which of the two materials should be on the front and on the back. The **Depth Offset** option can correct this issue, but this situation needs to be addressed when modeling to avoid having two surfaces on the same place.

Summary

We finally come to the conclusion of this chapter. It's true that we covered a wide range of aspects that can help us improve the quality of our project by working with Lumion's materials. We saw several ways to control and tweak them to meet a project's needs and explored some settings such as reflection, glossiness, and the Fresnel effect.

We can use Lumion's optimized materials and take the scene to the next level by producing accurate and realistic materials by creating our own textures and using the Standard material. Finally, we understood how easy it is to save our materials to be used in other projects and how to make a backup of the materials used in the entire 3D model.

With this topic covered, we are now ready to populate the entire scene with fantastic 3D models. For this, we can use the fully optimized, native 3D models available in Lumion and in the next chapter, we will see what is available and how we can control and tweak the vast 3D model library. Plus, there is a special section that shows how to create grass and scatter rocks, leaves, and other elements.

5
Creating Your 3D World

Throughout this book, we have focused and concentrated on the main protagonist of the project. The building is the motivation why we need to produce an architectural visualization, and it makes sense that a large effort goes into this subject. Nonetheless, the building also needs something extra, it needs life around it. One of the reasons why we produce visualizations is to display how the buildings and the environment will blend together and how people will enjoy living at or visiting the location. Lumion gives us a hand with additional details to make a scene believable by providing a wide variety of 3D models that are ready to use, along with some flexibility to manipulate and tweak the general aspect of these 3D models.

In this chapter, we will cover the following topics:

- The 3D models available
- Placing content
- Working with multiple objects
- Controlling the models
- Selecting different objects
- Editing models' properties
- Tweaking the grass
- Scattering elements

This chapter is the intermediate point of our project because we will cover everything we need to know to fully master Lumion's models. The bullet points provide a reasonable idea of what we will see, and by the end of this chapter, you will be able to think ahead and improve your workflow with what Lumion provides.

Lumion models – a quick overview

In *Chapter 3, Importing 3D Models*, we have briefly covered what Lumion has to offer in terms of 3D models that are tweaked and optimized to provide the greatest result possible. You have to keep in mind that different versions of Lumion dictate what models are accessible. There is a substantial difference between Lumion and Lumion Pro, but even if you don't have Lumion Pro, there are some places where we can get free and paid 3D models. Some of these websites were mentioned in the *Using additional models* section in *Chapter 1, Getting Ready for Lumion 3D*.

Different categories and what we can find

Let's have a look at what is available and for this, we have to open the **Objects** menu that will give us access to eight libraries, but we only need five of them, as shown in the following screenshot:

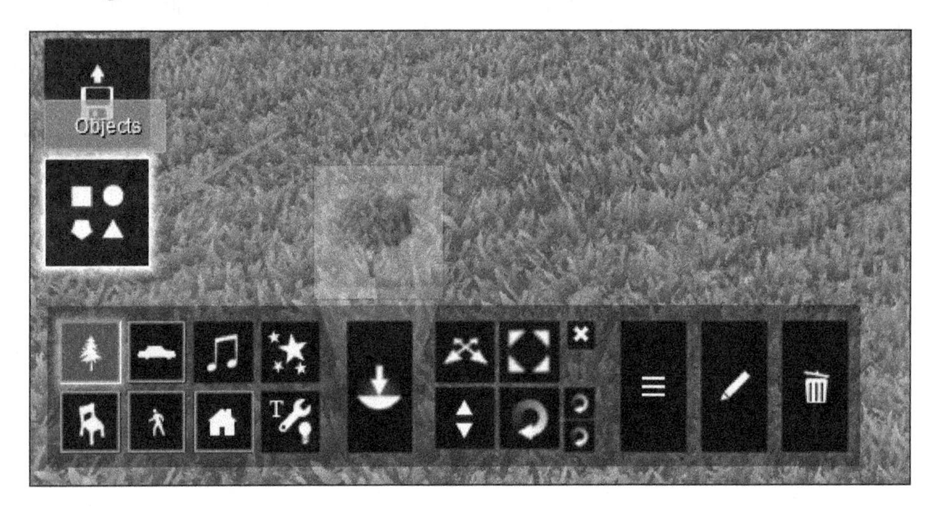

Each button represents a library where we can find different categories. The following list can give an overview of what each library contains:

- **The Nature library**: Inside this library, we can find several species of trees from Africa, Europe, and tropical trees, as well as grass, plants, flowers, cactus, and rocks.
- **The Transport library**: Here, we can find all forms of transport, from public transport to air balloons.
- **The Indoor library**: This is an important library that could be checked before modeling anything for interiors. We have the assorted objects, decoration items, electronics, appliances, food and drink, kitchen tools, interior lighting, taps, chairs and sofas, cabinets, tables, and utilities.

- **The People and animals library**: Here, we have people from different ethnic groups, 2D people, and animals. Please keep in mind that in this library, we have five types of objects: idle, walking, static, 2D cutout, and silhouettes. We will cover some of these objects in *Chapter 9, Animation Techniques*.
- **The Outdoor library**: Here, we have elements to populate exterior scenes with objects found in a normal daily life. Some of them can actually add interesting details to a scene making it look more believable.

These are the libraries that we will use to start populating the scene, but we still have to point out some differences between them, because not every model is 3D and not every model is static or idle. This knowledge helps us understand and make the decision of choosing the model that is appropriate for your scene.

Idle, animated, and other 3D models

As mentioned earlier, there are different types of models available in Lumion. We have 3D and 2D models and silhouettes, but the best way to comprehend the difference is by placing them in your scene and seeing how they behave.

Let's start by clicking on the **People and Animals** button to activate this library, but then we have to select the **Change object** button to open the library, as shown in the following screenshot:

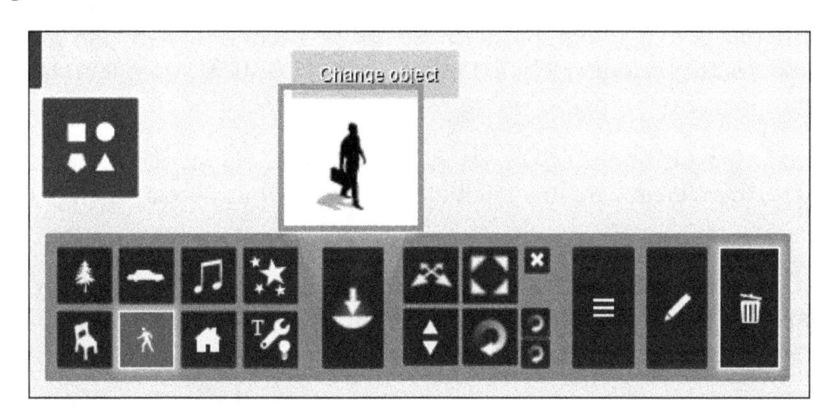

This button opens the library and we can start by selecting the **Men-3D** tab and select the first 3D model called **Man_African_0001_Idle**. Select this model or any 3D model with the idle suffix, and we are back to the **Build** mode where we have to click on the left mouse button to place the 3D model. Repeat the same step for:

- **Man_African_0001_Walk** under the **Men-3D** tab
- Any model from the **People - 2D - High Detail** tab

- Any model from the **People - 3D - Silhouettes** tab
- Any model from the **People - 2D - Silhouettes** tab

The idea is having something like this in your scene:

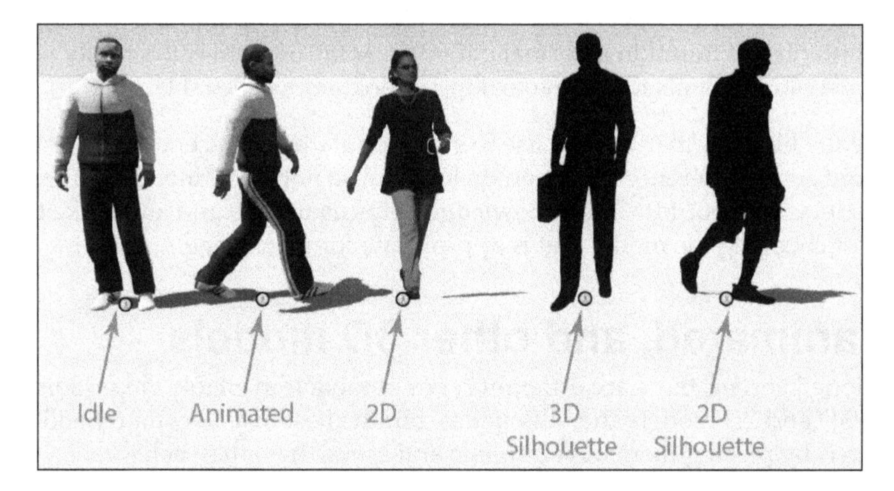

After placing these models, it is easy to understand the difference between each one. Perhaps the most significant aspect we have to point out is the different results we will get by using an idle or walk model. Both of the 3D models are animated as you can confirm while placing them, but with a walk 3D model, we can later animate them to walk around the scene. On the other hand, the idle 3D model is static, but we still have some loop animations that give life to the 3D model.

An additional aspect is that the 2D models are permanently facing the camera and unfortunately, there is no way to switch off this option, but we can change the color of the 2D model if necessary.

So, now that we know what is available, what is the next step? Start placing models and populate the entire scene with life, but let's have a look at some key points that will help you improve the workflow.

Project planning

While preparing the scene, there are a small number of aspects that need to be considered. Although variety is essential to add life to any scene, there is a difference between variety and pandemonium. We need to fight the temptation to start placing everything that is available in the Lumion's libraries. For example, there is no sense in placing European trees along with African trees or using a certain type of car that 'isn't correct for the type of project, just to mention a few aspects.

Usually, along with the CAD plans and depending on the size of the project, we have a landscape plan that shows where trees and other elements (if any) will be planted, as shown in the following screenshot:

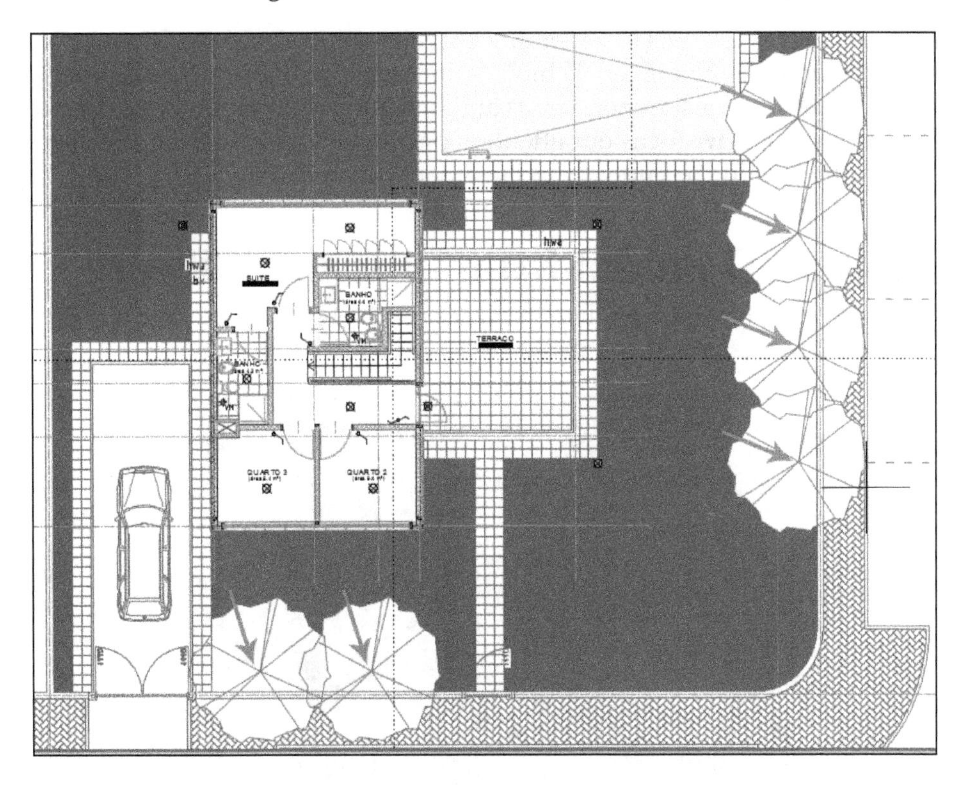

How can we translate this information from the CAD plan to Lumion? We will not have problems with the CAD plan shown previously because there isn't much information. However, with more complex projects we may need help and one easy way is by using a dummy object that shows where each element is placed. A small red cube can be used to represent a certain species of tree, while a blue cube can be used to indicate a shrub. Then, the 3D model is imported and this information is used as a visual aid to place the correct 3D models.

Another point that has been mentioned a few times in other chapters is the need for using layers to organize our scene. And this is something that needs to be addressed as soon we start placing content in the scene. Trees, shrubs, bushes, flowers, rocks, and grass are in the same library and this means that when we select the Nature library to tweak any of these 3D models, things can become really hard to manage because we could easily pick or delete the wrong 3D model until it is too late to amend. Have a look at the *Using Lumion's Layers* section in *Chapter 2, Creating a Project in Lumion.*

With these points in mind, let's start adding content to our scene.

Placing and controlling 3D models in Lumion

Where do we start? Well, this is something entirely personal, although it is a good idea to start working with bigger 3D models and then gradually moving down until the final 3D models are just minor details and touches to transform the scene into a professional project. If we focus our attention only in one section, the problem may be a lack of time to add the same quality to other areas in the scene.

Placing a 3D model from Lumion's library

The process of placing a 3D model is simple, as we can see from the following composition of images:

We will start by clicking on the **Objects** menu and choosing the correct library. As shown in the previous screenshot, we selected the Nature library and after that clicked on the **Change object** button to open the Nature library. Once in the library, we have to navigate to the desired tab and click on the thumbnail to select the 3D model. Back to the **Build** mode, we have to click on the left mouse button to place the 3D model.

> When placing a 3D model, Lumion recognizes surfaces and avoids any intersection between the 3D model and the surface. Sometimes, this feature can be in our way and cause some difficulties to place a 3D model. To bypass this problem, press and hold the *G* key, and then click on the left mouse button to place the 3D model in the terrain.

Great! We placed the first Lumion model in the scene. One model is placed and how many more do we need to place? It depends on what project you have, and if it is something small like the example shown in this book, placing 3D models is not a big issue. However, when working on large projects, placing the 3D models can be a massive and repetitive task, but don't forget that Lumion is a user-friendly application and provides tools that help with repetitive tasks.

Placing multiple copies with one click

Some 3D models may require several copies to create a more believable look, such as trees, bushes, flowers, and other elements. Imagine that you had to place tons of copies of the same model one by one. As mentioned, Lumion has some shortcuts that will help you save time and thereby not lose patience. What do we have to do? Before placing a 3D model, press and hold the *Ctrl* key, and then click on the left mouse button to place 10 copies of the 3D model selected, as shown in the following screenshot:

However, there is a slight downside to this technique as you probably must have noticed from the previous screenshot. The disadvantage is that we don't have control over the area where the 3D models are scattered and the distance between them; some of the 3D models may intersect with each other. With smaller 3D models, this technique is useful because the 3D models tend not to be far from each other, and with bigger 3D models, we can use the *Ctrl* key to place the 10 copies and then adjust accordingly.

Another shortcut that is worth keeping in mind is the *Z* key. If you press and hold the *Z* key and then click to place the 3D model and then click again, the next 3D model will have a different size. Consequently, a powerful combination is *Ctrl* + *Z* + the left mouse button to place 10 copies with different sizes, as shown in the following screenshot:

Why is this useful? This is a fair question. The best answer is to take some time to look away from the screen to outside and observe that we are surrounded by randomness. We hardly could find two trees with the same size and shape, even from the same species. Our eyes are a perfect mechanism to spot things that look repetitive.

However, we don't have the time and possibilities to create each tree different from the other, but we can cheat. Cheating is OK in 3D because it helps us gain time to concentrate our attention in other areas equally important to accomplish the perfect image still or movie. One way of cheating is by using the same tree, but changing the rotation, scale, and color. With the combination of *Ctrl* + *Z* + the left mouse button, we have the opportunity to at least change the scale of each copy placed in the scene.

If you look at the previous screenshot, the plants presented when arranged and placed in the correct location will look much more natural than using the same scale for the 3D model. However, how can we manipulate and control the 3D models placed in the scene?

Tweaking the 3D models

To place any model from Lumion's library, we have to use the left mouse button and if, instead of release, we hold the left mouse button and drag it, it is possible to change the location where the 3D model is going to be placed, as shown in the following screenshot:

However, we need more control than this and the previous screenshot also shows where we can find the tools to move, scale, rotate, and change the height of the 3D model. This is something we covered already in the *Rearranging 3D models* section *Chapter 3, Importing 3D Models*. The tools and shortcuts we use for imported 3D models are precisely the same for Lumion's native 3D models.

As a quick reminder, here is the list of the shortcuts to tweak the position, scale, and rotation of the 3D model:

- *M*: Move the 3D model
- *L*: Scale the 3D model
- *R*: Rotate the 3D model heading
- *P*: Rotate the 3D model pitch
- *B*: Rotate the 3D model bank
- *H*: Change the heights

However, there is an aspect that needs to be kept in mind all the time to tweak and control the 3D models in a project. This was addressed in the *Controlling 3D models* section in *Chapter 1, Getting Ready for Lumion 3D*. The example used in this section, with two trees and one car, showed that if we have the Nature category selected, we cannot select and control the car.

This is something that is crucial and if you are new to Lumion, it is perfectly normal that on the first few tries, you will get frustrated because you cannot select the 3D model. This may sound annoying, but in truth, this is a way Lumion helps us in not becoming overweight and confused when trying to select a 3D model by providing a narrow control.

With this in mind, the next section will show a few tricks and techniques that are useful with Lumion's models and techniques. This will help to improve the way we work with the 3D models and fully master this stage in the production.

Controlling the models

So, in what ways can we control a 3D model? Let's stop for a moment and think of one of the most important actions we can perform in almost any software: copy and paste. This is something indispensable for a smooth workflow that saves time.

Copying 3D models

Previously, we saw a way to copy and paste materials, but with 3D models, Lumion works a little bit differently. To copy a 3D model, we have to first select the Move object tool by clicking on the button or by pressing and holding the *M* key. Then, we have to select the 3D model by clicking with the left mouse button on the small icon that appears in each of the 3D models. Now that we have the 3D model selected, drag and press the *Alt* key, as shown in the following screenshot:

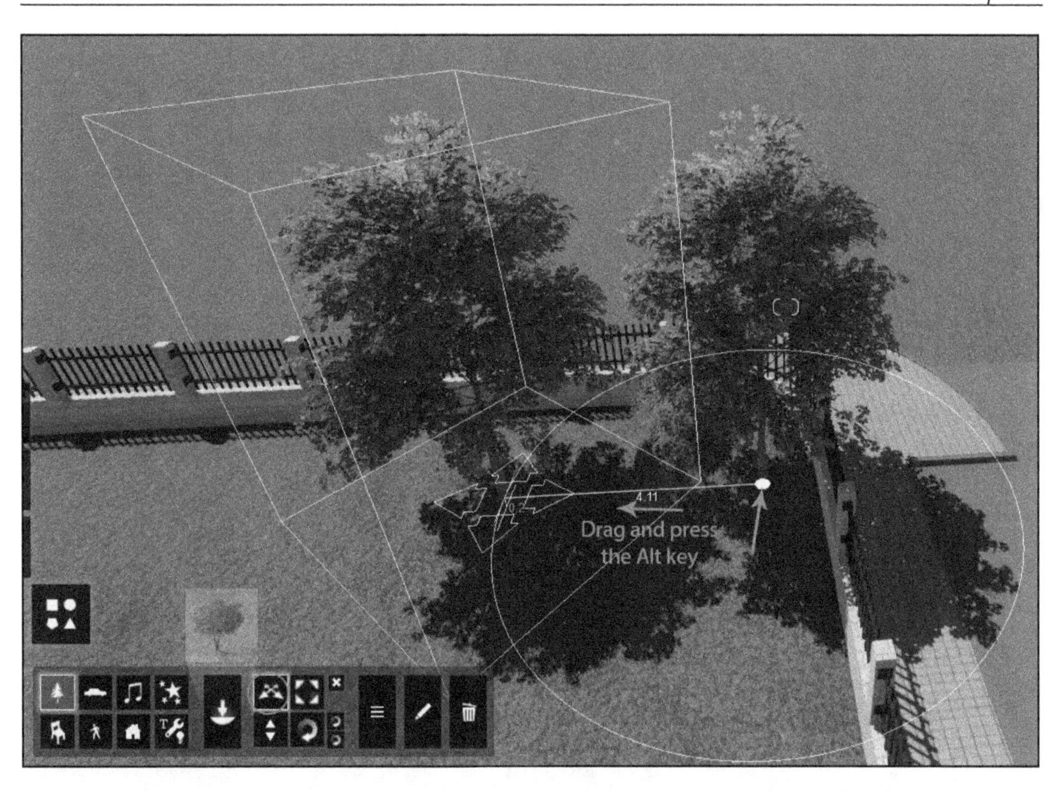

Even if by mistake, you have dragged the 3D model without pressing the *Alt* key, you still can copy it and a copy of the model will appear instantly. This technique is great to quickly populate the scene we have with loads of models, but this only works with the move tool.

When we memorize the shortcuts to control the 3D model and use the *Alt* key to copy 3D models, it is a question of minutes to fill the entire scene with a variety of 3D models. It is these small things that give the extra touch to a scene; so, things such as changing the model rotation and scale, particularly when working with the Nature category, is essential.

However, to fully control the 3D models, we will cover two important aspects that you'll need as soon you start to work with 3D models.

Selecting and deleting 3D models

One requirement that eventually begins to rise is the need to control several 3D models at the same time. Let's examine this situation: you just placed 10 trees, but they are in the wrong place. We have two ways to deal with this. The first one is to delete the 3D models and place them again, but how can we do this?

When we open the **Objects** menu, a toolbar appears at the bottom of the screen, and we can locate the delete button at the end of the toolbar. The process is simple—we click on the Trash object button and then select the 3D model to delete it, as shown in the following screenshot:

If we deleted a 3D model by mistake, there is always the **Undo** button that appears next to the trash button, but keep in mind that this button has some limitations because we can only undo one action. With the Trash object button selected, we can click on each model to delete it, but imagine having to do this for each 3D model. This is a tedious and unnecessary task because we can select multiple 3D models in one go. How? First, we draw a selection box around the 3D models we want to delete, move, rotate, and scale. To do this, we have to press and hold the *Ctrl* key and then draw a rectangle selection around the 3D models we want, as shown in the following screenshot:

However, this can produce some undesired results because we might end up selecting 3D models that are not desired. So, another option is to press and hold the *Ctrl* key and use the left mouse button to select each individual 3D model. However, this option doesn't inform us of the number of models selected, as shown in the previous screenshot.

Then, with the 3D models selected, we can do what we need, such as delete, relocate, or move models to another layer. We mentioned another option to select and control the 3D models present in the scene and the next section is going to introduce the powerful Context menu that will help us fully master Lumion.

The remarkable Context menu

We can call it remarkable because this menu gives us the full control and shortcuts to rearrange the 3D models present in the scene. This menu is divided into two very distinct sections: the **Selection** and **Transformation** submenus, as shown in the following screenshot:

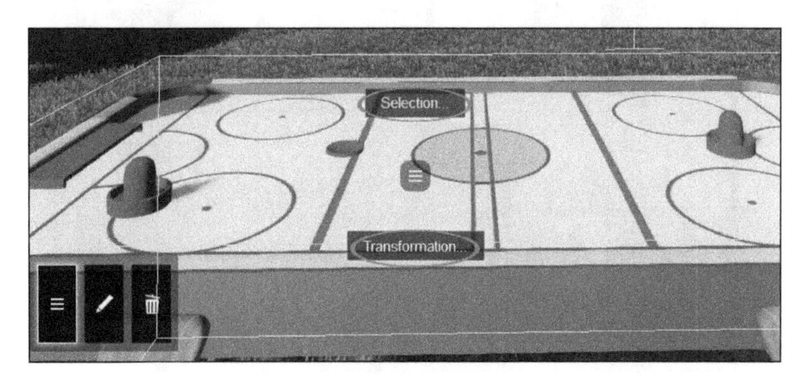

How can these menus be useful to your project? Let's start with the **Selection** submenu and when we select it the following options appear:

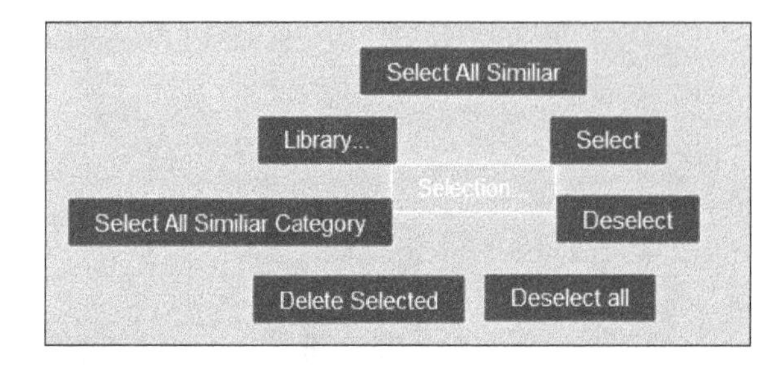

However, looking at these options doesn't help you understand how they can be so useful and powerful. Let's check how they work.

Selection – library

Working with the Nature library has some challenges and one of them is trying to identify a tree or other plant that we already placed in the scene. This can be really difficult, in particular when there are other models very similar to the one we are looking for. The **Library...** option found under the **Selection** submenu can give a hand with this task and will make your life easy. Locate the 3D model you want and using the **Context** menu, click on the **Selection** submenu. Select the **Library...** option and another two options appear. We need to choose the **Select in library** option and automatically the **Change object** button changes to the 3D model, as shown in the following screenshot:

Sometimes, when we click on the **Change object** button to access the library, we have to select each tab to find where the 3D model is, but once we have the correct tab, it is easy to recognize the 3D model because of the halo around the thumbnail.

However, there was another option called **Replace with library selection**. Now, this is when you start to see the full potential of Lumion and how these options will greatly improve the speed of your workflow.

Picking the example on the previous screenshot, we can see that the plant used is called **FicusElastica_001**. Then, we realized that this is the wrong 3D model, but on the other hand, the location is correct and we don't want to change the location even a few millimeters. The **Replace with library selection** option is our salvation; so, let's see how we can use it.

The first thing to do is to open the Nature library and select the correct 3D model, which in this case will be `FicusElastica_003`. After selecting this 3D model, we are back to the **Build** mode, but instead of placing the 3D model, we will select the **Context** menu and pick the 3D model that needs to be replaced. Then, click on the **Selection** submenu, next the **Library...** option and then click on the **Replace with library selection** button, as exemplified on the next screenshot:

In addition to this fantastic feature, Lumion will keep not only the location, but also the rotation and scale of the previous 3D model. Can you imagine how easy it is to replace a species of a tree or another model in the scene if the client doesn't like it? What about the other selection options? How can we use them?

Selection – all the Selection options

The options using which we have access to the **Selection** submenu are simple, particularly, the ones related to deselecting a 3D model. The **Selection** option is another way where we can select a 3D model, but using the *Ctrl* key is much faster. However, there are two selection options that can be used to select a wide range of 3D models or having a narrower control over what we select.

Let's say that we totally forgot to use a layer for the 3D models we placed and again we can pick the example that we have been using with the **FicusElastica_001** model. We need to place all the **FicusElastica_001** models inside a layer, but we have several models scattered around the scene. One way to tackle this issue is by selecting each model and then moving these to a new layer. The smart way is by using the **Select All Similar** option because when we use this option all the **FicusElastica_001** models are selected, as shown in the following screenshot:

In this case, we only have two copies of the **FicusElastica_001** model, but it is easy to understand how powerful this option can be and how easy it is to select a certain amount of 3D models in seconds. To know that a 3D model is selected, a blue wire box is drawn around the 3D model.

Eventually, we will realize that we need to copy every single tree, plant, flower, and rock from one point to another. This is a massive task to be accomplished using only the normal selection technique. If you think for a second all of these models are part of the same library, the Nature library. So, instead of using the **Select All Similar** option, we will use the **Select All Similar Category** option, as shown in the following screenshot:

As you can see in the previous screenshot, every single 3D model from the Nature library was selected and ready to be controlled in the way we need and want. To deselect the 3D models, we can make use of the **Deselect All** option, but a quicker way is by pressing and holding the *Ctrl* key and clicking wherever you want. However, what if we need to select models from different categories?

Selecting different categories

Selecting different categories is not something that we can find in the Context menu, but since we are talking about selecting 3D models, you may find this trick useful. Have a closer look at the following screenshot:

In the previous screenshot, we can see models from three different categories: Indoor, People and Animals, and Outdoor. How is that possible? It is easier than you think. Start by selecting the models found in the Indoor category. The next step is selecting the People and Animals category, and by pressing and holding the *Ctrl* key, select the 3D models you want in this category. Repeat the same step for as many categories as you like, but remember that you need to select individual models and not draw a selection rectangle. This principle also works if we select the models with the **Context** menu.

Another option to quickly select and transform a 3D model is by pressing the *F12* key. When we do this, every 3D model becomes available to be selected and we can change the location, rotation, and the height of the 3D model.

Now that we have the 3D models selected, what can we do with them? Let's explore the marvelous **Transformation** submenu.

Controlling 3D models with the Transformation submenu

Now, it's time to get more serious with the way we can use 3D models to push the scene to a more professional level. There isn't any special and hidden button in Lumion that will create a perfect and beautiful scene. Instead there is only patience, attention to detail, and a little bit of Lumion's help.

The options we have with the **Transformation** submenu are shown in the following screenshot:

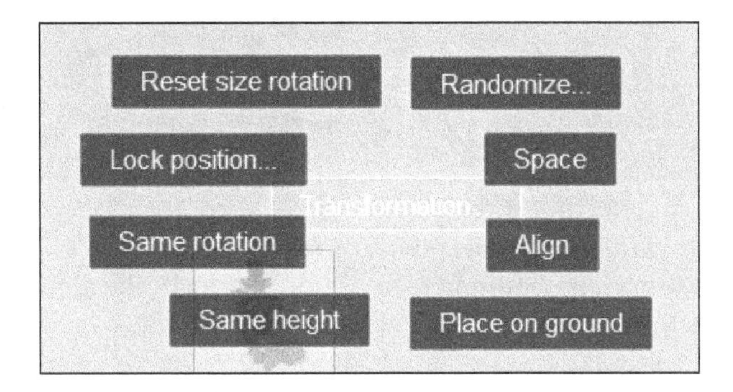

We already explored the **Lock position** option that gives the opportunity to lock or secure a 3D model avoiding any other change. And the **Place on ground** option does exactly what the name suggests. It puts the 3D model on the ground even if it is on top of another surface. Another simple option is the **Reset size rotation** option that when selected will reset the 3D model to the original size and rotation. So far, this is nothing special, but let's see what we can do with the other options.

Let's try to make this scene more interesting using the **Same rotation** option:

All the cars have the same orientation except one, which we are going to use to set the rotation angle for another three cars. The first thing we have to do is select all the cars we want to change including the car with the correct orientation and it doesn't matter in which sequence we select the cars. Now, we need to click on the **Context** menu and here is where we have to pay some attention and don't forget to select the car with the correct orientation. Then, select the **Transformation** submenu and click on the **Same rotation** option, as shown in the following screenshot:

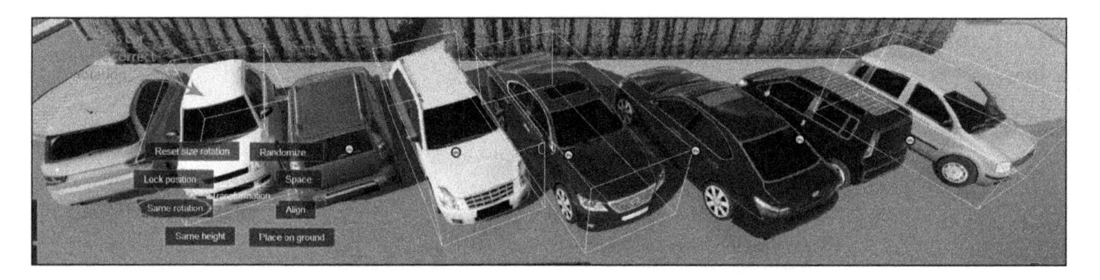

Again, for this to work, after selecting the **Context** menu, we have to select the model with the correct rotation. The **Same height** option works in the similar way, but in this case, it will change the height of the 3D model selected.

Several times, we mentioned the importance of adding randomness to our scene, particularly when working with plants. The **Randomize** option is a great tool that can be used to easily add variety to a scene because we can randomize the position, the rotation, and a combination of rotation and scale, as shown in the following screenshot:

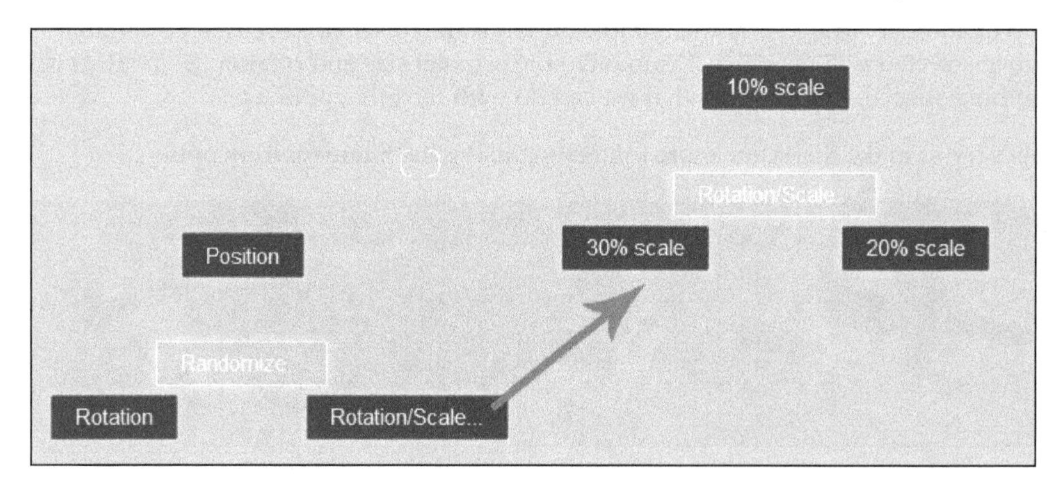

This is a powerful feature when well applied in a scene and this will save us time for more *important* tweaks, such as the special features that we are going to cover later in this book.

When using these submenus, to go back, we need to click on the rectangle in the center. In this case, we need to click on the Randomize rectangle in order to go back one level.

The next two options, **Space** and **Align**, can also be particularly useful in a situation like this:

We have these five planters, but we would like to have them evenly spaced on the path. Is this possible? The first thing we have to do, as exemplified in the previous screenshot, is to define the first and the last position. Then, we need to select all the planters and don't worry about the sequence in which you select the 3D models, but the most important aspect is that after selecting the **Context** menu we must select the planter or the model that sets the initial position, as shown in the following screenshot:

Easy as that, and we have all five planters with equal distance between them. Do you remember the fantastic **FicusElastica_001** model? They will look perfect on those planters. The **Align** option can give us a hand to perfectly align the plant with the planter, as shown in the following screenshot:

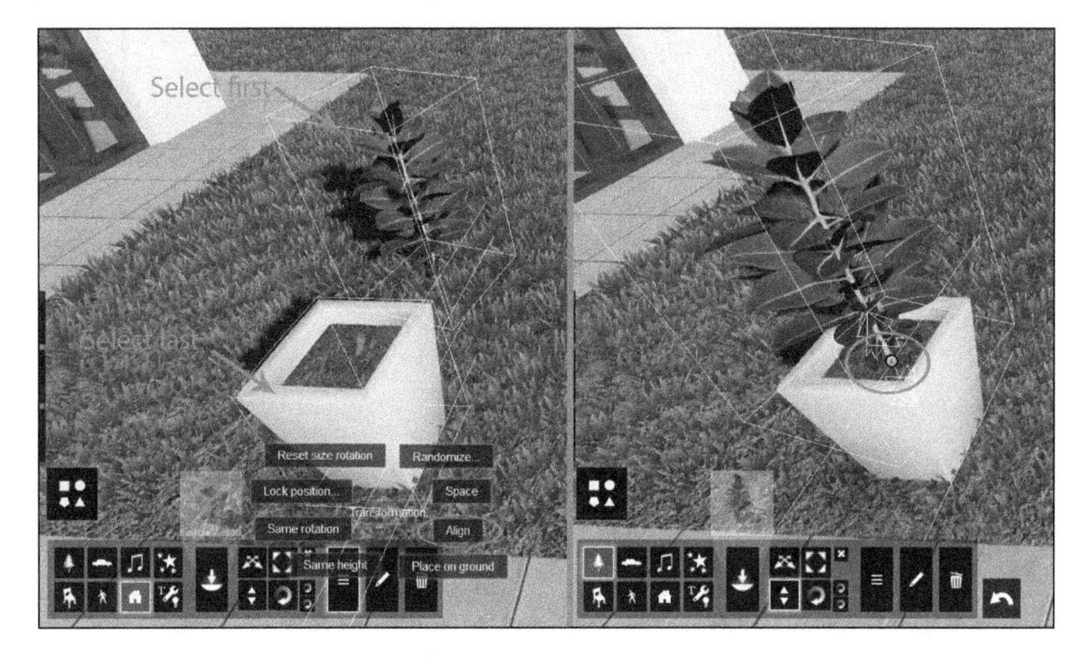

We have to first select the plant or the model we want to align and then select the planter and select the **Align** option. Although the plant will be right on the center of the planter, we still have to tweak the height of **FicusElastica_001**, but at least we avoided the effort of trying to pinpoint the center of the planter.

And with this, we will finish this section with several techniques to place and manipulate the 3D models we can find in Lumion's libraries. Placing 3D models is a stage that takes time, but these techniques can help us to cut some corners and improve our workflow. However, we still can go even further and give more dynamics to the scene with small adjustments and special 3D models.

Editing the properties of a 3D model

We can say that 90 percent of the 3D models available in Lumion have some properties that can be tweaked. For example, we can change a tree from spring to fall by tweaking these properties. This is something fairly easy, as shown in the following screenshot:

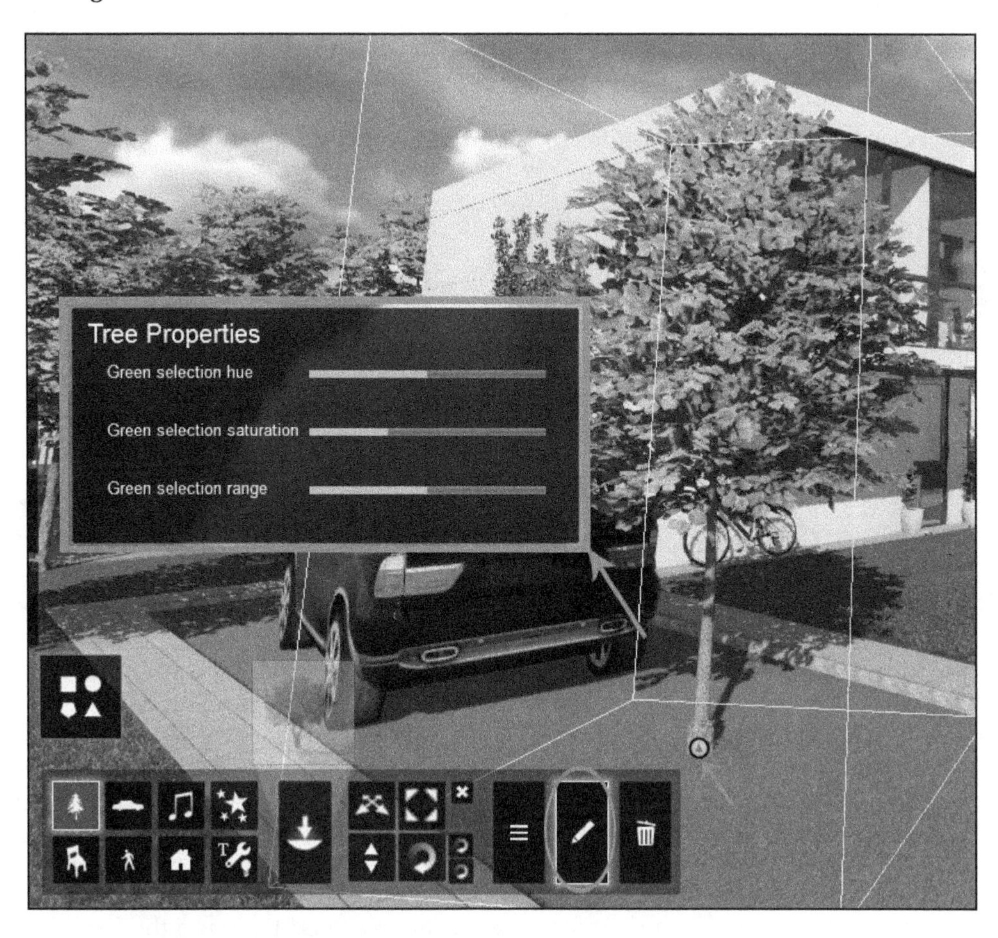

We have to click on the **Edit properties** button, select the 3D model and the properties of that object will appear if there is any. This is useful to tweak not only plants, but also a car's color, a flag, and in some more complex objects, the properties of the fire and other elements. The next topic is going to cover a final 3D model that we can add to the scene, and this makes all the difference.

Creating grass and using the Scatter elements

Since Lumion 4, we have the possibility to easily add grass to the terrain. However, this can be a double-edge sword because on one hand, we can add grass, but the downside is that the grass is created in the entire terrain. This is not useful, when we have an urban environment and the grass is constrained to specific areas. So, how can we solve this issue and where can we find this fantastic grass?

The **Grass** menu can be found under the **Landscape** menu, as shown in the following screenshot:

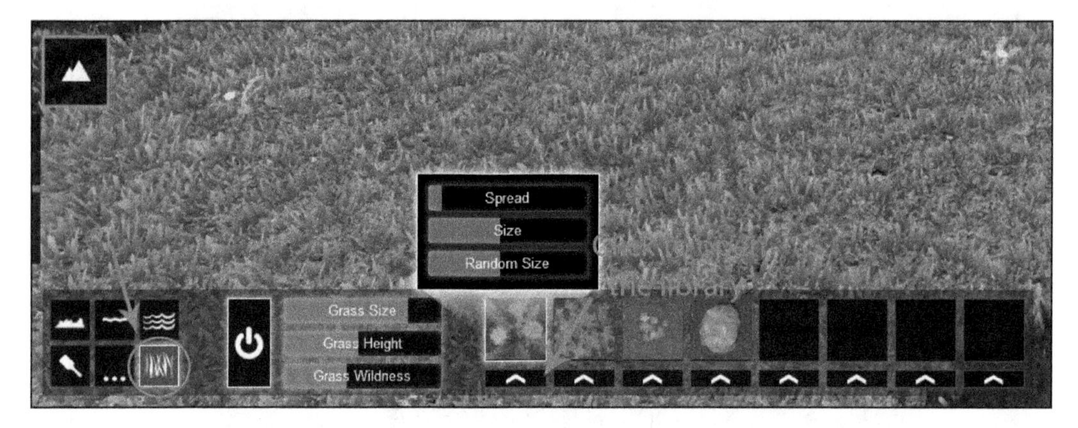

As we can see, adding grass is as easy as a click on a button. We need to tweak some settings to get the desired result by tweaking the grass size, height, and wildness. However, Lumion gives an extra detail to the scene, by giving us the opportunity to scatter flowers, leaves, small plants, and rocks all over the place. This in turn gives us the freedom of creating a perfect lawn or a wild field. However, what happens in areas that we don't want the grass? There are two ways we can tackle this issue:

- The first solution and perhaps the best one is by creating a 3D terrain with the roads, sidewalks, and green areas. Then, we need to assign the Landscape material and voilà, we have grass where we need.

- The second option is more difficult to perform because we have to paint the terrain with textures, as shown in the following screenshot:

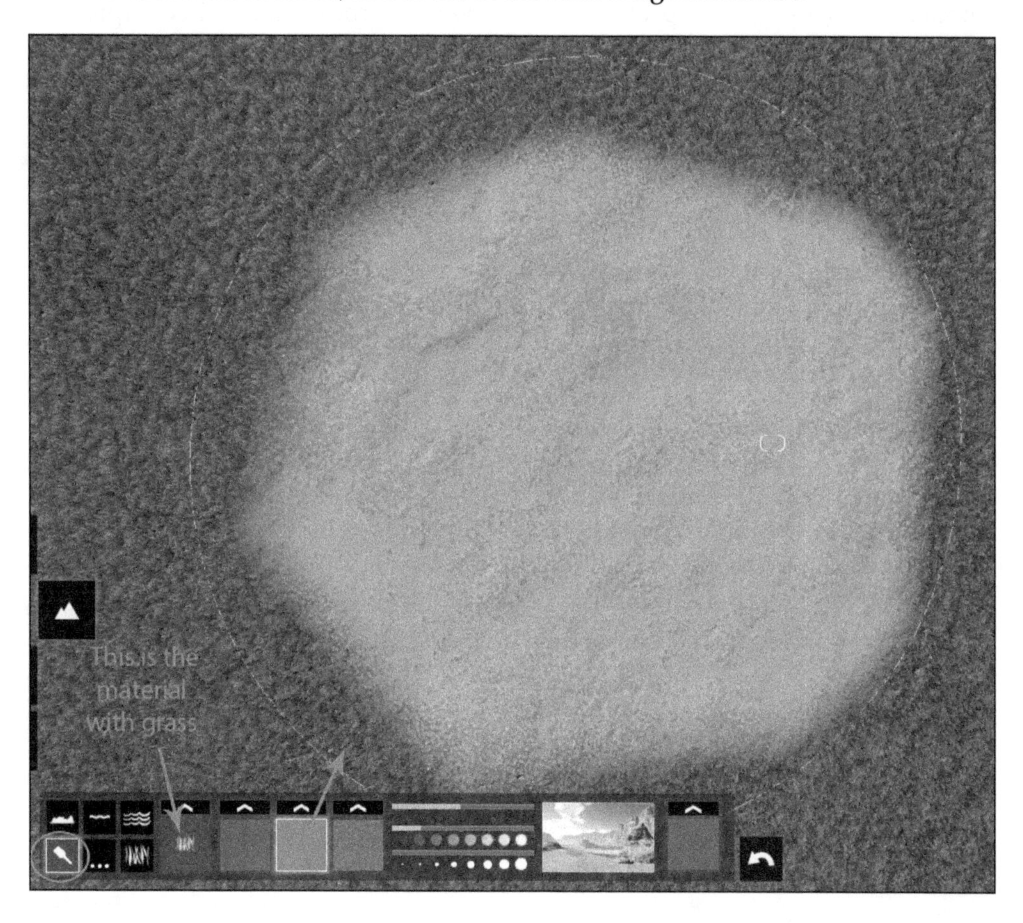

In the **Landscape** menu, we can find the **Paint** menu where we have the textures used for the terrain. The first texture is the one with the grass, so this means that in order to remove the grass, we have to paint another texture on top of it. And this is exactly what we did in the previous screenshot. The problem with this option is the lack of control because unfortunately, we don't have square brushes in Lumion to be more accurate.

Summary

3D models are an essential aspect of the scene we are producing. In this chapter, you learned what we can find in each category, those related to 3D models and the difference between the idle and animated 3D models. Then, you saw not only how to place 3D models, but also some techniques to place several copies, add randomness to them using the *Ctrl* + *Z* + left mouse button combination and copy 3D models using shortcuts. Plus, you learned that using the *F12* key can increase the speed when working with the different 3D models present in the project.

Another essential aspect you learned was the use of the **Context** menu, not only to select 3D models using different parameters, but also using the **Transformation** submenu to easily add life to your project. The final section covered the special touches you can give to the scene by using the grass and scattering different elements.

The next chapter is the final step before we start adding special effects. We will learn the basis to create different times of the day that can have a deep impact in the mood achieved in the project. And we will explore a not-so-well known area in Lumion—using spotlights, omni light, and fill lights to light interior scenes with a little bit of help from the Global illumination system.

6
Lighting in Lumion

Light is the most significant element to produce a good architectural visualization. We can have a detailed building with a beautiful landscape and spend hours tweaking and adjusting the materials, but without light, all those efforts are useless. This is because without light, we cannot see the materials, the building, and the environment. We may have the most incredible building and a stunning landscape, but without the right quality of light, the architectural visualization can still be flat, dull, and uninspiring. For this reason, lighting a scene is as essential as having a good 3D model. With the correct light, we can produce a warm and cozy scene or a cold and wet Monday morning. Lumion's primary concern is to create good visualizations in real time, and for this reason, some corners have to be cut, but looking at the bullet points related to the topics covered in this chapter, we still have a fair amount of control over the lighting in the scene.

In this chapter, we will cover the following topics:

- The Lumion weather system
- Lumion lights
- Interior illumination
- Tweaking spotlights
- Improving lighting
- Best practices with spotlights
- Improving reflections

Consequently, the main goal of this chapter is to introduce you to the **Weather** menu, which is the primary way to light the scene, and to the Lumion optimized lights, such as spotlights and omni and fill lights. However, you will notice that we are starting to change slowly from the **Build** mode to the **Photo** or **Movie** mode, where we have access to effects that can help us create a professional and fully optimized still image or movie.

Lumion lighting – a quick overview

One of the first steps when we are creating a scene in Lumion is choosing one of the nine different templates or presets. Although there are some differences between them, one aspect is certain in that the lighting is already set up for us. We don't have to worry about creating a sun or moon and then assigning an environment map to add some reflections and tweak the camera exposure. As we can see, there is a lot of work being done in the background, but how can we change the overall look of a scene?

Adjusting the Weather menu

An initial layer of control can be found in the Weather menu, and this menu is the first one found on the left-hand side of the screen, as shown in the following screenshot:

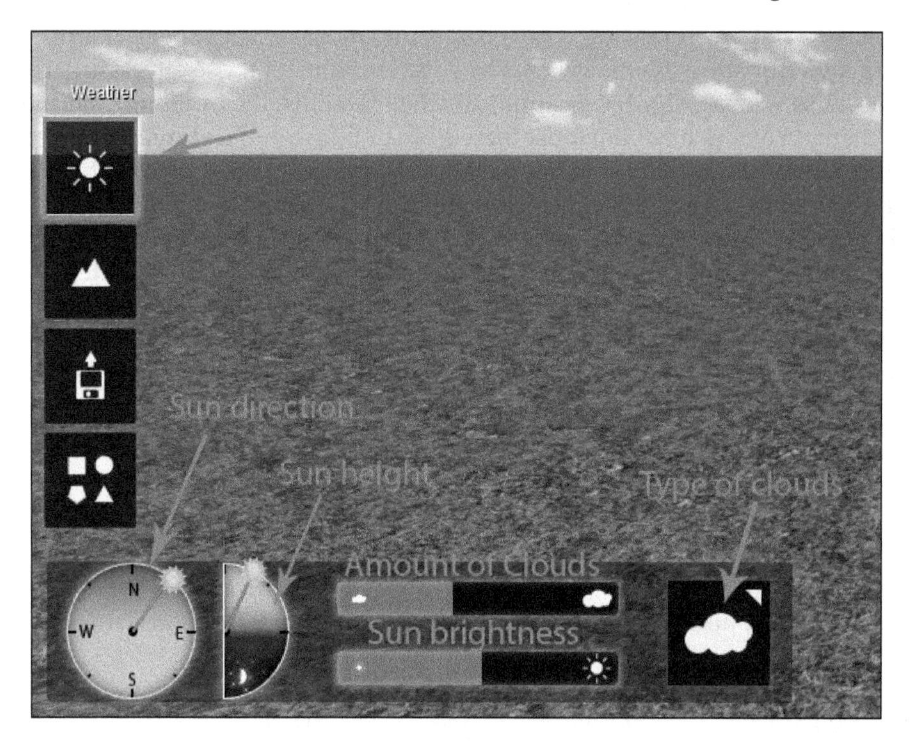

The level of control we have is smaller in comparison to other Lumion menus, but here we can find the main elements to tweak the lighting in our scene. It is possible to control the position of the sun and clouds in the sky along with the sun's brightness. Nevertheless, we don't have to stop here because lighting the scene is not constrained to the Weather menu or the effects found under the Photo or Movie menu.

Have a look at the **Objects** menu and find the Lights and special objects submenu, as shown in the following screenshot:

Let's have a look at the Lights and special objects library. In the first tab, we can find a wide variety of spotlights, and the thumbnail shows the light being rendered based on an IES light profile. The other tab has another type of light called fill light, and the third tab is called Utilities, where we can find a specific element to slightly improve the reflections in our scene, particularly the ones present in glass surfaces.

IES stands for Illuminating Engineering Society. An IES file is the measurement of distribution of light intensity stored in the ASCII format. In 3D software, it can be used to create lights with shapes in physically accurate forms.

Now that we know the tools, let's see how to tweak and control the **Weather** system to light the scene with the help of the additional lights.

Exterior lighting with the Weather menu

Remarkably, the position of the sun in the sky has a great impact on the whole scene. Take, for example, the golden hour, which is used in photography and cinematography; this is the period after sunrise or before sunset during which daylight is redder and softer. The reason why this particular time of day is so *famous* is because the Sun produces a soft, diffused light that is much more pleasant in contrast to the midday Sun.

We also have the sweet light or blue hour, which is the period of twilight every morning/evening and because of the Sun being below the horizon, the indirect sunlight takes on a predominantly blue hue.

However, why are we mentioning this here? Because now we are moving from a technical area to a more artistic stage where the choices we make are neither right nor wrong. There isn't any magic number that will create a beautiful visualization. Instead, we need to have a basic knowledge of how photography and cinematography work in order to create something pleasant and attractive to the viewer. Getting back to the golden and blue hour, it is here where we can start creating a similar lighting and run away from the common midday harsh light and shadow. However, before seeing how we can do this, let's have a quick look at the **Photo** and **Movie** modes.

Photo and Movie modes – a very quick introduction

Why are we talking about the **Photo** and **Movie** modes in this chapter? The reason is because we will start using more of these modes to enhance our scene. For example, what we will see in the next topic can also be accomplished in these modes. What are the benefits? The greatest benefit is the opportunity to keyframe the settings used in one shot, but this is something that we are going to cover in the next chapters, particularly *Chapter 9, Animation Techniques*.

To give an example, let's say we create two images and one needs to be at sunset and the other one earlier in the morning. If we only use the **Weather** menu, it means we have to change the settings every time we need to create an image, but using the **Photo** or **Movie** mode effects, we can easily switch from one setting to another.

With this in mind, we will cover a few aspects in the **Build** mode, but eventually, we will jump to the **Photo** or **Movie** mode, where we have more control over the settings and final output.

How to create a golden and blue hour

Let's open the **Weather** menu and locate the settings to change the direction and height of the sun.

In some projects, we have to be accurate to the point of which elevation is facing north. With the Sun direction tool in the **Weather** menu, we can easily see where north is in Lumion and rotate the 3D model to get a correct result.

The first thing we need to define is the sun direction, which is crucial because of the shadows and how they influence the project. It is always a good habit to aim in order to get a result where the shadows outline the building, but not in such a way that it distracts the viewer.

Now, the line between golden and blue hour is really thin, as shown in the following screenshot:

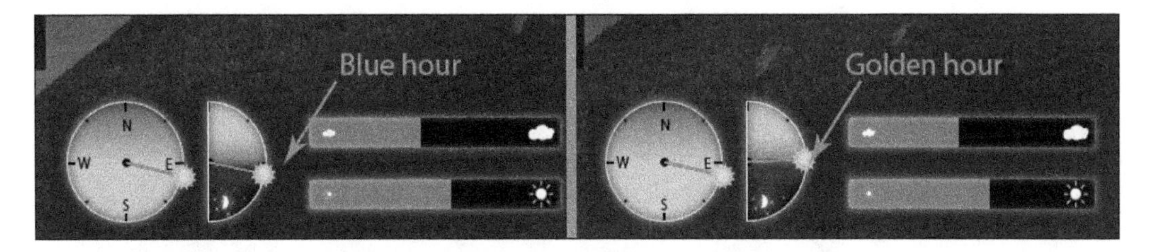

As you can see, it is really difficult to achieve the correct value, and we need a steady hand. As mentioned before, we can use the **Photo** or **Movie** mode to achieve the same result, but how?

Before we jump to these modes, it is useful to understand that in most situations, the effects we have in the **Photo** mode are available in the **Movie** mode. This means that what we learn in regard to the Photo mode can be applied and even copied for the **Movie** mode.

Creating a golden and blue hour with the Sun effect

Firstly, we have to open the **Photo** mode, and for this, we will have a look at the button on the right-hand side, as shown in the following screenshot:

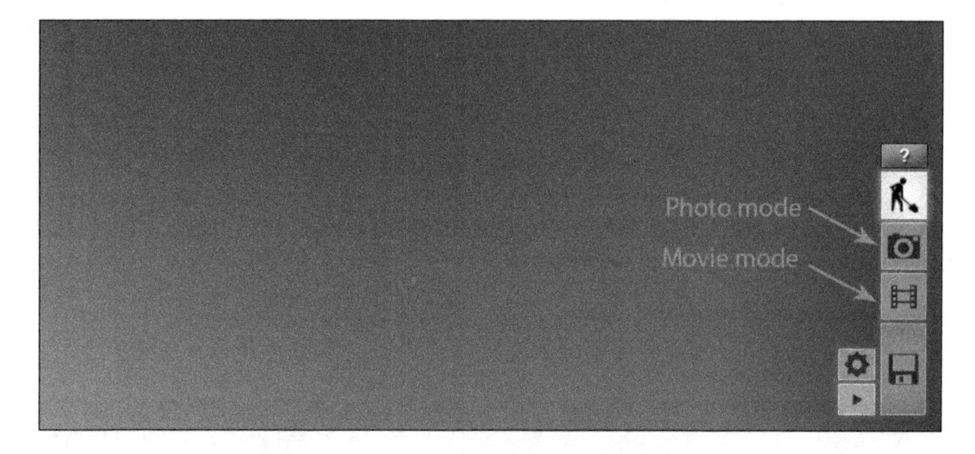

For now, we will use the **Photo** mode because it has a simpler interface, as we can see in the following screenshot:

To add the Sun effect, which is one of the effects to control the sun, we have to click on the New effect button, that in turn, opens the Photo effect library. Here, we have several tabs, but the one we need is already opened and all we have to do is select the Sun effect.

A new module is added to the Photo interface that will allow better control over the sun, as shown in the following screenshot:

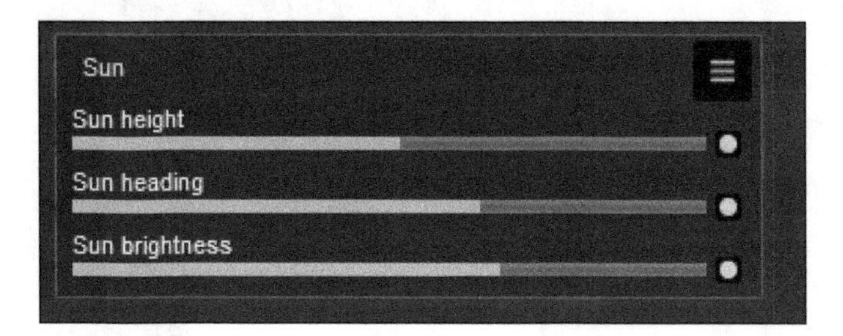

Interestingly, the settings available are precisely the ones we can find in the **Weather** menu, and in this case, we need to tweak the **Sun height** slider. Because of the narrow window we have between each special hour, the golden and blue, it is best to press and hold the *Shift* key to add smaller increments in the values.

Do you know what would help to create a more dramatic look? Some clouds to catch the light from the sun and sky. Since we are already in the **Photo** mode, why not add some clouds using another effect? We will later return to the **Build** mode and do the same thing on the **Weather** menu, which is a nice way to introduce another concept in Lumion. The changes we make in the **Build** mode can be easily overwritten in the **Photo** and **Movie** modes.

Adding realistic clouds using the Cloud effect

Again, the same process is used to add the Cloud effect. We have to click on the New effect button, open the **Weather** menu, and select the Cloud effect.

From now on, when it is mentioned to add an effect, the process is the one mentioned previously. We will mention the tab where the effect can be found.

With this new module, we have much better control over several aspects of the clouds, as shown in the following screenshot:

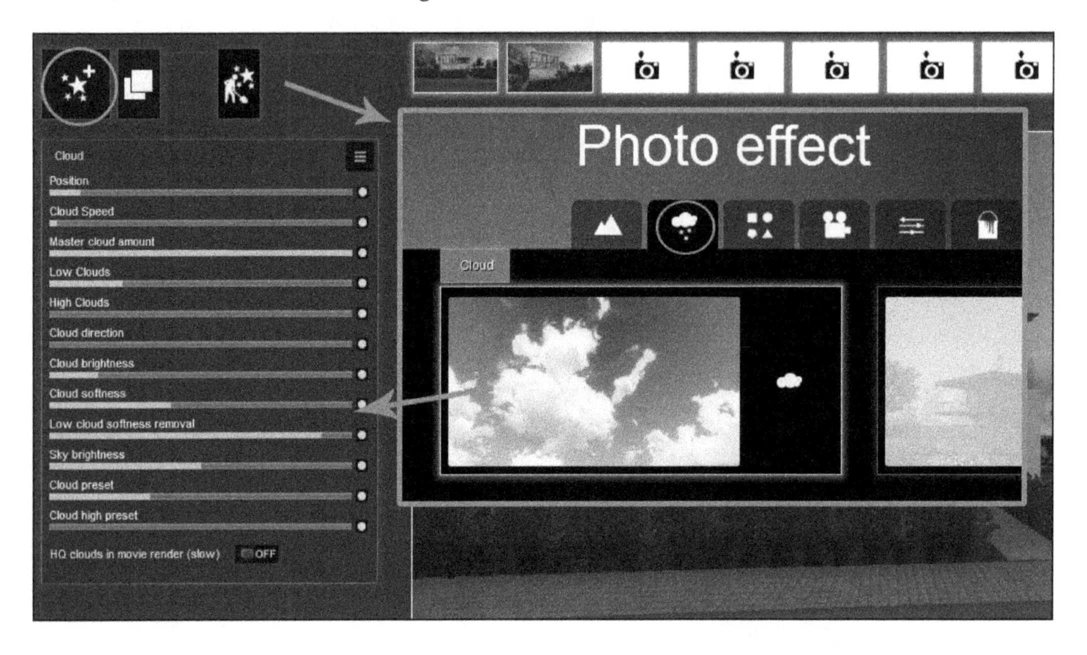

Some of the settings are self-explanatory, such as the **Position**, **Cloud Speed**, **Clouddirection**, and **Cloudbrightness**. With this effect, we have control over two layers of clouds: the low and high clouds, and these can be controlled using the **Low Clouds** and **High Clouds** settings. There are no correct settings for your scene, instead, we need to take a few minutes and test the best settings. Don't be afraid to try because you can always delete the effect and add a new one. To delete the effect, we have to click on the small icon found on the top-right corner, as shown in the following screenshot:

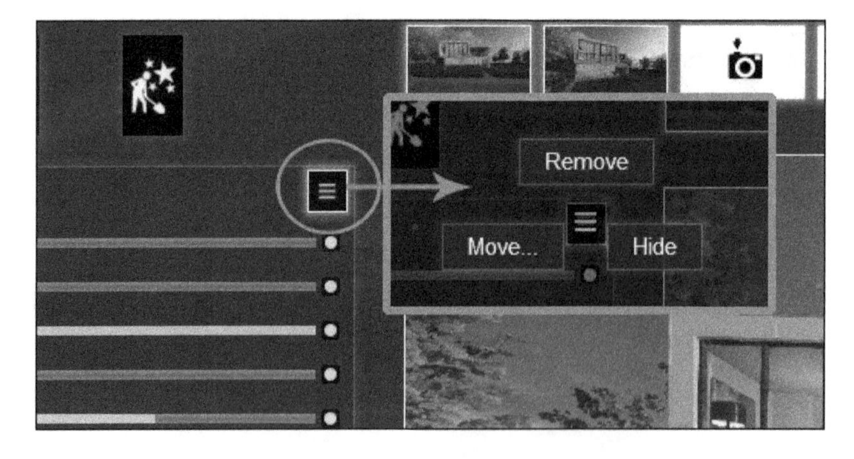

However, if we are looking for the nine clouds presets, we have to use the Cloud and Cloud high presets and the Master cloud amount to control the amount of clouds present in the sky.

Do you still want to know how to do the same thing in the Weather menu? Probably not, but here is a screenshot that shows where we can find almost the same settings:

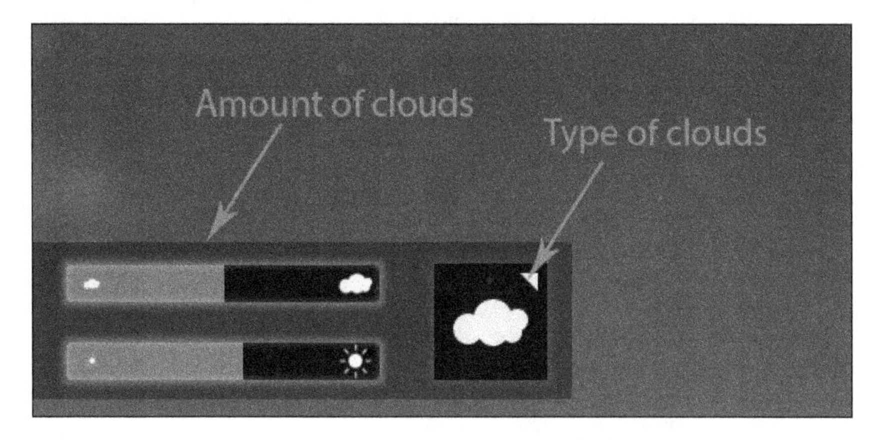

This is what we need to know to start tweaking the exterior lighting, but we also have some tools and lights available to create interior renders or improve an exterior render.

Interior lighting with Lumion's lights

Lumion is an application aimed more toward exterior visualizations, and if you check the model's library, it is easy to understand why. However, with each new Lumion version, new tools appear to create better interior renders, and with the real-time technology, the preview we get is very accurate.

The Lights and special objects library found under the Objects menu has all the tools we need to start improving the interior illumination, and that is what we will use for the next pages.

Spotlight, omni light, and fill light

When we open **Lights And Utilities Library**, there are at least two tabs related to lighting. The initial one, called Light, is probably what we will use most of the time because here we can find the most important lights such as the spotlight and fill light. What about the omni light on the second tab? Well, if you create a night scene and place an omni light and a fill light, you can easily see that the only difference is the intensity and color, and this is something that can be easily achieved by tweaking the properties of the light.

Let's place one of the lights and understand a difference between a spotlight and fill light, but before we start, perhaps it is a good idea to create a layer for these lights.

Placing lights

Let's open **Lights And Utilities Library** and select one spotlight. We will place a light in the same way we place a 3D model, and we can use the same tools to move, rotate, and scale the light. So, everything we learned in the previous chapters can be also used with lights. Once we select a light, we get back to the **Build** mode where we can place the light and see the shadows and intensity of illumination we get, as shown in the following screenshot:

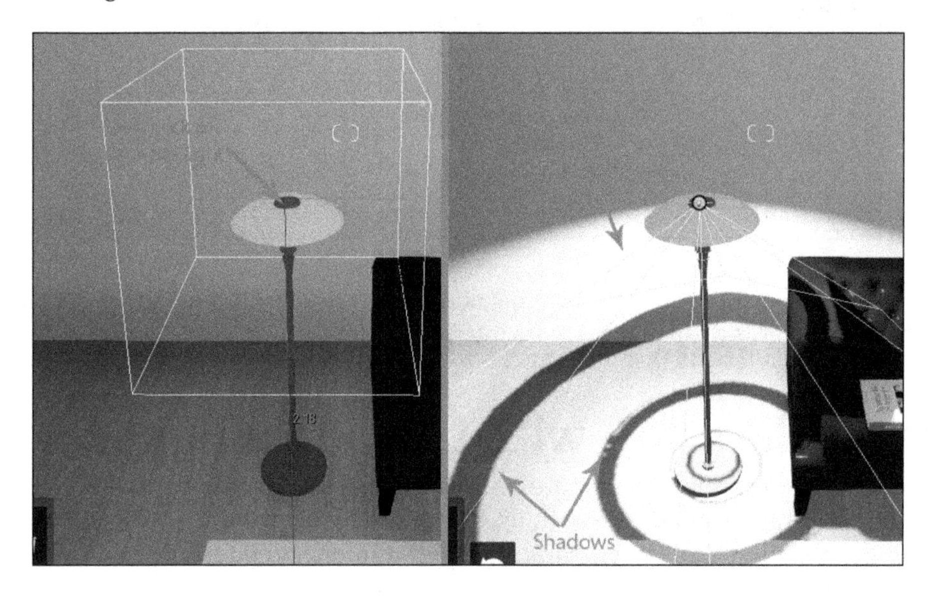

However, as soon as we lift the finger from the mouse button, the shadows disappear. Is there something wrong with our scene? Remember that Lumion's main goal is to provide the best performance possible while building our scene, and lights, in general, can be very memory-consuming. If we had 10 or more lights at full quality, the speed of our viewport would drop drastically, but there is also another side effect.

If you need to check the shadows produced by a light or set of lights, select them by pressing and holding the *Ctrl* key, and select each one to see the shadows produced.

When placing lights in our scene, it is important to remember that the more lights we have in the scene, the longer the render will take. So, we need to think carefully about our scene and try to optimize by checking if we really need those 10 or more lights. It is true that the light we get from a spotlight may not be sufficient to light the entire room, but there is a trick we can use to reduce the amount of lights present in the scene.

Using the fill light

Why might we use this light? This is a good question, and the answer is that with one fill light, we can create good illumination for the entire room. As the name suggests, it is a fill light, and the benefit of this light is that it provides a good illumination but doesn't produce any shadows. So, let's keep these points in mind because later we will see how to use the Global illumination effect to drastically improve the lighting in the scene:

- Lights, in general, are memory consuming and need to be used carefully
- The fill light can be used to provide a good overall illumination in one go
- The Global illumination effect reduces the use of lights

With these points in mind, let's have a look at another way to tweak and improve the quality of the lights in use.

Tweaking lights with the Properties menu

Let's have a look at the fill light. This light has the simplest settings to configure, as shown in the following screenshot:

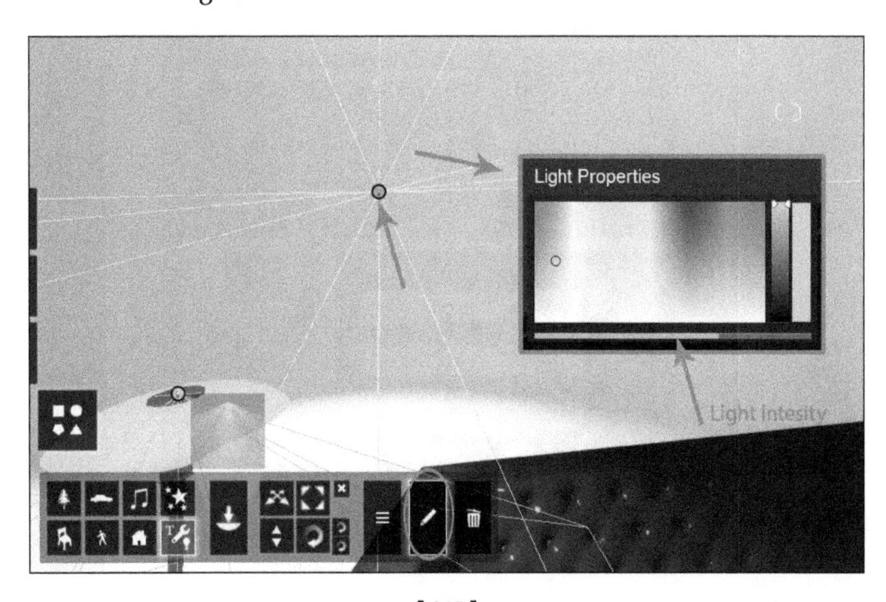

As we can see, the fill light has some simple settings where we can set the light color and more importantly, the light intensity. Before we start cranking up the light intensity, it is wise to first place all the lights we believe are fully necessary and then tweak the intensity of each light, so we can have a balanced scene with a pleasant illumination.

The fill light is a very simple light, but things are different when we open the properties of the spotlight. With a spotlight, we can configure the light color and intensity that is essential when talking about interior lighting. The temperature of a light is measured in Kelvins and a 2700 Kelvins light produces an orange light, a 3500 Kelvins light produces a yellow light, and a 5500 Kelvins light produces a more bluish light. These are just a few examples of how temperatures can produce different results, which also can reproduce several moods for our scene. A cold and bright light is more suitable for a medical environment, but on the other hand, for a cozy room, we want a warmer light. However, this is something that the fill light can also reproduce, so why is the spotlight so special? Let's have a look at the following screenshot and see what is available for us:

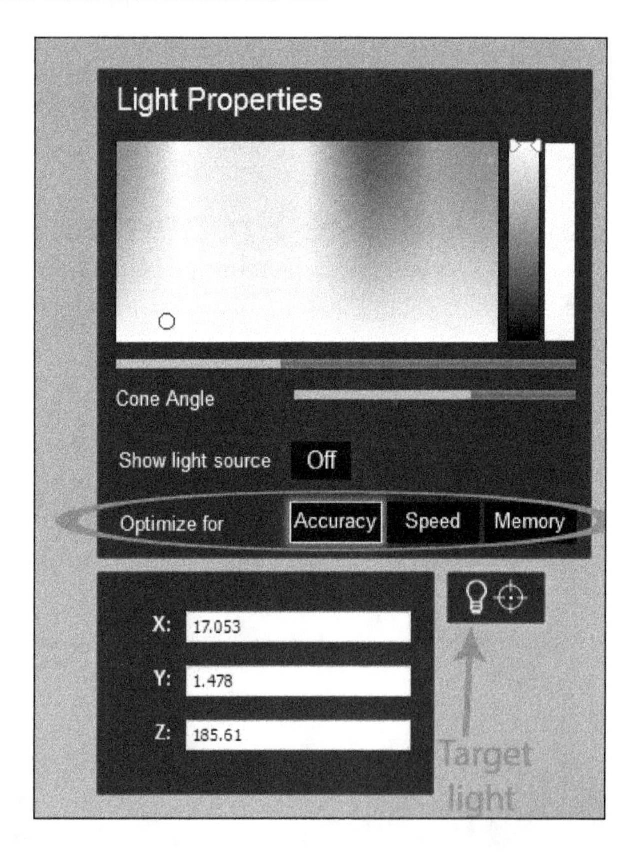

An important aspect that we can see on the screenshot is the possibility to tweak the **Cone Angle** slider, which in turn controls the area that is covered with this light. Initially, when we change the **Cone Angle** slider, there isn't any difference in the area covered, and the reason is because Lumion doesn't automatically update the light; we have to either select the light or move it to see the new cone angle. Keep in mind that the bigger value for the **Cone Angle** slider, the softer the shadows will be and the cone angle will lose detail.

The **Target light** option highlighted in the screenshot is also a useful element to control the light. For example, you probably noticed that in an art gallery, there is always a spotlight that points to the painting. With the Target light option, all we have to do is click with the left mouse button to specify where the spotlight should be pointing. To finish, click on the Back button to save the final position.

Now, the most important aspect when working with spotlights is the type and quality we will use. In order to improve the render time, we need to have a balance between shadow detail and quality.

If we start with the **Accuracy** option, the shadows created by the spotlight are updated every single frame. However, what does this mean? Well, if we have a spotlight with **Accuracy** turned on and an object is moving, the shadows produced are real-time shadows. This is obvious, but with the Speed and Memory options, the shadows produced are static. So, if we have a scene with people walking around, the quality we have to use is **Accuracy**; otherwise, the shadows will not be realistic.

On the other hand, every time we add a light with **Accuracy** turned on, it is another shadow that needs to be calculated at every single frame. The shadow has good quality because a 2048 x 2048 pixel shadow texture is used to create a very accurate and detailed shadow.

However, if we have a scene without life or a static image, we still have two other options.

The **Speed** option provides the perfect balance between render time and shadow quality because it only uses a static 512 x 512 pixel texture, and the shadow is not calculated at every frame.

The **Memory** option is the setting that probably doesn't increase the render time at all because it only uses a static 128 x 128 pixel texture, but the shadow quality is very low. However, there are some tricks to improve not only the interior lighting, but also the reflections. The following screenshot is the comparison between the three different options:

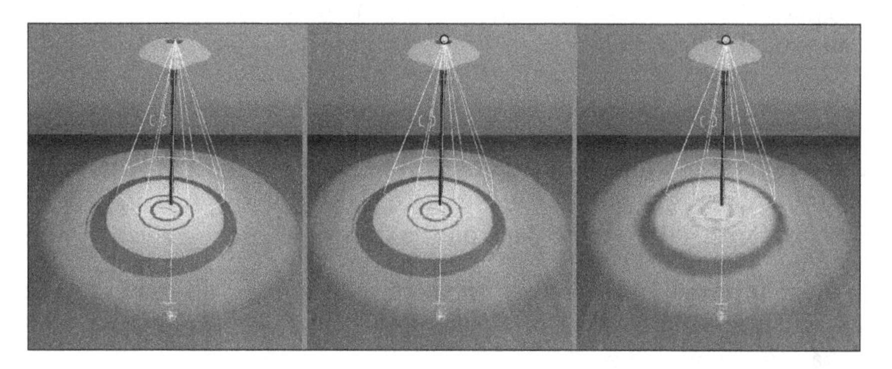

Working with Global illumination

Lumion is a real-time application, as mentioned several times throughout this book, and to keep up with this quality, some corners need to be cut out. Global illumination can include the darkening under an object and near edges and, color bleeding or, in other words, it simulates how light is transferred between surfaces in your 3D scene and it will greatly increase the realism of your scene. This is something that requires loads of processor power, and if Lumion did that in real time, we would need a super computer. For this reason, we need to simulate this global illumination to improve the quality of our renders, particularly when doing interior lighting.

Lumion has a way to simulate global illumination, and this effect can be found in the **World** tab under the name **Global Illumination**. This will add the following module to our scene, as shown in the following screenshot:

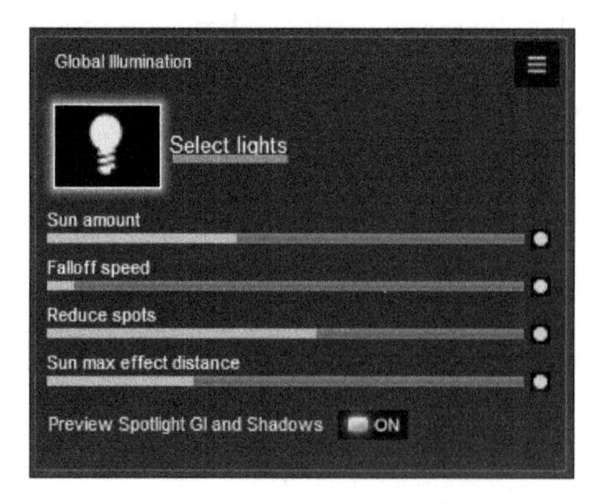

When working with a daytime scene, the first step is to increase the **Sun amount** slider. This action makes the sunlight bounce around the environment and automatically improves the light in areas where it is difficult for the light to hit. This will work fine for buildings with big windows and loads of light entering through the window, but in scenes where we have limited exterior light, there is a second option.

Have a look at the previous screenshot to locate the **Select lights** button. Click on this button, and for a few moments, we are back to the **Build** mode with a small change. Instead of controlling 3D models and other elements, we have the opportunity to select the spotlights with the left mouse button and then, using the Spotlight GI amount slider, start to adjust the spotlight's influence over the scene and the light produced.

The trick with this feature is to select just a few key spotlights and use this option to bring extra light into the scene. There is no need to add global illumination to every single light in the scene, because this will also increase the render time. The next trick is not directly related to lights, but lends an extra hand to improve the reflections.

Improving reflections with a reflection cube

A reflection cube is a feature that can be found under **Lights And Utilities Library**. This is the easiest way to add more accurate reflections to the glass and other elements with reflectivity without increasing the render time. Inside **Lights And Utilities Library**, there is a tab called **Utilities** and here, we can select **Reflection Control** to add reflection control to the scene in the same way we would add a 3D model.

The position and height of the reflection control can make all the difference and in reality, will produce different results. This happens because the reflections in Lumion depend on a panoramic reflection texture that is projected onto all reflective materials, and by specifying the position of the reflection control, we are dictating where the panoramic reflection texture should be rendered. We can use the combination of *Ctrl* + *-U* to update the reflection texture produced by this reflection control.

Summary

This chapter was no doubt an aid to start improving the look and realism of our scene. A correct light rig can make all the difference from an interesting image to an eye-catching and beautiful visualization. You learned how to use the **Weather** menu and some effects to create a good mood for the scene, and this helped introduce how the **Photo** mode works along with the effects available. Then, to bring the scene to the next level, you learned how to correctly use spotlights and fill lights to create an optimized render scene without increasing the render time too much. Finally, you understood how to use the reflection cube to quickly improve the reflection in glass surfaces.

What's next? In the next chapter, you will start the delicate task of tweaking and adjusting dozens of effects, particularly, the ones used with the **Photo** and **Movie** modes, which can make your scene unique. You will see how to use real camera and color correction effects to improve the realism of your project.

7
Creating Realistic Visualizations

Throughout this book we have mentioned several times that Lumion is not a photo-realistic application, and in order to deliver a real-time performance, some corners need to be cut and this can have an impact on the quality. Are we constrained by lack of quality after so much work? In the last chapter, we saw how we can use the Global illumination effect to substantially improve the lighting in the scene, and although there are some limitations of what we can get with Lumion, in reality, we have several elements that can be used to drastically improve the quality and realism of our project.

In this chapter, we will cover the following topics:

- Special effects—fire, smoke, and fog
- Applying and controlling the special effects
- The differences between the **Photo** and **Movie** modes
- Using the Sun Study for accurate lighting
- Tweaking shadows
- Creating realistic reflections
- Improving realism with camera effects
- Rendering still images

A good project, and consequently a perfect still image or movie, is made of the various elements. We need a good detailed model with perfect materials; the weather elements play their part too. However, it is in this chapter that we will start exploring the true potential of Lumion.

Special effects – fire, smoke, and fog

As mentioned in the introduction of this chapter, the eye for detail and the attention that we give to the details can make a massive difference between a reasonable scene and an eye-catching scene. This is not exaggerating the reality because if you have followed the instructions and techniques from the examples in this book, you have experienced this first-hand. After applying the techniques showed in this book, you may have made your visualization much more realistic. Now, let's see how we can use these effects and explore some practical applications.

Fire, smoke, and fog are elements that can be placed on the scene in the same way we place a 3D model. We need to open **Objects Library** and locate the Effects button to open **Effects Library**, as shown in the following screenshot:

It is amazing to find what is available inside this library, but it's also a word of caution! Although we have these fantastic elements ready to use, adding these special effects should be done in a reasonable way because if we overdo this, the result can be an unpleasant render that would look totally artificial.

Before we go even further, there is something we need to keep in mind. For example, select the Fire tab and see that there are 16 different types of fires. Great, but these 16 types of fires are just variations of the first fire. The same happens with the other elements. Perhaps the best example is the fog emitter that can be used to create several elements with endless variations.

However, instead of having one element of each, Lumion gives us a hand by providing shortcuts that can be easily tweaked to fit our needs.

A particle emitter is an essential element of a particle system. What is a particle system?

A particle system is a collection of many many minute particles that together represent a fuzzy object. Over a period of time, particles are generated into a system, move and change from within the system, and die from the system.

– William Reeves, "Particle Systems – A Technique for Modeling a Class of Fuzzy Objects," ACM Transactions on Graphics 2:2 (April 1983), 92.

The fire we see in Lumion in reality is a collection of images that when put together creates the illusion of fire. The same applies to the other elements and this happens because rendering these kind of elements is very time and resource consuming.

So, in what ways can we use these elements to enhance the scene and produce the best result possible?

Special elements – practical applications

Each project is different and what we will see now may or may not be useful for your present scene. Even if you are not thinking of using these special elements for your current project, it is at least a good idea to know how they work.

Fire – a practical example

Fire is perhaps the most applicable element among all the others. For example, you may be associating fire with a fireplace. Fair enough, but there are other useful and practical applications like the one exemplified in the following screenshot:

Of course, although the fire we used has the right area, the height is too big for the barbeque. What we have to do is select the **Edit properties** button and pick the fire so that we can have access to the following settings:

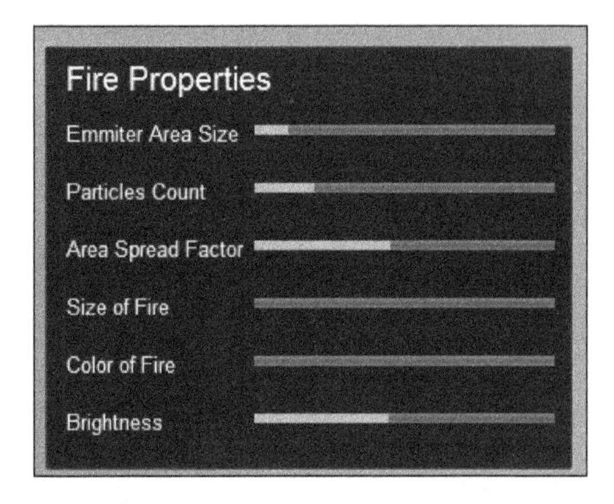

What can we say about these settings? The easiest way to explain these settings is by showing the result between values. Let's start with:

- **Emmiter Area Size**: This defines the area that is covered by the fire, as shown in the following screenshot:

- **Particles Count**: This defines how many particles of fire are created and this can be used to create a controlled fire (for example, a candle) and a wild and vivid fire (for example, an external fireplace), as shown in the following screenshot:

- **Area Spread Factor**: This setting works in conjunction with **Emmiter Area Size** and basically shows how tight the particles are in relation to the emitter, as shown in the following screenshot:

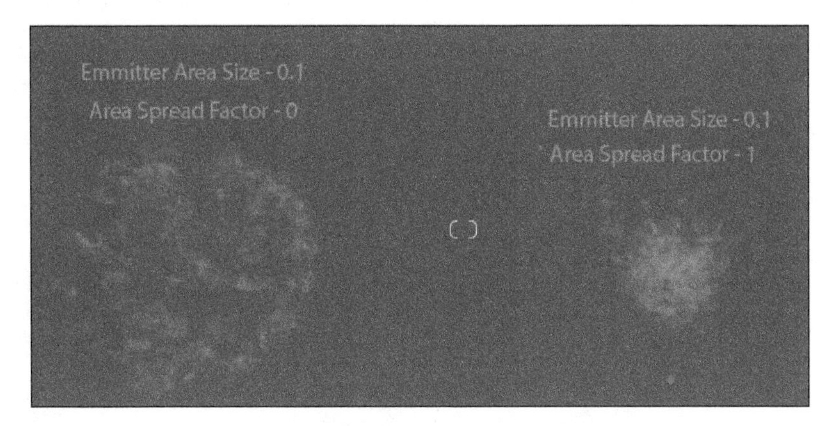

- **Size of Fire**: This, basically, shows how big the fire is in height
- **Color of Fire**: In case you want to create a fantasy environment here, we cycle between orange, green, cyan, blue, and purple
- **Brightness**: This basically can create a dull and an ending fire to a vivid fire, as shown in the following screenshot:

There is an extra touch we can add to slightly improve the look of our fire. If you look closely at the fire that you placed in the scene, you can see that although we have a fire, this doesn't emit any light. In this situation, it is not a big deal, but when we move to an interior scene adding a fill light, or even a spotlight with an orange color it can totally transform the living room into a cozy and welcome environment. Again, small details can make all the difference and since we mentioned this, let's get back to our barbeque and add an additional element that is missing and we are not referring to the meat.

Smoke – a practical example

Let's have a look at the following screenshot and see how adding smoke to the fire helps to increase the level of realism, as shown in the following screenshot:

Again, we need to tweak this element so that it blends nicely with the scene. So, what can we accomplish with the settings available and what are the differences between them? Yes, you are right because we will use examples to explain how it works:

- **Color and Overbright**: These are the initial settings we need to tweak if we want to change the color and brightness of the smoke
- **Density**: This is where we can define the opacity for the smoke, but keep in mind that high values may not produce the best results, particularly for close-ups, as shown in the following screenshot:

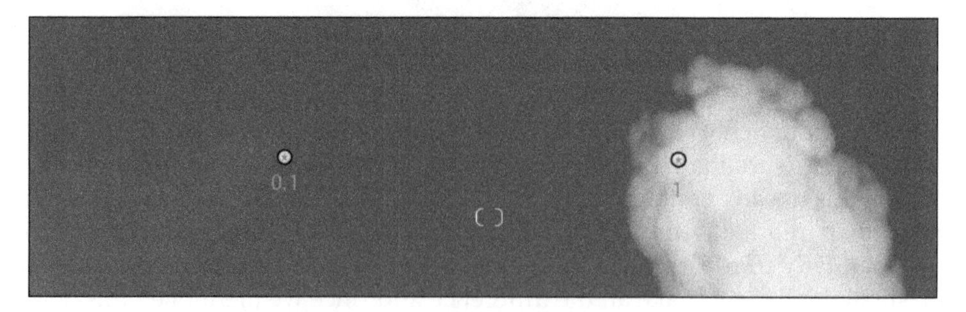

- **Column Size**: This basically increases the height of the smoke's column, but if we start to increase this value, it is also essential to work with the next settings to create a believable smoke column

- **Particle Size**: This is a useful setting to tweak the thickness of the smoke column, as shown in the following screenshot:

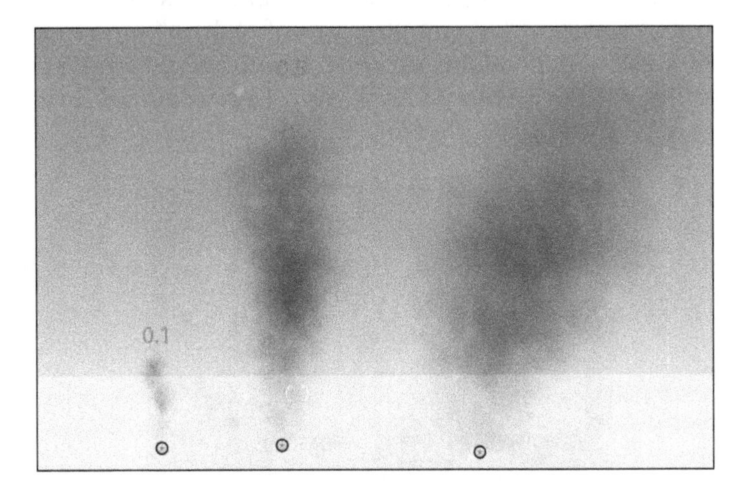

- **Randomize**: In scenes where we will see smoke from a long distance, this setting can be used to add some variation on how the smoke column rises to the sky, as shown in the following screenshot:

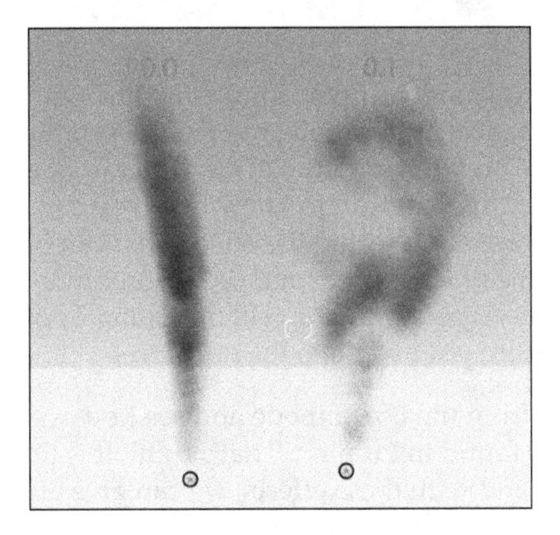

Smoke is something we can also add to a chimney or to mimic the vapor that comes from an underground grid.

What about the **Fog** tab? Is there anything useful inside this tab for our scene? Once again, it depends on the type of project we will work on, but let's have a look at this final special element and then we can jump to a much more creative area.

Fog – practical examples

The first thing we realize when we open this tab is that we not only have fog, but also dust, steam, and water dust. If you place one of each on your scene and open the **Properties** panel, you can see that the fog, dust, steam, and water dust use the same properties. In reality, the **Properties** panel is called **Fog Properties**, even if you are using water dust, as shown in the following screenshot:

Definitely, after all the explanations given for the fire and smoke, these settings are self-explanatory. The practical application goes from reproducing mist in the early morning; mimic the haze on the horizon with the water dust and create a hot tub with the steam. However, the best way to know how you can apply these special effects is by giving them a go and seeing the effects that can be created. Don't be constrained with the name of the emitter and see if you can use these elements in a totally new way. With the experience, you will find good opportunities to use all of these elements and enhance your scene to the next level.

Now, it is time to move from the **Build** mode and see how we can use one of the most powerful elements found in Lumion. That's right, it is time to start working with the camera effects, and with these effects, we can give an extra level of detail that otherwise would be difficult to achieve.

Photo and Movie effects

Although this is a fundamental aspect to work with Lumion, the truth is that this is nothing new for you by now. The *Photo and Movie mode – a very quick introduction* section in *Chapter 6, Lighting in Lumion*, gave a fair introduction to the **Photo** mode.

We have already mentioned the benefits of using effects in the scene and exemplified how to add the global illumination effect to the scene to achieve a fantastic result in the lighting area. Although we started to cover some effects in the previous chapter, here is the official start of how to use Lumion's effects. This chapter is aimed at providing you all the information you need to fully and completely master Lumion's camera effects.

What are the effects and how can they help me?

What are the effects and how can they help me is a fair question because the way Lumion is presented is that we can easily create a movie or still images in a relatively short period of time. Some will even say that they can have a movie ready to render in 15 minutes. However, this *help* from Lumion can be a reason why our projects don't look so great because we forget to add layers of detail, which in turn, will contribute to create a believable and more realistic image.

Now, getting to the point, Lumion has some camera effects that assist in adding realism to our scene. The artifacts and errors that the photographer wants to remove, such as chromatic aberration, vignette and noise and lens distortion, are precisely what we want to add to our scene to improve the realism, but why? Pick a camera, take a photo, and then look at it closely. Can you see what looks like grain in the picture or the dark corners around the picture? Can you see the purple line close to the edge? These are elements that help our brain to tell: I am looking at a picture and not at a 3D image.

This is what we can add to our scene, but don't overuse it.

Let's establish a golden rule: if you start to see the effect clearly, it is time to stop and go back one or two values depending on the effect. We don't want to see the effect, we want our brain to perceive the effect.

We need to fully understand first about the effect so that we can correctly apply it because in some situations, this effect doesn't happen and will look artificial. So, take some time to test and fully understand how they work and what they can be used for. Only then you will fully master Lumion's camera effects.

Things needed for this chapter

For now, we will focus our attention only at the **Photo** mode. So, why is the main topic mentioning the Movie effects? The reason is because all the effects we will see here can be applied both to a static image (the **Photo** mode) and to a movie (the **Movie** mode). For this reason, it is good to keep in mind that all you will learn here can also be applied into the Movie effect, which is going to be covered in *Chapter 9, Animation Techniques*. Are you losing something for not using the **Movie** mode?

The difference with using the Movie mode

The difference between the **Movie** and **Photo** modes is that the **Movie** mode is designed to create small clips that when combined creates a movie.

> The truth is that we can also create static images using the **Movie** mode, although the control we have might not be the best, the benefit is that we have access to more options. This includes the opportunity to export render passes that can be later used to tweak the image.

The **Photo** mode on the other hand gives a quick access to output a single still image, as shown in the following screenshot:

Let's say we tweak an effect in the **Photo** mode, and now that we are working in the **Movie** mode, we want to use the same effect to achieve the same result. Do you have to grab a pen to write down the values used in the **Photo** mode? Thankfully, the answer is no because Lumion allows us to copy some effects from the **Photo** to **Movie** mode and vice versa. This is something we will cover in *Chapter 9, Animation Techniques*, so that we can focus our attention on the effects.

Sun study – what is it and how can it be useful

One of the first things defined right from the start of the project is where the building is going to be located. This has a massive impact on how we develop the scene in Lumion and as an example, just think of the native plants found in Africa and the ones found in Asia. These kind of aspects need to be prepared through the project, but there is something else with a big influence in the scene. In this instance, we are referring to how the Sun and shadows affect the building and the surroundings, and this is so important that it can force the designer to change where certain trees will be planted.

In Lumion, we have an amazing and useful effect called **Sun study** that can be found on the **World** tab, and with this effect, we have access to the following settings:

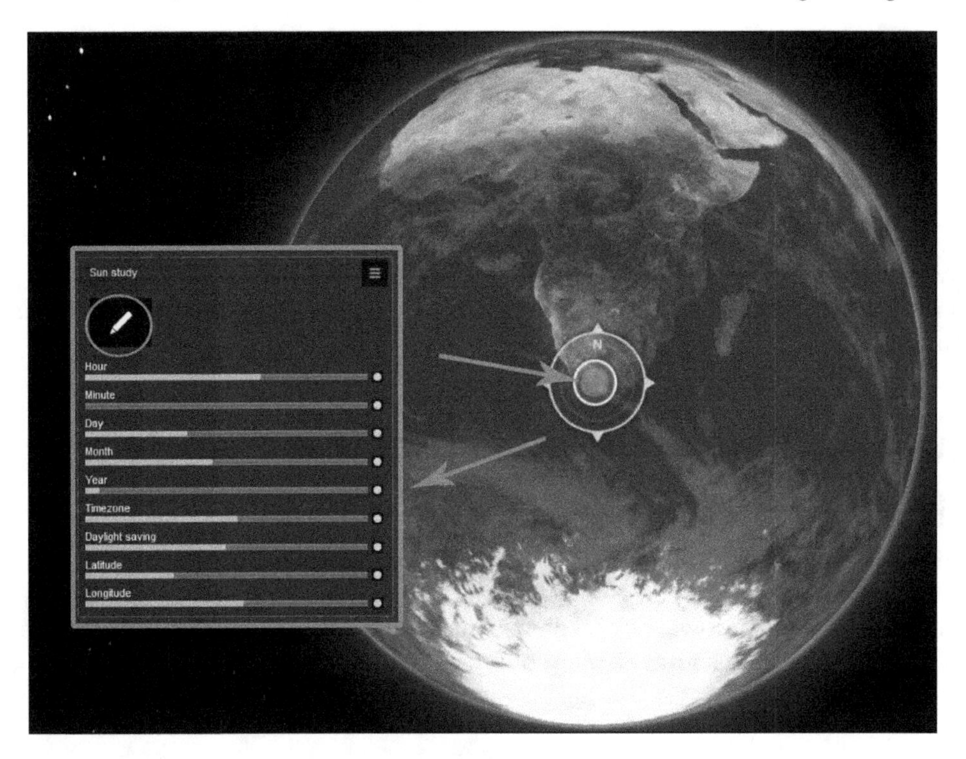

As you can see, the concept of this effect is simple and intuitive. The first step is to select an approximate location where the building is located and for this, we have to use the following:

- **The right mouse button**: Click and drag to orbit around the globe
- **The mouse wheel**: This is used to zoom in and out to be more accurate when selecting the location
- **The left mouse button**: This is used to select the location

This is the most intuitive and direct way to pinpoint the location of the building, but if we need to be very accurate, there is the possibility to use the latitude and longitude values.

To help you get the exact location of the building, refer to `http://www.latlong.net/`

The rest of the settings are self-explanatory and the beauty of using these settings is that one can create a time lapse movie, but that is something we will see further in this book. So, for now, just tweak the settings according to what you need. Try different values to see which one produces the most pleasing and eye-catching look.

You may wonder what the **Daylight saving** setting is. The daylight saving time is the time that is adjusted to achieve longer evening daylight in summer by setting the clocks an hour ahead of the standard time. This gives us the opportunity to make better use of daylight, although not all the countries follow this rule.

Now, that we took care of the sun, there is something else that could be tweaked and most of the times, we don't even realize how important they are. We are talking about shadows.

Tweaking shadows using the Shadow effect

Shadows are an essential element to create a believable environment and if you don't understand why, just try to press the *F1* key and see your scene without any shadows. Without shadows, our scene becomes very dull and lifeless and this shows why shadows are such a vital element of our scene.

However, you may be asking: aren't the default settings good enough? Well, you probably will be able to answer that question after this reading and applying the techniques covered. Let's add the **Shadow** effect that can be found under the **World** tab. However, before we move further, there is something we need to understand.

Working of shadows in Lumion

In order to correctly tweak the shadows and spot any issues, we need to understand how Lumion works with shadows. Once again keep in mind that Lumion is a real-time application and to prevent flickering or any other shadow artifacts, Lumion applies the shadow on top of every surface with a small offset. It may happen that we are creating a close-up of some 3D models to look as if they were floating with no contact with a surface. This is when we need to correct or tweak the shadow.

Correcting shadows

As explained in the previous topic, in some situations, when the camera is close to a 3D model, the shadow has an offset in relation to the 3D model giving the impression that we have a serious case of floating objects, as shown in the following screenshot:

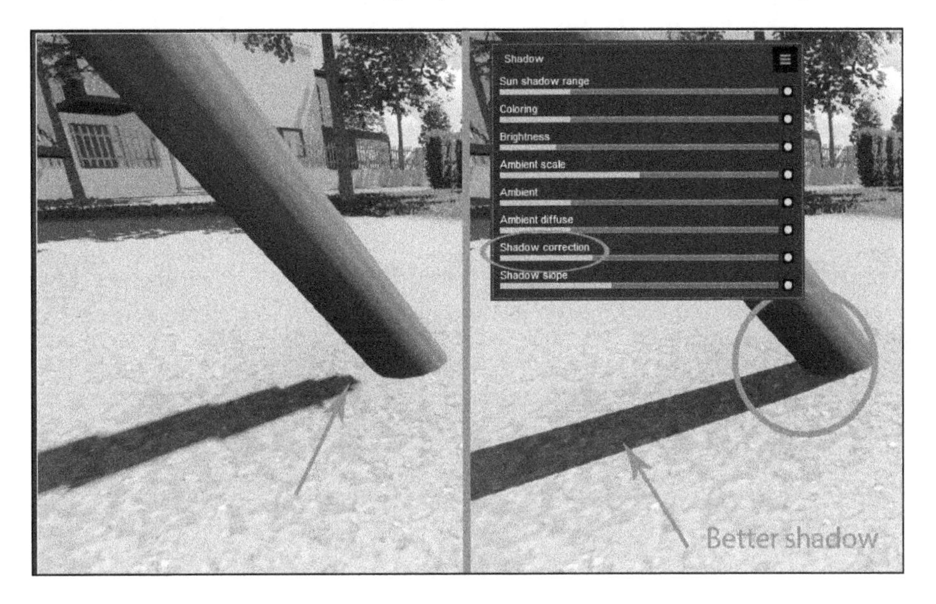

The image on the left clearly shows the offset between the 3D model and the shadow, but the image on the right side is correct because we used the **Shadow correction** setting as highlighted in the screenshot. This is the first step to start correcting some issues with the shadows, but if you look closely at the previous screenshot, there is another aspect that needs to be taken into consideration.

There is a massive difference between shadows when we compare the right-hand side image with the left-hand side one. So, what happened? On the left side, the Sun shadow range was tweaked in order to increase the quality of the shadow, but we need to be reasonable. Why? We may want to play safe and decrease this value in order to get the best shadows possible, but on the other hand, this will make objects far away from the camera causing the loss of shadows. And if you increase the Sun shadow range to the maximum value, it is true that we recover the shadows, but the quality drops quite substantially. This is more of a problem when creating movies, but can be tackled by animating the effect. That is right, we can animate effects and this is something that we will be covering in *Chapter 9, Animation Techniques.*

Is there anything else we can do to improve the quality of the shadows and the sunlight?

Coloring and tweaking soft shadows

In an exterior daylight scene, the main light source is the sun, but then there is another element that also influences the shadows—the sky. Comparing with the sun, the light from the sky is soft and diffuse giving a different tint to shadows accordingly to the weather. A clear sky can make the shadows darker and bluer, but on the other hand, when the sky has more clouds (overcast), the shadows become grayer. Can we mimic this effect in Lumion?

Once again, the **Shadow** effect has the answer with the **Coloring** setting. A value close to 1 will increase the bluish look and a lower value creates a warmer color. Keep in mind the guidelines already mentioned to use the correct color accordingly with the weather and lighting you have.

Before we move to a more artistic section, let's talk about soft shadows and how they can be both good and bad to our scene. It may happen that our scenes in some areas look something like this:

This scene is full of blotchiness where two surfaces are close to each other. In real life, we have these kinds of soft shadows that are produced by light bouncing of the elements in the world. So, in one way, these shadows are great to improve the realism when applied in a subtle way, but on the other side, the image above is not acceptable. How can we solve this? The **Shadow** effect has three settings to control these shadows, as shown in the following screenshot:

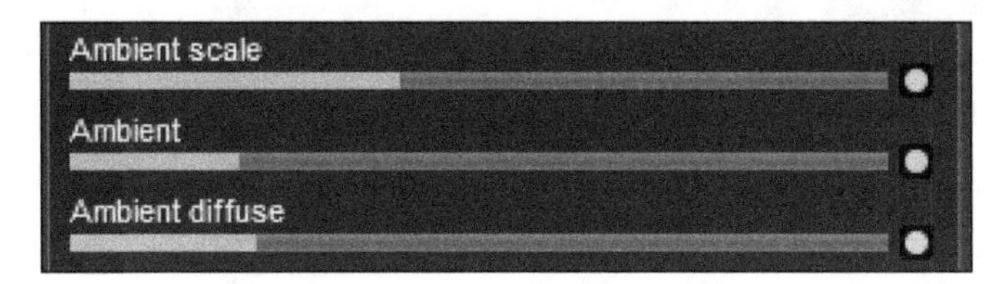

Firstly, we need to start by tweaking the **Ambient** slider because this controls the intensity of soft shadows, while the **Ambient diffuse** slider allows us to control the brightness or darkness of the shadows. The final point is the **Ambient scale** slider that needs to be tweaked, taking into consideration the size of our 3D model and the objects around it.

Working with these settings is not a bad idea to render a small preview in order to check how the effect is working. Lumion viewports can give you an idea, but this often proves not to be enough to check the effect.

So, we have defined a location for the building in order to get accurate shadows. We have also tweaked the shadows, so what's next? Next, we have to improve reflections with the **Reflection** effect.

Creating realistic reflections

Reflections are another essential aspect that needs to be tweaked and controlled. We saw how to control the reflections in materials and also mentioned how to slightly improve the reflection in glass surfaces. However, it is natural that even when using a **Reflection** control, the reflections don't meet our requirements in terms of accuracy. The effect we need is the **Reflection** effect, which is found under the **World** tab.

The following screenshot helps understand how this effect works:

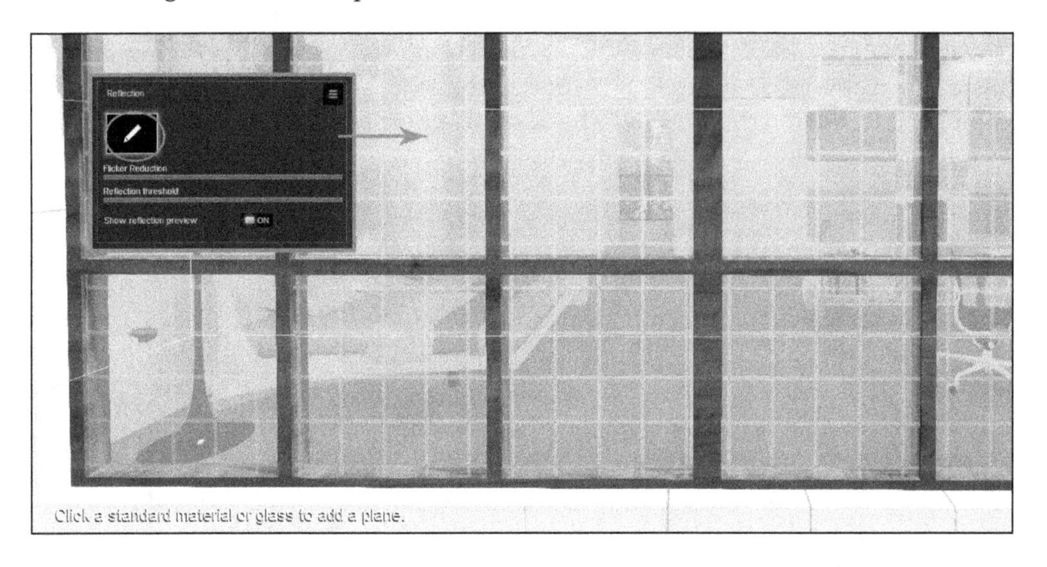

After selecting the **Reflection** effect, we need to click on the button with the pencil. This will get us back to the **Build** mode where we need to select a **Standard** or a **Glass** material to add a plane. After adding a reflection plane to a glass surface, we have to click on the **Back** button and the difference between the default Lumion's default reflections and the reflections obtained by the **Reflection** effect is immediately noticeable.

Great, so let's add reflections to all the surfaces! This is when we receive the bad news and the bad news is that we can only add 10 reflection planes in each scene. Even so, we need to use these reflection planes with prudence and wisdom. The reason is because every time we have a reflection plane, the entire scene is mirrored to produce those nice reflections. Now, imagine your scene mirrored 10 times and it will start feeling the massive impact on the performance of the viewport and not to mention the increase of render time.

How can we tackle this problem? By planning carefully where we need good reflections, by using surfaces with a low polygon count, and by tweaking the materials the best way possible.

Due to Lumion's limitations, we cannot add this reflection plane to elements such as the ocean, water surface, grass, and other special elements.

The control we have over the reflections is limited. We can reduce flickering, which is noticeable in movies; the other essential setting is the **Reflection** threshold. In this setting, let's adjust the distance at which nearly-co-planar surfaces are included in the reflection plane. This is very important to use when surfaces close to the reflection plane aren't reflected.

After all this hard work, it is time to be more artistic and start to explore the effects we can find at the **Camera**, **Style**, and **Artistic** tabs.

Improving the realism with Camera effects

Before we jump to this fantastic effect, there is something that needs to be discussed. Throughout this book, we have been using a scene as an example to show how to fully master Lumion, but the main purpose of this book is not for you to create a perfect copy of the example you see here. Instead, the information and techniques showed are aimed to provide everything you need to apply the same techniques to your own project creating a unique piece of work.

So, you may find the next topics somehow subjective and it may seem like some lack of information or guidelines. Let's face it—if you're ready to add Chromatic Aberration with 0.2 of **Dispersion**, 0.9 of **Affection Area**, and 0.5 of **Safe Shadows**, this is not going to help you to master Lumion's effects and know what they are and how to use them. You need to apply them and tweak them over and over again until you understand what can be accomplished with each setting. Besides, it is important to apply these effects using photo references in order to achieve a natural look.

Camera effects – what are they and how to use them

For the next effects, we will first learn what they are and how they work in the real world. After this, we will have an overview of how to use them or what the different settings can do with the help of close-up screenshots highlighting specific areas. Let's start with depth of field.

Depth of field

The easiest way to explain what **depth of field** (**DOF**) is, is by having a look at the following screenshot:

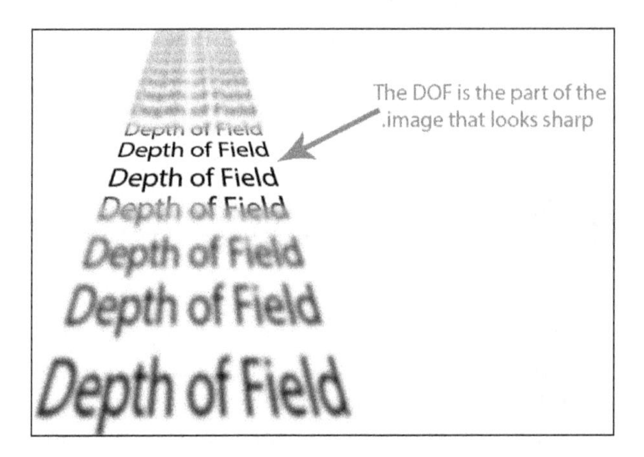

Why is this effect important? When using DOF, the viewers' attention is grabbed by the area that is in focus blurring any distractions. When correctly used, DOF can have a deep impact both on the art and quality of the image or movie.

When we add this effect to the **Photo** mode, these are the settings available:

- **Focus distance**: This specifies where the camera should focus
- **F stop**: This removes some of the blur, but most importantly creates a gradual transition between sharp and blurred areas
- **Smoothness**: This is used to create sharper edges, but you probably should leave this at `1`
- **Isolate foreground**: This controls the layers of DOF in front of the camera, but `9` out of `10` doesn't produce a good result
- **Expansion**: This works great for close-ups to get a sharper look of the 3D model in focus

This effect is very sensitive, so don't forget to use the *Shift* key to make smaller increments.

Creating lens artifacts with the Lens Flare effect

If we take a photo against a direct source of light, like the sun, some lens artifacts will appear later in the picture. These artifacts can be added to our scene using the Lens Flare effect, but we need to do it in a very subtle way. There isn't anything more 3D than the overuse of lens flare, and for this reason, we should take some time to understand the different situations where these artifacts appear, but also artistic ways to enhance our scene. The following screenshot shows the artifacts we can add to an image:

The settings highlighted in the screenshot are the artifacts that can be produced with this effect. All the other settings are involved with the intensity and quality of these artifacts. Use them wisely. Don't forget to check your references for similar photos.

Balancing the Bloom effect with the Exposure effect

The camera lenses can never focus perfectly and this is fine in most situations. However, when we take a photo with an intensely bright light, all these imperfections are perceptible, particularly, the halo effect around the bright areas. The **Bloom** effect can be found under the **Style** tab and when this effect is added to the scene, we only have to control one setting to increase or decrease the amount of bloom in the scene, but this will make our scene too bright in some situations.

This is when the **Exposure** effect comes into play to save the scene because with this effect, we can define how light or dark an image will appear. This also helps to understand another important concept—layers of effects. When working with effects, we need to keep in mind that some effects can null a previous effect. For example, if we first added the **Exposure** effect and then the **Bloom** effect, probably, we needed to go back to the **Exposure** effect and tweak it again.

The combination of these two effects can be used to reproduce what happens when we shoot inside a room and a window to the outside is over-bright with bloom around the window.

Noise

Adding noise to our image may sound strange, but the noise we are referring to describes the flecks or grains that appear with low quality cameras or when we shoot in low light. This is something that when added to a 3D image can help to make the image more believable, but we need to add just a small amount and not exaggerate like we did here:

The **Noise** effect can be found under the **Style** tab, but don't copy the previous screenshot because the main goal of this image is only to show what noise is. The trick with this effect is going back a few values once the noise starts to be noticeable. Too much noise will distract the viewer, but the correct amount will trick the brain to think that the image is a photo. However, if you are creating a night time scene, adding a little bit of extra noise will actually help to sell the image or movie.

Changing the saturation with the Selective Saturation effect

Under the **Style** tab, we have another effect that initially may not look useful at all. **Selective Saturation** is one effect that when applied will create an oversaturated image that doesn't look natural. So, how can we use this effect?

One application is using this effect to actually remove saturation from the scene. This may happen because of the previous effects we used and this effect can be used as the final way to bring a more natural look to the image. For this, you need to bring the **Range** slider to 0 and work only with **Residual Color Desaturation**.

Another application that is more artistic than realistic is using this effect to isolate colors. Is this useful for a project? For example, perhaps the scene we are working on has loads of vegetation and this can distract the viewer from the building itself. The **Color section** setting is the key to isolate or remove colors from the image. A value of `0.3` will bring the green color and the different hues, a value of `0.5` isolates the blue color, and finally, the value of `0.9` isolates the orange\red\brown color.

Color correcting in Lumion

The next step to enhance the image or movie is by color correcting the scene. Although this expression can have many meanings, usually when we color correct, it will repair or remove problems with the colors in an image by tweaking and changing the pixels that make the image.

In Lumion, we need to use the Color correction effect once again found under the **Style** tab, but keep in mind that this doesn't mean you can change a blue pixel to red or vice versa. Although we have many settings, you will eventually work with just a few of them such as:

- **Enhance contrast**: This is used to make the shadows darker and bring more contrast to the image
- **Gamma**: This is something you don't want to change for now unless you want to change the gamma later in an application such Photoshop
- **Saturation**: This can be a replacement for the previous effect if you are only looking after changing the saturation of the entire image

As you can see, there is no magic number to color correct an image because every image or movie is different from the previous one. The main goal of this effect is to improve some elements in our scene or to do some color grading.

Color grading usually is the final step when correcting an image because we are giving the final look to the image or movie. We have stopped at the **Saturation** setting because the next settings are the tools you need to give the final look to the scene.

How do **Red Shift** and **Blue Shift** work? Both these settings are going to remove some colors from the scene. For example, if you use a negative value for **Red Shift**, the image will get a Cyan tint, but if you use a positive value, the image will get a purple tint. **Blue Shift** works in the same way, but in this case, a negative value creates an image with a yellow tint and a positive value will create a blue tint.

Great, but how can we apply this to give the final look? For example, if you set **Red Shift** to `0.6`, this will add more red color to the image. If we set **Blue Shift** to `-0.3`, the blue color will be removed from the image. What is the final result? You created a warmer mood that will work great for sunny days or to create a cozier environment. So, why don't you try to invert the values for both settings and see the final result?

Adding vignette

What a strange word—**vignette**. In reality, this is a French word to describe different things, but in photography and in 3D, this word is used to describe an undesired effect caused by camera settings. When the corners of an image are darkened, which can be very strong or hardly noticeable when compared with the center, it is called vignette, as shown in the following screenshot:

This effect can be found under the **Artistic** tab and is called vignette. The settings are very simple; we have **Vignette Amount** to control the quantity of vignette and **Vignette Softness** to control how strong the vignette is.

However, why do we want to use this effect in our scene? Firstly, because this is something that occurs naturally and consequently when the correct amount is applied, the image becomes more realistic. The second reason is to pull the viewer's attention to the center of the image hiding any distractions. Once again, there isn't any correct value for this and the other effects because only the experience and references will tell you how strong and how discrete the vignette is going to be in your scene.

Lens' errors – chromatic aberrations

The best way to explain what is a chromatic aberration is by having a look at the following screenshot:

It is painful to watch an image like the previous one, but the effect was exaggerated in order to be visible. So, the purple fringing, distortion, and the blurred edges are a combination of errors that are called **chromatic aberration**.

This effect can be found under the **Artistic** tab and is called **Chromatic Aberrations**. Once again the same question appears: why should we use this effect? The reason is that these errors are common in photos or movies and adding the correct amount will help to increase and enhance the realism of our scene. However, we really need to be cautious with this effect because too much will ruin the image making the viewers feel repulsed instead of getting attracted to what they are seeing.

A practical application for the God Rays effect

God Rays is one of those effects that can only be used from time to time. Is this true? Although the **God Rays** effect found under the **Artistic** tab is used primarily to create, that is right **God Rays**, in reality, we can reproduce a haze. Haze is an atmospheric phenomenon where dust and other particles change the clarity of the sky. The settings available with this effect are **Decay**, **Length**, and **Intensity** that need to be tweaked according to your scene in order to create this effect, as shown in the following screenshot:

Before we move to the final topic about *Rendering still images*, let's have a look at two final effects that can also help to enhance the scene.

Working with Horizon and Volume Clouds

The first effect that we will see is called **Horizon Cloud** and can be found under the **Weather** tab. The settings available are very simple because we can only change the amount and the type of clouds and add some softness to the clouds, but the final result will be something like this:

What is the benefit of using this effect? In some situations, we may not have enough environments to be reflected into glass surfaces and instead of having an ugly reflection of the horizon line, with this effect, we can add a nice cloud to break that line. If you find it difficult to see the clouds, press the *U* key to render it with high quality.

The other effect is a little bit more complex and is called **Volume Clouds**, which creates a really 3D cloud. The benefit of using these types of clouds is the opportunity to create animations flying through the cloud. The other benefit that helps improve the realism is that these types of clouds produce real-time shadows, as shown in the following screenshot:

Render still Images with the Photo mode

Now that we applied all of these effects, there is something we need to do and that is rendering or exporting the images of the scene. Doing this in the **Photo** mode is very easy because all you have to do is select the size of the image and this will open the Windows Explorer to specify the folder to save the image, as shown in the following screenshot:

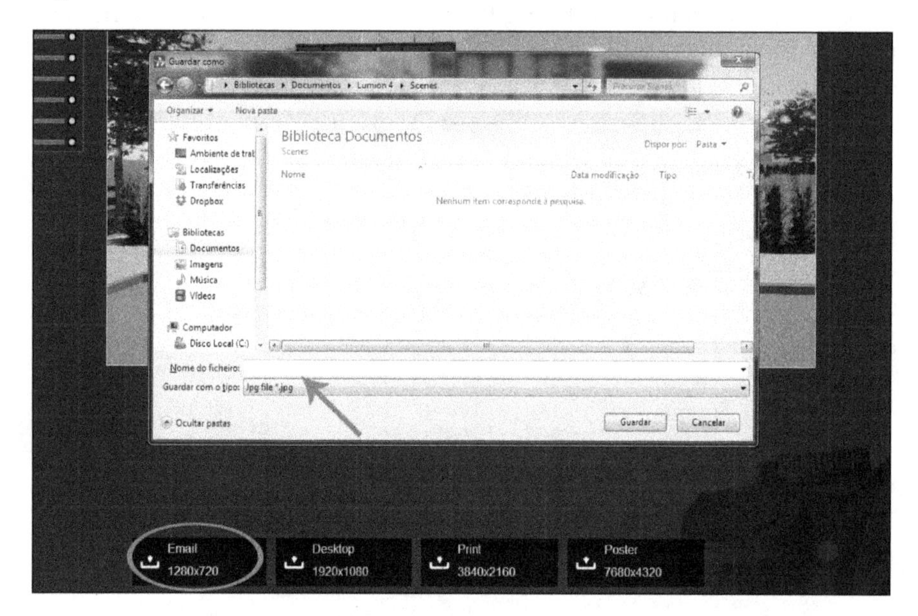

Then, just click on **Save** and enjoy a cup of coffee while Lumion renders the final image.

Summary

This chapter was the cornerstone for your project. Here, you learned the magic of adding special elements such as fire, smoke, and fog along with practical applications for real projects. Then, you jumped perhaps to a more exciting topic: **Photo** and **Movie** effects. You learned not only what they are, but also how they can be used to improve the realism of your project. You didn't find any magic formula for these effects because as mentioned several times, each project, each image, and each camera position has its own needs. However, with all the knowledge and techniques covered, you will be able to fully master Lumion's effects.

In the next chapter, we will carry on exploring these effects, but in a more artistic way by mimicking some art techniques. You will see how to use them to create technical and conceptual illustrations. You will learn how to combine effects and manipulate them in order to achieve beautiful nonphotorealistic renders.

8

Non-photorealistic Visualizations with Lumion

For the majority of architectural visualizations, we are advised to create realistic and believable images or movies. However, in particular situations, the client or company may not want to be too detailed with materials and other elements essential to create an accurate 3D visualization. From time to time, the client may instead want something relatively simple or more artistic, and we may feel anxious to meet these types of requirements. The previous chapter was dedicated to creating believable architectural visualizations and for that, we covered a wide variety of camera effects and other elements to build layers and layers of detail contributing to a realistic render. Still, it is normal to enquire if Lumion can help us with a different approach to architectural visualizations.

The answer is yes! In this chapter, we will take a step back from the realistic region and move to a more technical, conceptual, and even artistic side.

In this chapter, we will cover the following topics:

- Non-photorealistic Render
- Using NPR visualizations
- Creating NPR using Lumion
- Artistic effects—what is available
- Controlling Lumion's effects
- Exploring artistic effects
- Creating conceptual visualizations
- The Painting and Watercolor effects
- The Sketch effect

- Creating technical illustrations with the Manga and Cartoon effects
- Correcting perspectives in Lumion
- The Sharpness effect

As you can see from these bullet points, we will explore what NPR is and why to use it. Then, we are back to the **Photo** mode to explore the effects that can be used to create such visualizations. Nonetheless, what is NPR?

Non-photorealistic rendering

Non-photorealistic rendering (NPR) is the use of artistic techniques to create an image or a movie without the realism component. In other words, the image or movie still represents the structure or the environment, but not in a photorealistic way.

What are some artistic ways to create NPRs? There was life before 3D and proof of this is the fantastic paintings from some famous artists that represent buildings and places. With just a few strokes and much less detail, these artists managed to bring to us beautiful places and times that otherwise would be lost forever.

> If you are interested in seeing some examples of paintings of buildings, search for works from the following artists:
> Perrot Ferdinand-Victor, Beggrov Karl Petrovich, Paterssen Benjamin, and Grekov Alexei Angiliyevich, to mention a few.

What did the artists use to produce such beautiful pieces of art? We do not have only oil paintings, but also impressionism, cell shading, stippling, cross-hatching, and outlines, just to mention a few techniques. However, by now, you might wonder why we should use this artistic approach. And what are the benefits?

Benefits of using NPR's illustrations

One element that characterizes NPR's illustrations is the free style, without any constraint to precision, perfection, and fidelity. We don't paint each leaf on a tree or every grass blade, because we only want to convey the idea of a tree or a grass field. This is perfect for scenarios where the client only desires a simple representation of the building or site. This kind of illustration is useful during the conceptual design or for an outline application where no commitment to materials or other elements is required. The only intention is to provide an idea of the conceptual design.

So, when a client wants a visualization of a conceptual design, our best solution sometimes is not to provide a complex and realistic architectural visualization, but instead an NPR that will still be a useful piece of information. Sometimes, an NPR is a breath of fresh air among all the realistic renders, and when well-performed, can stand out of the crowd.

By now, the question still hangs in the air: is Lumion a capable application to produce such artistic renders?

How can Lumion help us?

"How can Lumion help us?" is a fair question because the initial idea we had of Lumion was that this fantastic application lets us create amazing 3D visualizations in minutes. Lumion has effects that can imitate some of the techniques previously mentioned, and this can provide us with a good head start. Nevertheless, there is something we have to keep in mind: there is no such thing as automatic art. In the previous chapter, while covering different effects, we didn't have any secret formula or settings to improve the realism of the scene. Why? Because each scene is different and it is only by experimenting and playing with the effects that we can fully grasp what is possible to accomplish and when an image or video is perfect with the correct combination of effects.

However, enough talk! Let's see the available artistic effects in Lumion. The following screenshot gives an overview of the effects:

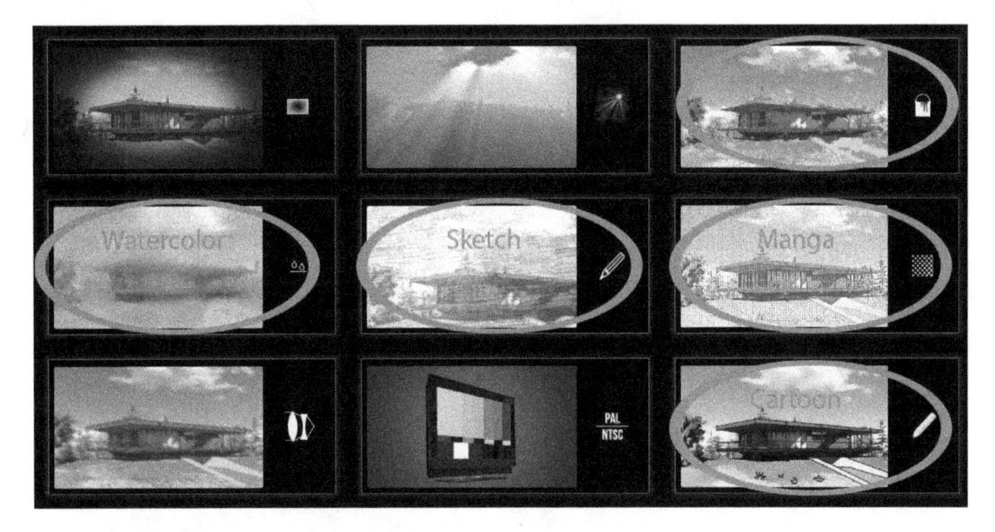

As highlighted in the previous screenshot, we have five artistic effects available that can be found under the **Artistic** tab.

Similar to the effects covered in the previous chapter, these effects can individually add a nice touch, but we can create a more professional and eye-catching look by combining them. However, did we mention that if we stack an effect over another effect, we can nullify effects?

That is correct, and this is an aspect we need to keep in mind while working with these effects. Another word of caution is that the effects we will cover do not always produce the best results when combined with the depth of field, chromatic aberration, and other effects associated with realism. This means that we have to delete, hide, or even move the effects. But how?

Moving, deleting, and hiding effects

To take the best of what Lumion's effects have to offer, we need to understand how to stack effects on top of each other, removing or changing their position. While adding effects to your scene, you probably have noticed that this small button that is available with every single effect, as shown in the following screenshot:

This small button with no name is the way we control effects in Lumion, as exemplified by the following screenshot:

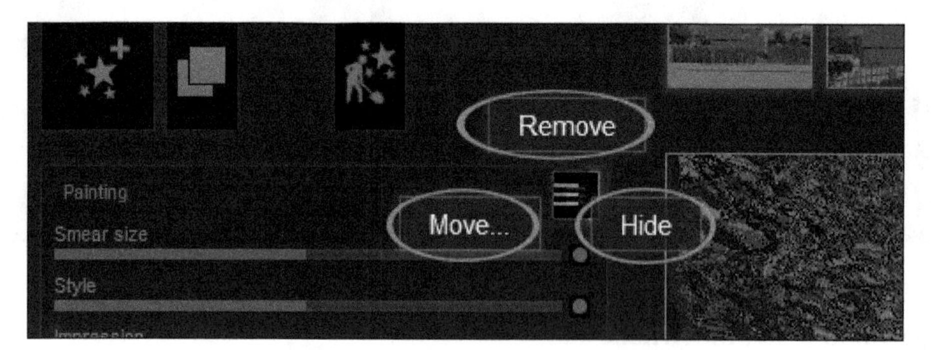

When we click on this button with the left mouse button, these three options appear:

- **Remove**: As stated, this option removes the effect from the stack
- **Move**: When we select this option, another two appear, giving the opportunity to move the effect up or down in the stack
- **Hide**: This option hides the effect and can be useful to check an effect before and after being applied

And to wrap up this section, let's have a look at another essential feature that can control the effects in the **Photo** or **Movie** mode. What happens when we have 10 effects and we have to go back to check or change something? Lumion creates new pages with effects so that all the effects can be displayed. So, when we have more than one page, we can navigate between pages using the arrows that appear above the stack of effects, as shown in the following screenshot:

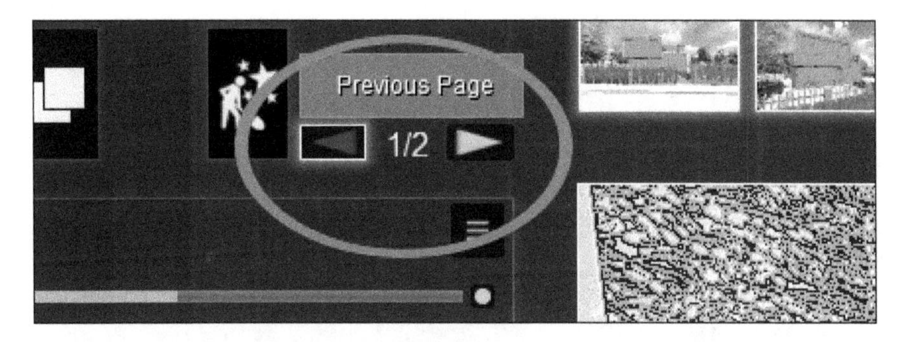

This is something essential to comprehend since we will make good use of this feature to combine and check the effects and how they behave when mixed.

How to use the artistic effects

To start working with the artistic effects, let's again open the Photo effect library and select the **Artistic** tab. We have some effects available that were covered previously, but the ones we will use for this section, as mentioned previously, are the Painting, Watercolor, Sketch, Manga, and Cartoon effects. These five artistic effects can be divided into two separate areas:

- The artistic side with the Painting, Watercolor, and Sketch effects
- The illustration side with Manga and Cartoon

What is the best way to learn these effects? To fully understand and master these artistic effects, we will use two examples to explain how an effect works and secondly, how this can be combined with other effects. The first example that we will see can be used to create a conceptual visualization, and the second example can be used to create a technical illustration. Without further ado, let's start with the conceptual visualization using the Painting, Watercolor, and Sketch effects with the help of a few extra effects.

Conceptual visualization with the Painting, Watercolor, and Sketch effects

Our goal with this topic is to introduce the Painting, Watercolor, and Sketch effects and show a useful application to help you understand how these effects can be combined. By the end of this section, you can achieve something like this, or even better:

To lay the foundation for this visualization, let's start by covering the first effect.

The first layer – the Painting effect

Impressionism was a 19th century art movement that was started with a group of Paris-based artists. Some of the main characteristics of this art movement are the use of small but visible brush strokes, and sometimes, they even create small points using the tip of the brush. The visual impact we get from this painting doesn't come from the fine detail, but instead from the composition, color combination, and visual depth that is created with layers and layers of paint. This brief explanation serves to introduce the Painting effect in Lumion that mimics this impressionist technique.

By now, you probably have added this effect to your scene and have started exploring how it works. The result by default is already amazing, and the effect becomes more noticeable when we are using materials with textures and lots of variations. The likely question in our head is: how does each setting affect the scene?

Although we could read a long explanation for every setting, perhaps the best way to understand how each setting works is by playing with the values, and in this case, we will see comparisons between different values and how they change the image. The Painting effect is created by the combination of five different settings.

The first setting we need to set from the beginning is not **Smear size** but **Impression**, and the following screenshot helps us to understand why:

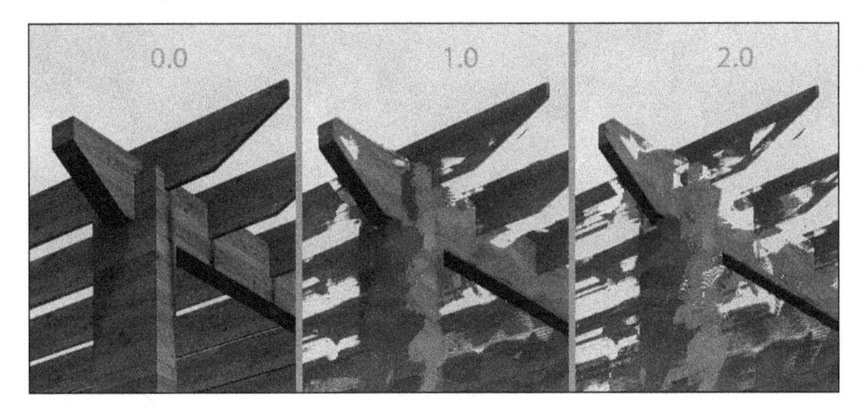

The **Impression** setting is the one that defines the strength of the effect, which means that if you feel the scene would be enhanced by reducing a little bit of the Painting effect, **Impression** is the setting to use.

Now that we have set the mood, we can start tweaking the different elements that create the painting. The first setting is **Smear size**, and the values we can use go from `0` to `2` and the following screenshot shows the difference between each value:

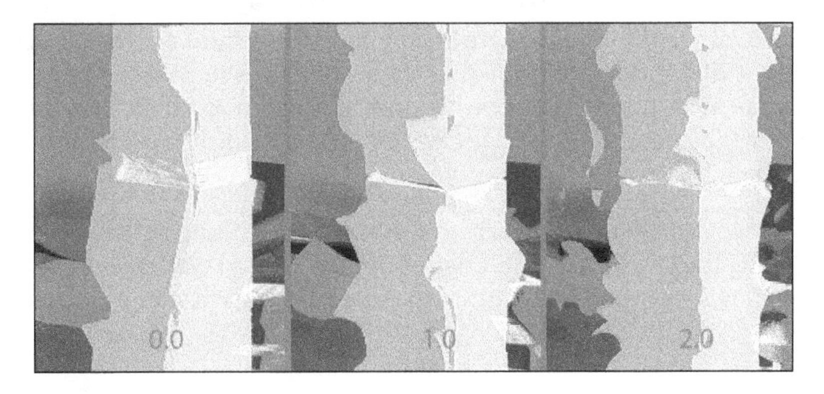

What is the conclusion we take from the previous screenshot? With a value close to `0`, the image loses detail because the paint strokes are bigger, while a value close to `2` creates a more distinct shape. Once again, there are no correct values, and while a value close to `0` may be extreme in some scenarios, it can be perfect in another case.

Now, one thing you will find out while playing with **Style** and **Details** is that these two settings can add or remove details. So, for example, we can remove a detail by lowering the **Details** slider, but gain some of that detail again with the **Style** setting. The next screenshot helps to understand what can be accomplished when we use the same value for **Smear size**, **Style**, and **Details**:

What about the **Random offset** setting? Because what we are using is an effect and not real painting, some images will be looking similar. So, we can add some randomness to the set of images by using a different value in the **Random offset** slider.

There is an extra touch we can add to the final image, but this needs to be done with an external application such as Photoshop or GIMP.

Best practice – adding a varnish layer

The next step is not required, but there is only one way to add an extra touch that can make all the difference. Traditionally, we used canvas to paint and even after adding some layers of paint, the canvas texture was still noticeable. Lumion doesn't have something like this; however, we can add a fake varnish layer to mimic the canvas texture.

In this section, we need to use Photoshop or other image editing tools such as GIMP that allows using the layer's effect. In Photoshop, we have a layer effect called **Bevel & Emboss** that allows us to add this illusion that the painting was done on a real canvas.

After rendering the image, we need to open it in Photoshop and use the *Ctrl* + *Shift* + *N* combination to create a new layer on top of the image. Give a name to the layer, something like varnish layer and press *Shift* + *F5* to open the **Fill** option, as shown in the following screenshot:

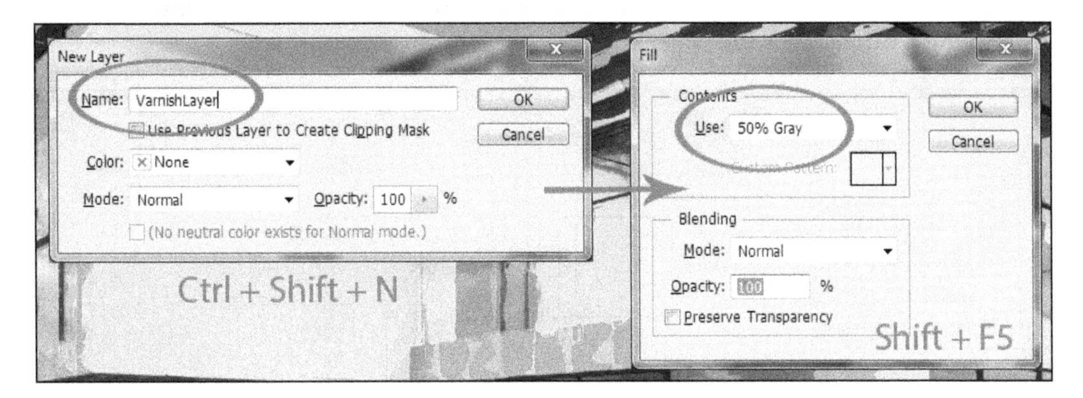

With the **Fill** window open, select **50% Gray** as the color to fill the new layer in the **Contents** field. This new layer with the 50 percent gray color is useless unless you change the blend mode to **Overlay** and for this, you need to select the layer and press *Shift* + *Alt* + *O*. This also sets the **Overlay** blending mode.

The next step is to use a layer style to recreate the canvas texture. Once again, select the varnish layer and go to the **Layer** menu, and under the **Layer Style** submenu, select **Bevel & Emboss**, as shown in the following screenshot:

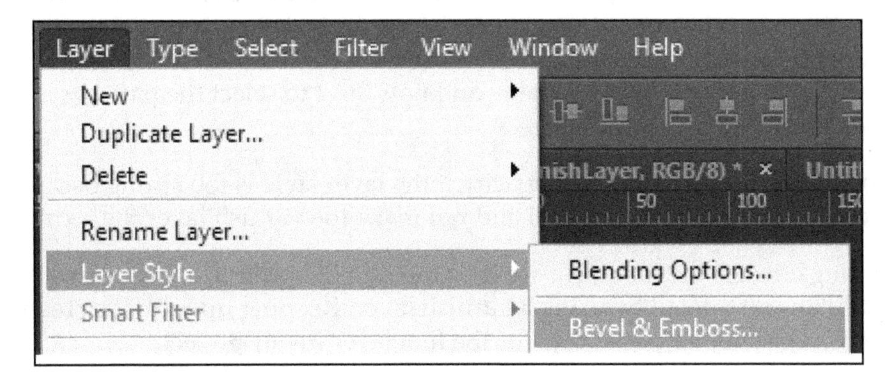

This particular layer style gives access to two additional options, and the one that is essential for us is **Texture**. After selecting the **Texture** option, the window changes to another area where we can tweak or change the texture in use. Next to the thumbnail is a small arrow that allows us to change or load a new image. The following screenshot shows the steps to load **Artist Surfaces** that contains several textures resembling a canvas texture:

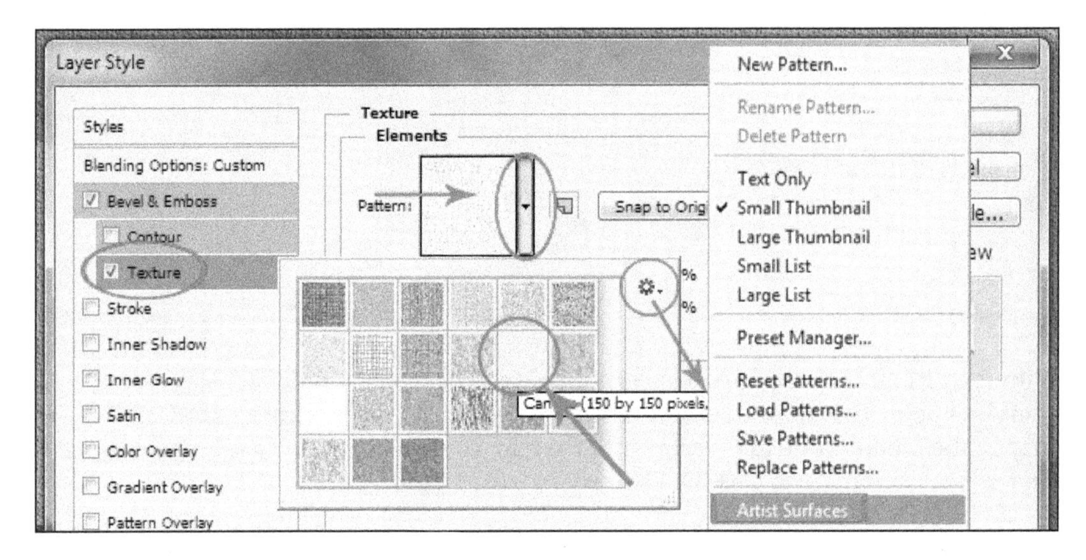

The first step is to click on the small arrow to open the pop up with the textures. Next, there is a small gear that when clicked, opens another pop-up window with several options, but the one we want is **Artist Surfaces**. When you click on this option, Photoshop asks: **Replace current patterns with the patterns from Artist Surfaces?**. Click on **Ok** to replace them, and now start to select the patterns and see which one looks better to your image.

It is a good idea to lower the layer opacity if the layer style is too strong because the goal is to add an extra layer of detail and not make the varnish layer the focal point.

The Painting effect is the first layer we are added to the project, and now, we saw how to add an extra detail by using a varnish layer. Keeping up with the creative side, we will see another possibility for the first layer in our project.

The first layer – the Watercolor effect

It is good to know we have a second option to use in a project. Perhaps, the first question is: what is Watercolor? Watercolor is a painting technique that uses water-soluble pigments. What are the benefits of using this technique? In real life, the colors appear to glow on the paper and because of the pigment's sediments, each painting has its own uniqueness.

In Lumion, the Watercolor effect does a good job reproducing this painting technique, but we can give it extra help by using additional effects, which we will see later in this topic. For now, let's start by adding the Watercolor effect and have a look at the settings available.

The **Accuracy**, **Radial accuracy**, and **Depth accuracy** options work together to create a painting that is somewhere between a loose painting and an accurate painting, but to be more specific, let's have a look at each of these, as follows:

- **Accuracy**: This deals with the detail accuracy in general and affects the entire image
- **Radial accuracy**: This controls the accuracy of the objects close to the camera
- **Depth accuracy**: This controls the accuracy of the objects in the distance

However, to have a better understanding, the following screenshot shows a comparison between these three values when all are at `0`, `1`, and `2`:

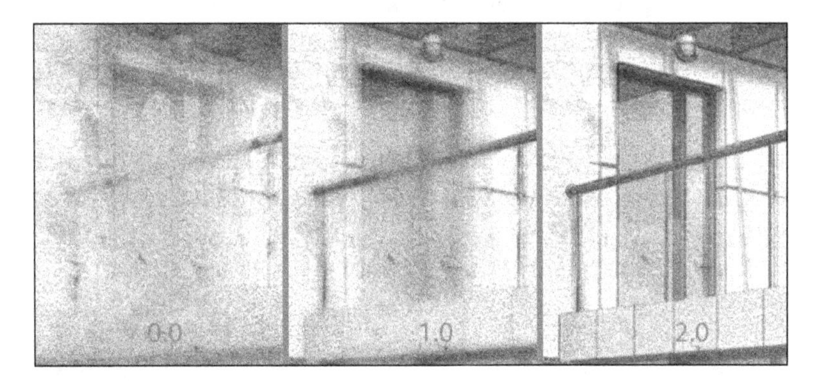

Moving on to the next settings, the **Distance** setting can work as a depth of field and a value close to `0` puts everything in focus, but on the other hand, if we crank up the **Distance** setting to `2`, the entire image appears blurred.

The **White out** option can be used to reproduce when the artist puts the focus on the center of the image and the borders lose contrast and color. Remember the Vignette effect? This one works the same way, but instead of darkening the corner, the **White out** option removes the color and contrast.

Finally, the **Dynamic** option is similar to the **Random** offset found on the Painting effect, where we can add randomness to the image, making each render different from the previous.

What we can get from this effect is going to depend on how we tweak the settings, but eventually, the final render will have this Watercolor effect. However, we can substantially improve the render by using some extra Lumion effects.

Best practice – improving lighting and color

The effect we will use to improve the render output is the Bloom effect. Although we can apply it on top of the Watercolor effect, the best results come from combining these two effects in an image editor such as to Photoshop or GIMP. After saving an image with the Watercolor effect, we will add the Bloom effect. The strength of the Bloom effect is going to depend on the final look, but usually a value between `0.6` and `0.9` produces a good result.

So, now we have two images: one with the Watercolor effect and a second one with the Watercolor and Bloom effects.

You can try to export an image with just the Bloom effect and see how it works in your scene.

Getting back to Photoshop, let's open the watercolor and the bloom image, but we need these two images together on the same file. In the bloom image, press *Ctrl* + *A* to select the entire image and then *Ctrl* + *C* to copy. Open the watercolor image and press *Ctrl* + *V* to paste the image.

The next step is easy; we need to change the blending mode of the Bloom layer to **Soft Light** and change the opacity to reduce the strength of the effect, as shown in the following screenshot:

Of course, we are not limited to the **Soft Light** mode, there are some other options such as **Multiply**, **Lighten**, **Overlay**, and **Color** that also produce nice results. The benefit of using this Bloom layer on top of the watercolor is that we can get much more vivid colors and a better contrast. However, we don't have to stop here.

Best practice – the Watercolor Painting effect

Similar to the Painting effect, we can add an extra touch to our render when using the Watercolor effect. Once again, we have to go through the process of creating a 50 percent gray layer, change it to overlay, and add the **Bevel & Emboss** layer style. If you can't remember the steps, have a look at the *Best practice – adding a varnish layer* section found in this chapter.

However, in this instance, we need to locate the watercolor texture present in **Artistic Surfaces**, as shown in the following screenshot:

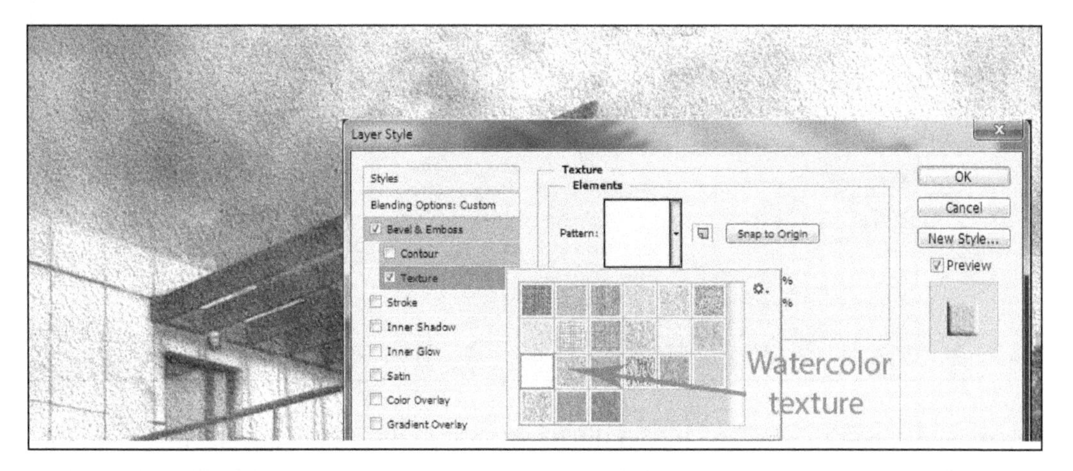

Adding this extra detail to our image greatly creates the sensation that we are looking at a painting. The grain that is added really mimics the sediments that are left when the pigment is diluted and applied to the paper.

However, did you know that there is an extra layer of detail that can be added to both the Painting and Watercolor effects? This second layer is produced by using the Sketch effect to boost the image and give a better outline to the building and other elements.

The second layer – the Sketch effect

The Sketch effect is another fantastic Lumion effect that mimics a drawing made by hand using a pencil. This is perhaps the oldest and mostly used method of expression used throughout the centuries and that till today has the power to communicate ideas in a simpler and more efficient way. Lumion does a really good job with this effect, getting almost a realistic handmade drawing. Firstly, let's see how we can use this effect alone.

Let's begin by adding the Sketch effect to our scene and the first thing we notice is that we have an amazing colored sketch. This effect can deliver mainly two outputs, as shown in the following screenshot:

It may be difficult to perceive this in the hard copy of this book, but the image on the right is a colorful drawing, while the image on the left is a black and white drawing.

This can be achieved by using the **Coloring** setting that removes or adds color. The value in the middle creates a perfect balance between the two options and works fine in most cases.

What else can we take from this effect? The possibilities are endless, but before we show some of those possibilities, let's have a look at the **Accuracy** setting, and the best way to understand what this setting can do for us, have a look at the following screenshot:

This perhaps should be our second or even first step when working with the effect. Are you trying to have a loose drawing or a very technical illustration? With this in mind, we can then jump to the other settings.

Really, the best way to learn this effect is by trying all the possibilities, but the following guidelines can help you to know which setting to use:

- **Sketch style**: This setting, with a value close to `0`, will have the fill of the surfaces and no outline, while a value close to `2` will create only the outlines.
- **Contrast**: This makes the line darker or if you are using some color, this will make the colors brighter or darker.
- **Outline fadeout**: This is one of the settings in which you will only see a change within value between `1.9` and `2`. This setting can be used to create very thin outlines.
- **Dynamic**: This is a key setting to create a more believable drawing. It is similar to **Accuracy**, but while **Accuracy** removes details, this setting keeps the details but makes it less perceptive, as shown in the following screenshot:

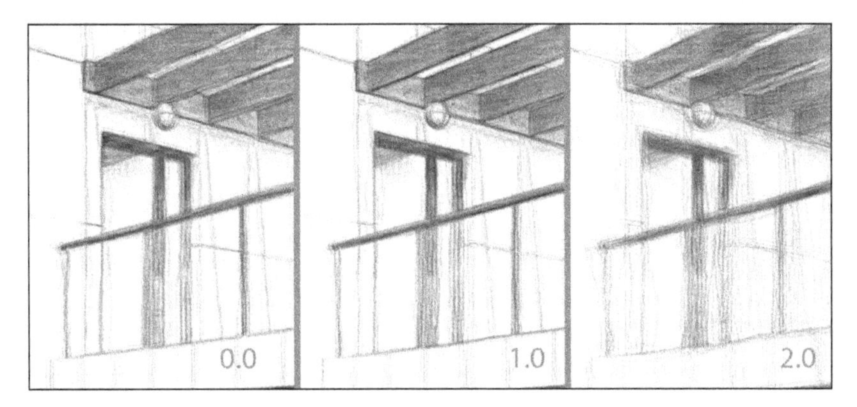

As we can see, **Dynamic** is very important to add the extra touch that blurs the line between CG and manual work.

Now that we know how to use this fantastic effect, the question in our minds can be something like: why is this effect the second layer to create a good conceptual visualization?

The reason is that we can substantially improve the shadows, giving an extra contrast to certain areas and adding more detail without compromising the Painting or Watercolor effect.

For this, we can export different images with the Sketch effect. The first image is just the outlines without color and the second image is color without any outlines.

For the outline image, you may want to try these settings:

- **Accuracy**: `1`
- **Sketch style**: `2`
- **Contrast**: `1.7`
- **Coloring/Outline fadeout**: `0`
- **Dynamic**: `1.4`

And for the colored image, try these settings:

- **Accuracy**: `1`
- **Sketch style**: `0`
- **Contrast**: `1.6`
- **Coloring**: `1.9`
- **Outline fadeout**: `0`
- **Dynamic**: `1`

Now, we should have four images: one with the Painting effect, another with the Watercolor effect, and finally, two images with the Sketch effect. In what ways can we improve each effect?

Best practices – enhancing a Watercolor/ Painting render

The output we get from the Painting effect can be greatly improved when combined with the Sketch effect. Unfortunately, Lumion doesn't have the feature to blend effects; so, we need to export each effect as an image and then combine them in an application such as Photoshop or GIMP. In what ways can we improve an output from the Painting effect? Do we need it?

It is true that Lumion does a good job, but creating an architectural visualization is not only about applying a pretty effect to the scene. One benefit of using the Sketch effect with the Watercolor and Painting is the opportunity to enhance the quality of the shadows, which in turn gives more contrast and depth to the image. Another benefit is an option to boost the colors in the image. However, this doesn't mean we are stuck with the Sketch effect, because we can always try other effects. So, how can we combine them?

Although we will use Photoshop to combine these effects, the same principles can be applied with other applications. The first step we need to take is to open the following images:

- Painting render
- Sketch colored render
- Sketch outline render

We need to stack them so that the painting render is the bottom layer, the second layer is the sketch colored render, and the final layer is the sketch outline render, as shown in the following screenshot:

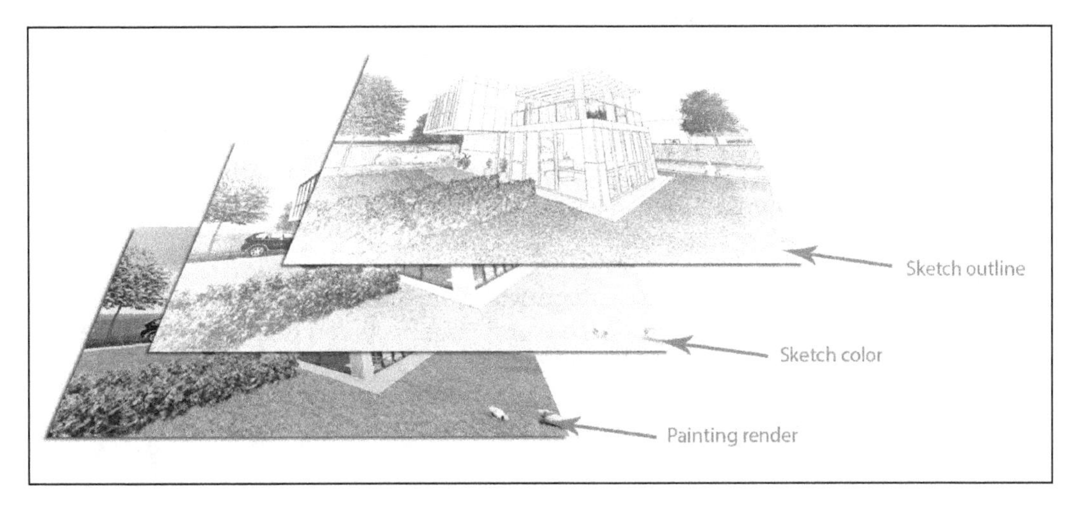

However, if we do this, the result will be an image with the sketch outline on top, and this is not an improvement. Let's start by switching off the Sketch outline layer and focusing our attention on the Sketch color layer. With this layer, we can give a boost to the color by setting the blend mode to **Color**. Setting the blend mode to **Color** doesn't mean that it is the only possibility because in fact, **Soft Light** also produces a good result; so, always try the other blending modes.

We need to reduce the strength of this layer, but before we do this let's add a switch on the Sketch outline and set the blend mode of this layer to **Multiply**. You also can try this with **Linear Burn**, **Soft Light**, and **Pin Light**. Using the **Multiply** blend mode helps us to add more black shade to the shadows and more contrast to the image.

This simple technique can also be applied to the Watercolor effect or to other effects. Again, this is just one possible combination of effects and nothing should stop you from trying different effects and blend modes and see in what ways you can enhance the renders you get from Lumion with this easy technique.

Now, what about the other two effects we mentioned: the Manga and Cartoon effects?

Technical illustrations with the Manga and Cartoon effects

What is a technical illustration? Technical illustrations are drawings that are used to illustrate how something works or is assembled. The goal is to visually communicate and explain information of a technical nature to a nontechnical audience. This is often accomplished by using conventional drawings, exploded views, and cutaway drawings. Is this something useful?

Technical illustrations, as the name states, are not architectural visualization, but they are an essential part of any project. Most clients will not ask for this kind of information, but with the use of applications such as Revit, it is not difficult to provide sections, elevations, and even plants with a nice effect, and this can give you an edge to the services you provide.

Two effects that are perfect for these categories of illustrations are Manga and Cartoon, with the help of other effects. One of these effects can help us correct the perspective of our camera by providing straight lines. What do we mean by this?

Correcting perspective with a 2-point perspective

Lumion uses a 3-point perspective to present the 3D models, and this sometimes can create a camera angle that makes the building and other objects look taller and stretched. There is no issue if this is something you want, but to produce a nice technical illustration, we need the vertical lines to remain vertical irrespective of the camera angle. This is possible with an effect that, when applied, transforms our scene to a 2-point perspective where two vanishing points are used to create the image.

The effect we will use is the 2-point perspective that can be found under the **Camera** tab. However, when we apply this filter to the scene, nothing changes, and this is because we have to tweak the value in order to switch this effect on or off. The following screenshot shows how this effect can change the scene drastically:

As we can see, there is a massive difference between the lines on the left image and the ones on the right side. And with this, we have everything we need and we can start working with the Manga and Cartoon effects.

Exploring and using the Manga effect

The Manga style is characterized by the use of clean and perfect lines, which in turn can be filled with color. Lumion has something similar that can be found on the **Artistic** tab and is called **Manga**. The best way to learn this effect is by applying it to our scene, and immediately, there is a drastic transformation from a believable environment to a cartoonish scene.

Like the Sketch effect, we also can produce two kinds of outputs with this effect: outline and colored renders. This is very obvious when we look into the settings and see the **Outline vs fill** setting, and with this setting, we can go from an image with only color to just an outline, as shown in the following screenshot:

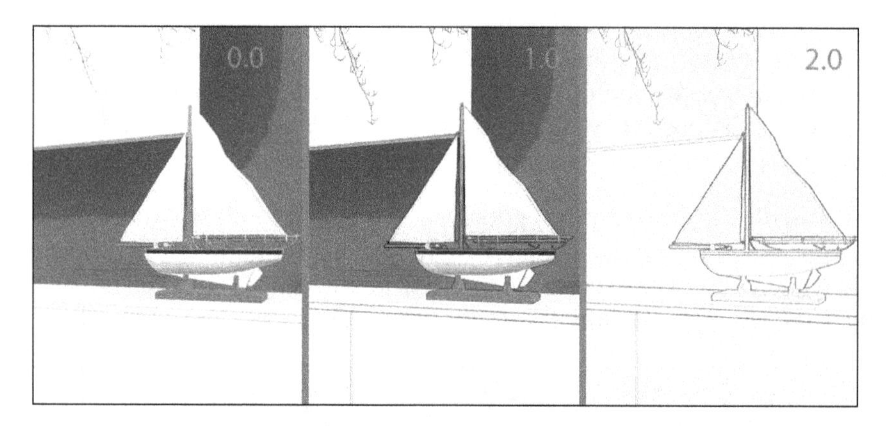

This is what is going to set the mood for our illustration, and while working with this effect, it is easy to see it is a special feature. This effect blends so perfectly with the scene that it preserves a good amount of detail found in the textures. The frame on the wall is a good example of how even when using the full outline, we can see the picture, and this can be perceived in all the texture we use for the project. This is good because it adds a nice effect to the illustration. However, what if we want to use some color?

The **Fill** method, **Tone count**, and **Coloring** are the settings that control the working of the color, and here is a brief explanation of how they work:

- **Fill**: This can be used to create a nice transition between colors or to create harsh areas of color
- **Tone count**: This increases or decreases the amount of tones in the scene, which affects the color detail available
- **Coloring**: This creates a black-and-white image when close to `0`, or an over-saturated image when close to `2`

What about the **Pattern** setting? This is an interesting setting because it adds a nice stippling texture to the entire image and, in some circumstances, can remove blotchiness in some dark areas. Keep in mind that this setting only affects the image when we are using color and not an outline image.

You probably are thinking whether we can also combine this effect with other effects. This is one of the most important aspects to create something unique: the ability to question and explore additional possibilities. The answer is yes, we can combine this effect like we did with the previous ones, but let's introduce the next effect before showing some of the possibilities.

Working with the Cartoon effect

The final effect related to NPR is the Cartoon effect. This effect is a great tool to produce a quick illustration of an architectural design, and at the same time, a very economical way to communicate concepts and ideas. One of the benefits of using this effect is the clean and clear 3D model's outlines. Where can we find it? This can be found under the **Artistic** tab and close to all the other artistic effects we saw previously.

However, when we apply this effect, the initial look is peculiar because here we don't have a clear outline neither a good or strong color and the final result is very dull. Like the Sketch and Manga effects, we can also have two different images as the output: one with just outlines and another with color.

Some of the settings are easy to understand; for example, **Fill to white** adds or removes the color from the image. Let's set this setting to `2` and play a little bit with **Outline width**. The **Outline width** setting is the one that we have to tweak to control the thickness of the outlines, as shown in the following screenshot:

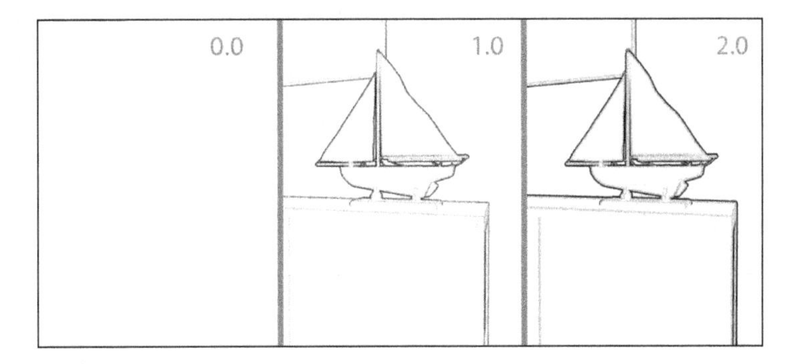

So, as we can see, a value close to `0` entirely removes the outline, but when we increase this value, the thickness and consequently, the detail, increases. On the other hand, if we are working with color, we need to balance the **Alteration curve**, **Saturation**, and **Black level**. Both the **Alteration curve** and **Black level** deal with and control the contrast in the scene, and in most cases, we have to increase these settings to avoid having a washout image.

Don't you feel that there is something missing? Could we benefit from tweaking and combining different outputs? The principles we applied for the Painting and Watercolor effects can also be applied here.

Best practices – combining different outputs

Are we going to combine different outputs again? Yes, because this is one of the best ways to fully take advantage of what these effects have to offer. However, there is an extra touch we can add to our image when working mostly with outlines, and that is removing the blur for the lines, making them crisper. How?

Sharpening lines

One of the simplest effects we can find in Lumion is the Sharpness effect that can be found under the **Style** tab. This is simple because we only have one setting to tweak, but although simple, this effect has a deep impact on the scene. Why?

Sharpness can bring out the quality of the details in the image, and this is because we improve the borders' distinction and create sharp transitions between edges. This means that we can give a much clearer look to an image. This effect can also be used to produce believable renders, but use a small amount; otherwise, the image will lose the realism. With an NPR, we can use this effect to have clear lines and a good distinction between colors.

Improving the Cartoon effect

Now that you know how to improve the quality of the image using the Sharpness effect, it is time to see how to tweak the images we get from the Manga and Cartoon effects. For example, with the Cartoon effect, we could create a much better image if it were possible to blend the outline with the color. It is true that with the settings set to `1`, we can create a balance between these two components, but the result is so dull and lifeless. The question is: can we increase the detail in the outlines and maintain the color? Not in Lumion, and this means that we need to export one image with color and the second with the outlines, as shown in the following screenshot:

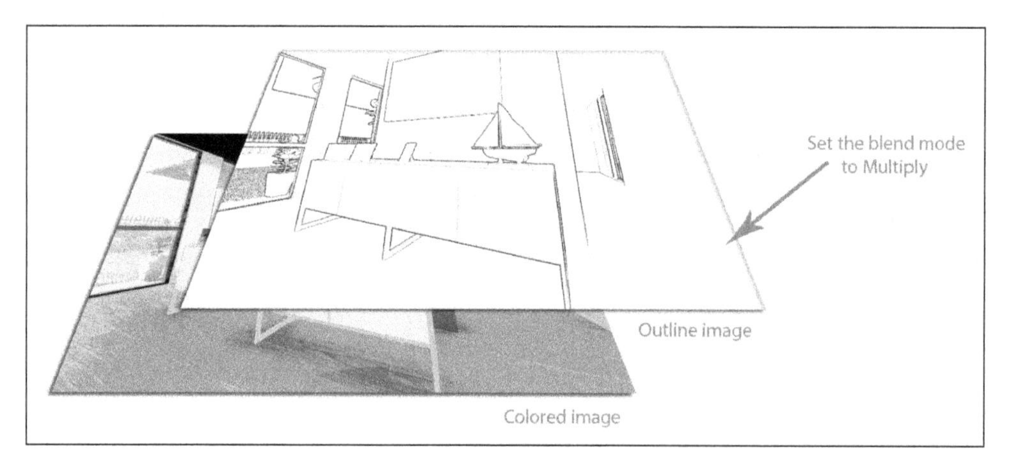

As we saw with the other effects, we can take advantage of blending modes to tweak and greatly improve the final look of an image. The same principle applies here and we need to set the outline image to **Multiply** in order to see the lower image shown in the preceding screenshot.

However, we can add more contrast and improve the color in the image if we duplicate the colored image and set the blend mode to **Soft Light**. Using the copied image with the **Soft Light** blending mode increases the overall contrast of the image and gives a slight boost to the color saturation.

Creating a colored drawing with the Manga effect

With the Manga effect, we can create an interesting effect by exporting two images again: one with color and a second with just the outlines. However, we will not set the outline image to **Multiply**, but instead create a mask by going to the **Layer** menu and under the **Layer Mask** option, select **Reveal All**.

With the layer mask selected, press *B* to select the brush and set the color to black. Remember those books with the outlines; your job is to fill the areas with color? In this case, we don't need to fill them with color, but instead mask areas to reveal the color below, as shown in the following screenshot:

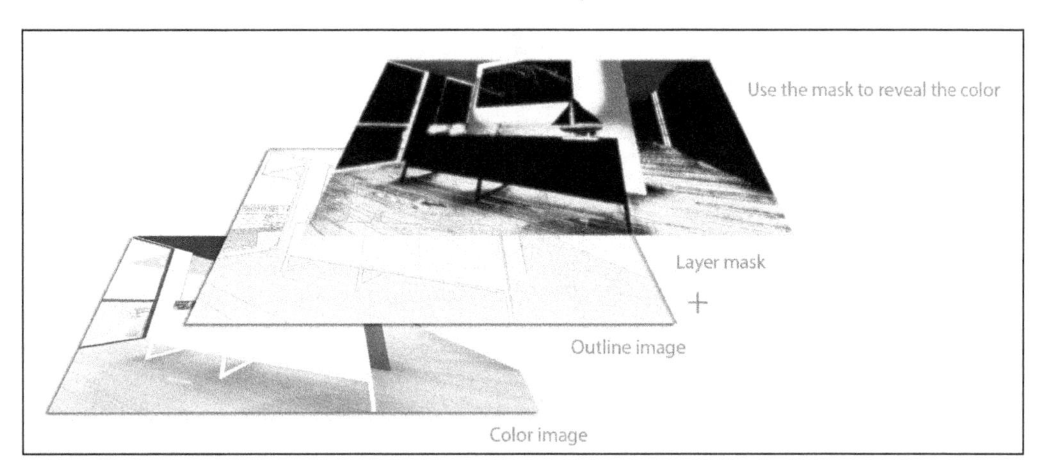

It's not a bad idea to set the opacity of the brush to something like `50%` and start painting or masking the areas where you want to show the color from the preceding image. This is shown in the preceding screenshot. You can try different brushes and see the result you can get with this technique. The idea behind these topics is not to provide one certain way to do it, but instead show one possibility and give you room to explore and develop your own techniques.

Summary

This was another chapter dedicated to working with effects and certainly, you began to understand that Lumion is a powerful application. Here, you learned everything related to creating non-photorealistic renders and the benefits of using this approach. Then, we introduced, one by one, the artistic effects. Painting, Watercolor, Sketch, Manga, and Cartoon are the main NPR effects that Lumion provides. However, you also learned that there is always room to improve the final output by combining these effects and also by using additional effects such as the 2-Point perspective and Sharpness.

From conceptual visualizations to technical illustrations, you saw how Lumion can help, and hopefully understood that there is no magic button to create beautiful renders. Although our attention is focused on using Lumion, the truth is that we can export the results achieved with these effects and combine them using an external application such as GIMP or Photoshop. A good way to explore different techniques is by using the various blend modes found in these applications.

In the next chapter, we will see how to bring our scene to life using animation techniques. Animation can seem like a very complex and difficult subject, but the next chapter will teach you not only how to control and use the camera to create a movie, but also some composition techniques that can definitely increase the quality of your movie.

9
Animation Techniques

Why did you choose to work with Lumion? Was it because of the vast and diverse 3D model library? Was it because of the simplicity of creating and tweaking materials? Or, was it all the effects that transform the scene into a beautiful image? Probably, all these aspects led you to try Lumion, but certainly, one crucial aspect is the technology that permits us to create a movie easily and effortlessly. This is one of Lumion's strongest features, but possibly, it is also one that might give the impression of being complex and difficult to master, especially if you don't have much experience in animation or a 3D background. Nevertheless, it is important to conquer your fears and master this area of Lumion, as well.

In this chapter, we will cover:

- Lumion animation—a quick overview
- Planning your movie
- Working with cameras
- Creating a camera path
- Composition and how to use it
- Editing clips
- Changing the length of clips
- Camera-filming techniques
- Deleting and controlling multiple clips
- Animating effects and layers
- Using layers to control objects

So far, you have learned how to create images in Lumion, and all our concentration was on the **Photo** mode. Just a reminder: all the effects we covered in the **Photo** mode can also be used in the **Movie** mode; the concept is not very different, and keeping this in mind will help you comprehend not only how Lumion's animation system works, but also how to grow in confidence and master this area of Lumion. Therefore, let's start with a quick overview of the **Movie** mode.

Lumion's Movie mode – a quick overview

First things first: where can we find the **Movie** mode? In the bottom-right corner, there are several buttons. By now, it is not that challenging to find the **Photo** mode button and, consequently, the **Movie** mode button, which is just next in line. Click on this button to open the **Movie** mode. The **Movie** mode is the heart of all the animations we can create in Lumion. The interface of this mode is relatively simple, as shown in the following screenshot:

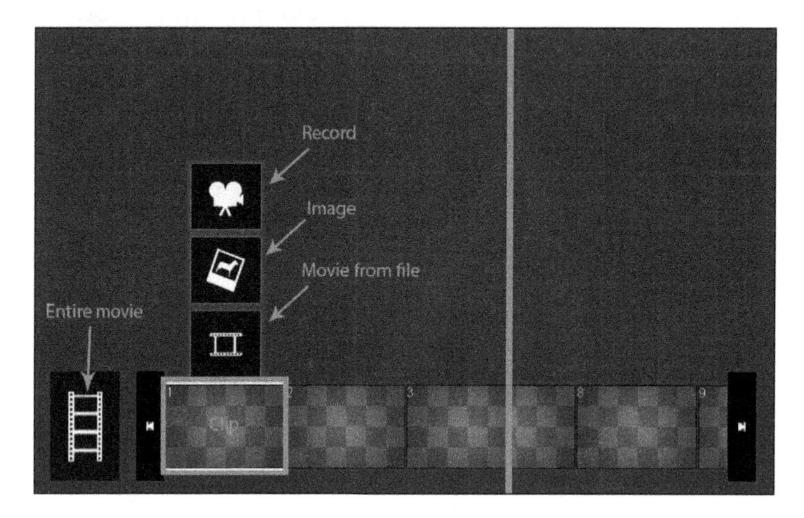

For now, let's keep in mind that we have three options to create a movie in Lumion:

- **Record**: This option is the only one that gives you access to the scene created in Lumion
- **Image**: Click on this button to load an image that can be used as part of the movie, but you need to keep in mind that the image imported needs to match the resolution of the movie; otherwise, it might look distorted
- **Movie from file**: This loads an MPEG-4 video that can be used as a section of the movie

When we mention animation perchance, our first reaction is complete panic, since all this sounds too complex and difficult. If you are creating a camera path, animation using curve paths and effects could sound too challenging. However, remember that Lumion does a fantastic job in making all these tasks straightforward, and this is patent when we jump to the **Movie** mode.

Subsequently, by now, we are probably thinking, "I have no idea how this works!," "Where do I start?," "Why can't we have a magic button to create animations?" Once more, the technology itself doesn't produce inevitably stunning movies. In reality, the process to create a movie doesn't start at the **Movie** mode.

Creating a movie in Lumion

It isn't our goal to cover filmmaking in this book for the simple reason that it is something out of the scope of this book, but then again, we cannot jump straight to Lumion and start shooting a movie. Well, we can jump to Lumion and start generating a movie, but there is a massive difference between a clumsy/unplanned movie and a proficient 3D one.

What are the requirements to start creating a movie in Lumion?

Motive and the need to create a storyboard

A motive is the reason why we are producing a 3D walk-through. If you think about it, if we are deprived of a motive, we wouldn't know exactly what to show and how to present the project. For instance, for a particular project, the client might need to display how the planned building interacts and blends with the environment, and this could be what he or she needs for a planning application. For another project, we might have a real-estate agent trying to show his/her customers how one would be living in the house they are promoting.

The approach and techniques used for the first instance have nothing to do with the second example, and this demonstrates why a motive is the first step to create an expert movie. Now that we have the motive, there is a need for an extra step: creating a storyboard. Do you really need a storyboard? And what is a storyboard?

A storyboard is a graphic representation of how your video will flow, and it can look something like this:

What we have here is a series of numbered images of illustrations representing the different shots, and we can also add some notes to clarify what we need to show in each shot. So, why do we need this?

The reason is that it saves time and money. A storyboard can help you explain to others how the movie is going to be and what it will look like, and provides a solid shot list that makes the creation process smooth. This can also work as a safeguard for you, because if the client agrees with the storyboard, any additional changes can be charged as extra work.

You can easily find some storyboard templates using Google. Type `storyboard template` to see some examples.

Even though this is not something that is essential to work with Lumion's **Movie** mode, you should take some time to think and plan the movie before starting the recording in Lumion.

Lumion's Movie mode – the workflow

What is the procedure to create a movie in Lumion? We need to start by creating clips using the three options mentioned earlier, and once we've finished recording and creating these clips, we can add effects. So, we have two options:

- **Applying the effects to each individual clip**: The benefit here is that we have the opportunity to give specific attention to each section of the movie, but the disadvantage is that we might have to use the same effect in several clips, which means we have to copy and paste the effect over and over

- **Condensing all the clips into a movie**: The advantage here is that we have the opportunity to use effects with consistency throughout the movie, but it doesn't allow us to have accurate control in specific sections of the movie

After adding these effects, we can start working with animation, which means we have to use the specific effects found in Lumion. Once everything is prepared, we can check and edit the clips and, finally, export the whole lot as a movie file or a sequence of images.

While it might seem intricate and confusing, Lumion's **Movie** mode is very intuitive, and in the upcoming sections, we will break down the entire process into small steps. This will help us understand how each stage works and will also help us fully master Lumion.

Step 1 – shoot the movie!

In real life, an essential element to create a movie is a camera. Likewise, in Lumion, the camera is the most important element to capture the beautiful scene created, and it is with this camera that we can start recording clips.

> A clip is the smallest element that can be created to produce a movie. A movie can have just one clip, but it is a good habit to create several clips to improve the workflow.

The process is called creating a camera path, and what we need to do is set multiple snapshots that define the different camera positions, as shown in the following screenshot:

At this instant, you might think that creating a storyboard is not such a bad idea after all, because we are not dealing with a physical path, so we do not see anything that will aid us in creating this camera path. How does it work then?

Creating a camera path

Let's start by opening the **Movie** mode and selecting an empty clip. As already shown in the previous screenshot, three options appear, and in this instance, we will select the Record button. When this option is selected, a new interface appears where we can start taking photos to create the camera path. Do you see the preview window with your scene displayed? This is your camera, and you can control it using the same shortcuts used in the **Build** mode, but just as a reminder, here are some of the most used shortcuts to navigate the Lumion camera:

- *WSAD* or arrow keys: These move the camera forward, backward, or to the left or right
- *Q*: This moves the camera upward
- *E*: This moves the camera downward
- Spacebar + *WSAD* and *QE*: These slow down the camera speed
- *Shift* + *WSAD* and *QE*: These increase the camera speed
- *Shift* + Spacebar + *WSAD* and *QE*: This is an option to choose a high-speed camera
- The right mouse button: Press this and move it to look around
- The middle mouse button: Press this and move the mouse to pan

Now that we have placed the camera at the initial position, what is the next step? Have a look at the following screenshot:

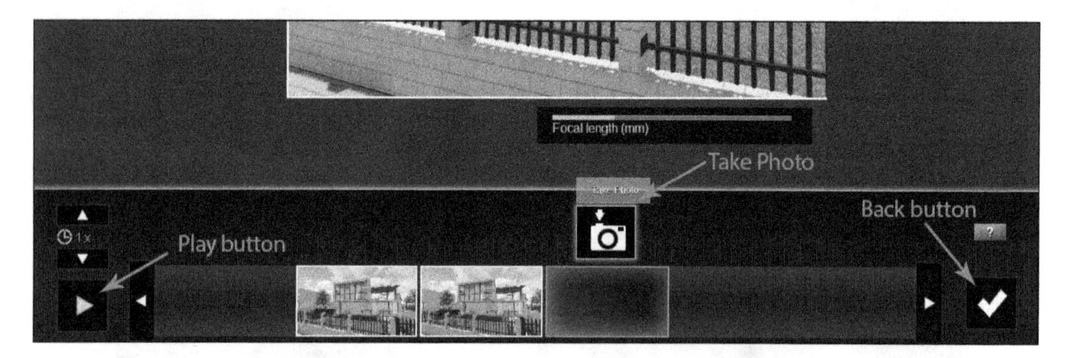

After all, creating a camera path is not that difficult. Use the **Take Photo** button to create a snapshot or photo of the camera position, move the camera to a new location, take another snapshot, and so on. While recording the clip, it is always a good idea to use the Play button to check the camera animation, and if you are happy with the result, click on the Back button to save this clip and return to the **Movie** mode.

Remember the camera positions that you store using *Shift* + *0*, *1*, *2*, to *9*? While recording the clip, you can use the shortcuts *Ctrl* + *0*, *1*, *2*, to *9* to load those camera positions and use them as a starting point for a great camera angle.

On the other hand, does this mean we have to create every single frame to create a clip? Will three or four photos be enough to generate a clip?

The camera path – how it works

Initially, this might cause some misperception and lead us to take piles of photos to create a clip, but in the end, the result will not be satisfactory. We don't need to create almost every single frame of the clip. Why? Have a look at the following screenshot:

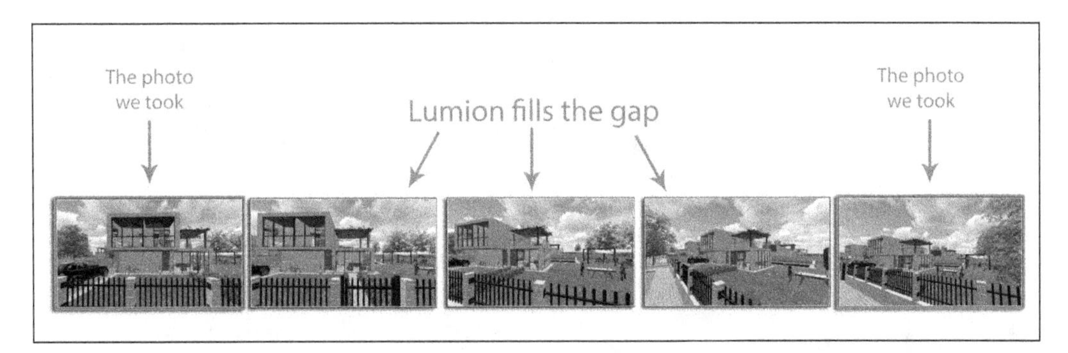

As exemplified, we can see that we took two photos in two different locations in the **Movie** mode. However, Lumion knows that you just don't want these two frames, because if you use them, the clip will be extremely short, and the animation will look odd with jumps between locations. Consequently, what Lumion does is fill in the gap between these two frames with additional frames in order to create a smooth transition between the two camera locations. Technically, we only need to worry about the camera locations and the length of the movie, because Lumion is in charge of making everything else work.

What is the length of my camera path? Every photo you take is equivalent to 2 seconds. This means that every time you press the **Take Photo** button, you are adding another 2 seconds to the animation.

Why did we use the expression *technically* in the previous sentence? There is something we need to know. Though the concept of creating a camera path is easy to understand, once more, we need time and patience to produce great results. Lumion does a fantastic job filling in the gaps between locations and creating the best smooth result possible, but we also need to create a good transition between locations.

Best practices – creating a smooth camera path

The problem is not when we are shooting in a straight line, but when we start to rotate the camera, at which point we might experience some *strange* jumps. To better comprehend the problem when using abrupt camera changes, have a look at the following screenshot:

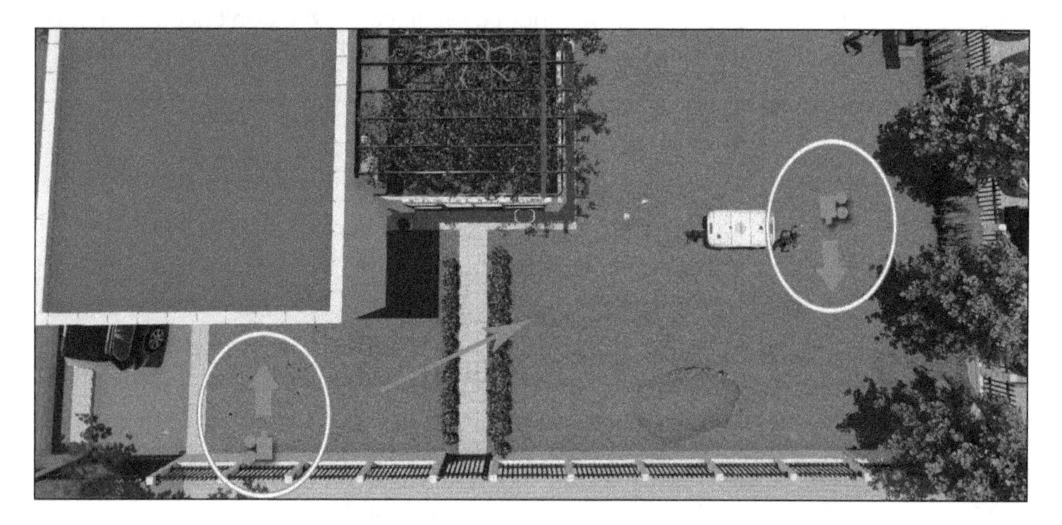

What happened there? We took our first photo looking straight at the house, and then, we moved the camera to another location with a rotation of 180 degrees. Do you want to try this with your scene? Now, play the clip and see how Lumion adjusts the path between the two camera positions. However, the result is so clumsy and strange that it is difficult to understand what is happening.

We definitely don't want this kind of camera path in our clip, but on the other hand, this might be exactly what we need for the project. The client specifically told us that they want a clip just like this. Are we doomed failure? Let's have a look at the same scenario, but with a different approach:

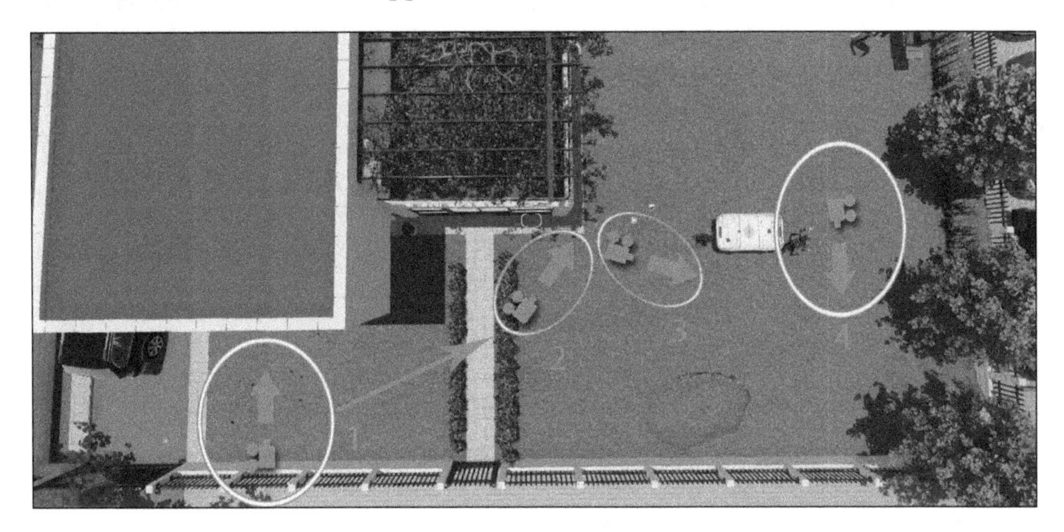

If you try applying this technique now that Lumion has more information or camera positions, it will create a smooth transition between the first and second positions, then another transition between the second and third positions, and, finally, another one between the third and fourth positions. The end result will be a smoother camera path.

However, if you followed precisely what is shown in the screenshot, there is a slight problem. The camera's speed between the first and second positions is very fast when compared to the camera's speed between the second and third positions. Why?

Think in this way: the speed you need to cover 10 meters in 2 seconds is not the same as when you need to cover 1 meter in 2 seconds. Lumion has 2 seconds to cover the distance between the first and second positions, and as it is a big distance, the camera needs to be faster in comparison to the distance used between the second and third positions. Is there any solution to this problem? Try to keep the same distance between the camera positions, and Lumion will be able to use the same camera speed between each position.

But then again, we have a problem because we already took the photos. Is there any chance to tweak the camera positions? Of course there is; after all, Lumion is user-friendly and always eager to help us.

However, before we go further, let's have a conversation about the composition that you will certainly find useful while tweaking the camera path.

Best practices – composition and its importance

This small section serves only as a quick guideline to help us understand what composition is and how we can apply some of the techniques in our project. Also, almost everything we will cover here can and must be applied when we are creating still images with the **Photo** mode. However, why is this subject so important? First, let's see what composition is.

Composition

Composition can be found in almost every type of art and, in simple terms, can be described as the way you frame your scene. Composition is the placement or arrangement of objects and forms in a way that guides the viewer's eye to the subject, making it attractive and pleasant.

A great way to familiarize yourself with composition is searching for examples of good composition in photography and cinematography.

Importance of composition

Pointing the camera to an eye-catching element and shooting a photo or recording a frame doesn't necessarily create a prodigious photo or movie. Things are not so simple, and this can initially be a great frustration for someone who is just starting to take the first steps in this area. Why is composition so important?

Not only can we guide the viewer's eye toward the most important elements in the scene, but likewise, we can also reveal things that the viewer doesn't necessarily notice in the first instance. The power of composition lies in the fact that we can transform a trivial and ordinary element into something interesting just because of the way we arrange it within the frame. Your scene can be extremely interesting, but the final viewer will only see the contents within a frame, and they need to recognize and understand what is being shown to them.

Composition is important because it enhances the impact of a scene by creating compelling images or movies with a natural balance and draw attention to the important parts of the scene.

Getting a good composition

Simply put, a good composition guides the viewer's eye to the subject and doesn't let them wonder what the purpose of such a photo or frame is. Nonetheless, in order to achieve a good composition, we need to follow some composition guidelines. These guidelines can fluctuate depending on who you ask, but usually, they are as follows:

- **Rule of thirds**: Take your frame and divide it into nine equal segments by two vertical and two horizontal lines. Our eyes are naturally drawn to a point about two-thirds up a page, and we can make an image more pleasing to the eye if we focus the subject on one of the intersecting points created by these imaginary lines. Also, the horizon needs to be placed on the upper or lower third of the photo. All these points are exemplified in the following screenshot:

- **Leading lines**: The goal of using lines is to help the viewer's eye move from the foreground to the background. We can use straight, diagonal, and curved lines to create depth and a sense of movement.

- **Cropping**: The goal here is to cut out all the unnecessary details to keep the viewer's attention on the subject. In Lumion, this can be achieved using the **Focal length (mm)** parameter that appears in both the **Photo** and **Movie** modes.
- **Point of view**: This is one of the factors that can have a massive impact on the scene and affect the way the viewer sees the subject. Changing the point of view can completely change the sense of scale and the message we are trying to transmit.
- **Background**: When shooting an image or movie, the camera has the tendency to flatten the foreground and background by removing the depth, and this happens because the camera is a two-dimensional medium. However, we can make the subject stand out from the background using the depth of field to blur the background. This is something we will cover later in this chapter. Another option is to include objects in the foreground, middle ground, and background, and as our eye recognizes these layers of information, we can create an image with more depth.
- **Framing**: This involves using foreground objects to work as frames for our subject. For example, in the previous screenshot, we used some trees to naturally create a frame for our shot.

As you can see, composition is not a linear and easy subject to be explained in just a few pages. Take some time to understand how composition works and the best way to use it in your scene, because we can hardly use all these elements in just one frame. A good composition can only be achieved by experimentation and experience; therefore, try, and if a guideline is not working, just ignore it.

Step 2 – editing the clips

Now that we understand how the composition works and why it is so important, we might see the need to change and tweak the camera path created. It is very demanding to create a perfect clip on the first try, and even if we are happy with the results, the client might want some changes.

It is also time to explore some techniques to create interesting movies by combining not only what we learned about composition from the previous sections, but also some movie techniques.

Editing a camera path

Editing and changing a camera path in Lumion is easy and very intuitive. The first thing we need to do is double-click on the clip or use the **Edit clip** button, as shown in the following screenshot:

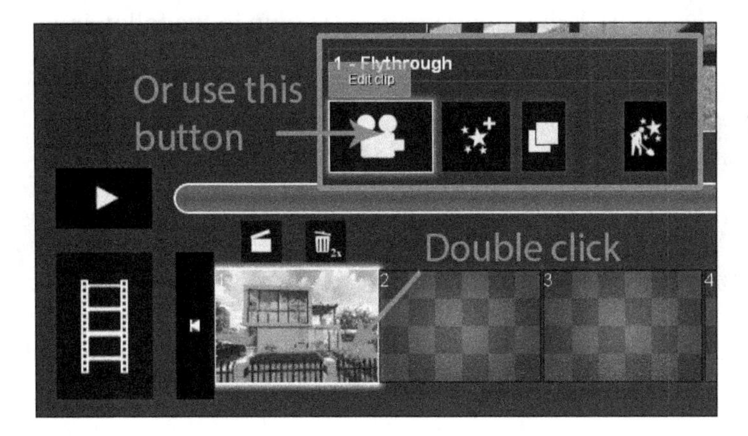

Both these options will take us to the same interface where we recorded the clip, but now, we will tweak the photos taken. As we are focused on editing the camera path now, the options available are slightly different, as shown in the following screenshot:

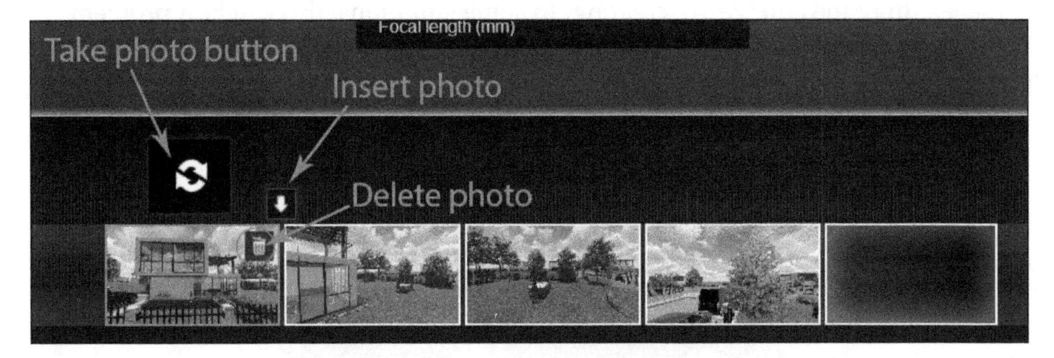

Again, what is the workflow to retouch a camera path? The first step is selecting the photo or snapshot that needs to be corrected or adjusted. Then, we can use the same navigation system that we used to navigate the camera in the **Build** mode.

For a more accurate control of the camera, we can use the Spacebar key to slow down the camera speed and then use *Ctrl* + *H* to level the camera.

As soon as we are happy with the adjustment, we can click on the **Take Photo** button, which has a different icon to represent the overwriting we are about to do. Adjusting the camera path is easy since we have the Play button to check how the animation is working. There is a better way to see the places where some adjustments are required. If we press and hold the left mouse button in the area above the snapshots and then drag the clip, we can check the camera path, as shown in the following screenshot:

Additional actions that we can perform while tweaking the camera positions are inserting a new photo and deleting a photo, which will, in turn, change the length of the movie.

Changing the video length

The fact that we added or removed a photo from the camera path has an impact on the length of the clip we are creating. In some situations, this can be a problem because of certain requirements, but yet again, Lumion provides all the tools to tackle this issue. When recording or tweaking the camera path, we can see the Play button, a small clock with two arrows, as shown in the following screenshot:

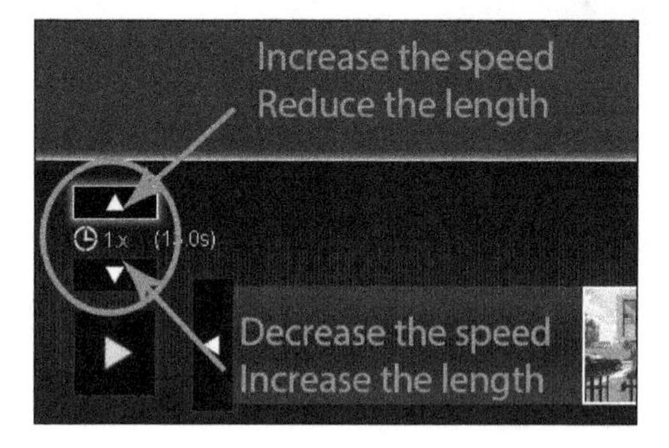

This is where we can change the length of our clip by increasing or decreasing the clip's speed. If you hover the mouse over one of the arrows, some information appears, informing us of the current length of the clip. Then, as shown in the previous screenshot, when the speed is increased, the length of the video is reduced, and vice versa.

Best practices – camera-filming techniques

To create a great movie, we not only need a good composition, but also good filming techniques. This section covers some techniques that can be used to produce a good architectural walk-through.

Tilt

A tilt shot involves tilting the camera up or down, and this technique also needs to be combined with a good action; otherwise, it will lose its power and impact.

This can be easily done using the *Q* and *E* keys to move the camera up or down.

Panning

While a tilt shot is in a vertical movement, the panning shot is precisely a horizontal equivalent of this. The trick to achieve a good panning shot is to use precise timing and framing accuracy to match the camera's movement with the action.

Zoom

There isn't much to say about this kind of shot. Although it seems simple, we need to make it absolutely smooth and not too fast; otherwise, the zoom will look jerky and strange. How can we do this in Lumion? It is really easy to create these types of shots, because when we record the clip, there is a feature called **Focal length (mm)** that can be used to add zoom. How? Have a look at the following screenshot:

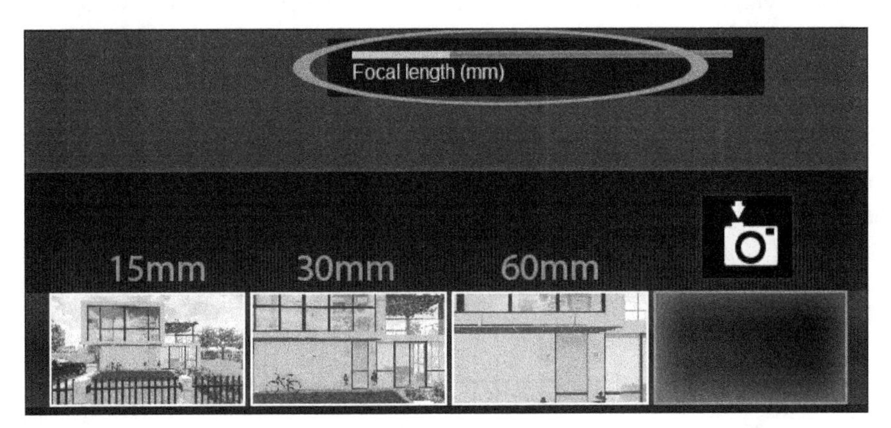

In the first photo, we used the default value for **Focal length (mm)**, which is 15 mm; in the second photo we used 30 mm, and then, in the final photo, we used 60 mm. When we play this animation, we can see if we need to insert another photo with a different focal length or use the clip's speed to create a slower zoom.

Tracking

A tracking shot is a sideways camera movement that is slightly more complicated than creating a tilt or zoom shot. The basic idea is to go from point A to point B in a straight line, but instead of looking straight ahead, the camera is looking sideways. These kinds of shots need to be combined with foreground objects between the camera and the subject. The following screenshot will give you an idea of how this works:

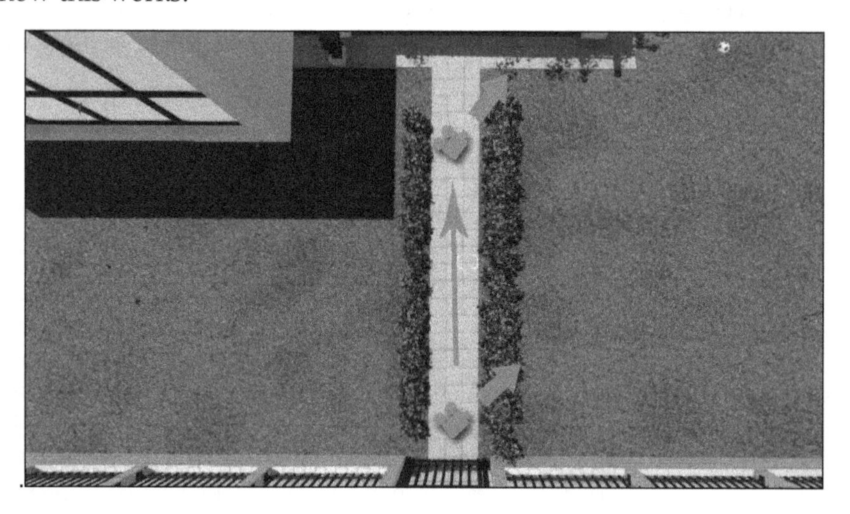

This technique can be combined with other techniques such as zoom to create a great impact on the viewer. We will track along a path and use a slow zoom to focus the viewer's attention on the main subject.

Conclusion

These are just a few techniques that can be used while recording a clip. We can obviously merge different techniques, such as using a tilt shot and zooming in on the subject. Once again, the best way to learn these techniques is not only by applying them to your project, but also by taking some time to study how other artists have applied similar techniques.

A great example of camera shots can be found in the movie *The Third and The Seventh* by Alex Roman. It is a masterpiece not only in cinematography, but also in composition rules.

Also, it doesn't hurt to explore the techniques used by filmmakers Steven Spielberg, Ridley Scott, and Martin Scorsese, just to mention a few.

The next stage in this workflow is organizing and controlling the clip or, hopefully, the clips in the movie.

Step 3 – organizing the movie

As mentioned earlier, a movie can be made up of a single clip, but often, we might find more advantage in creating more than one clip. Why is this? Creating a fantastic movie in Lumion is not something that happens by chance. We need to think about the objective of the movie, how we are going to use composition, and, finally, how we are going to shoot the movie to make it appealing. Imagine managing all this information in just one clip, and you can easily see the nightmare in tweaking the camera's speed and the clip length.

On the other hand, the benefit of using several clips is that we have the freedom to stop one shot and move to another area, and we have the ability to apply different effects according to our needs. Are you convinced?

Handling clips

What do you think should be our priority when organizing the clips created? That's right! We need to give a proper name to each one, because the name that Lumion gives is too generic.

Renaming clips

Where can we check the name for each clip? The easiest way is by hovering the mouse over the clip; a small label appears showing the name for this clip, which, in your case, might be **1 - Flythrough**, as shown in the following screenshot:

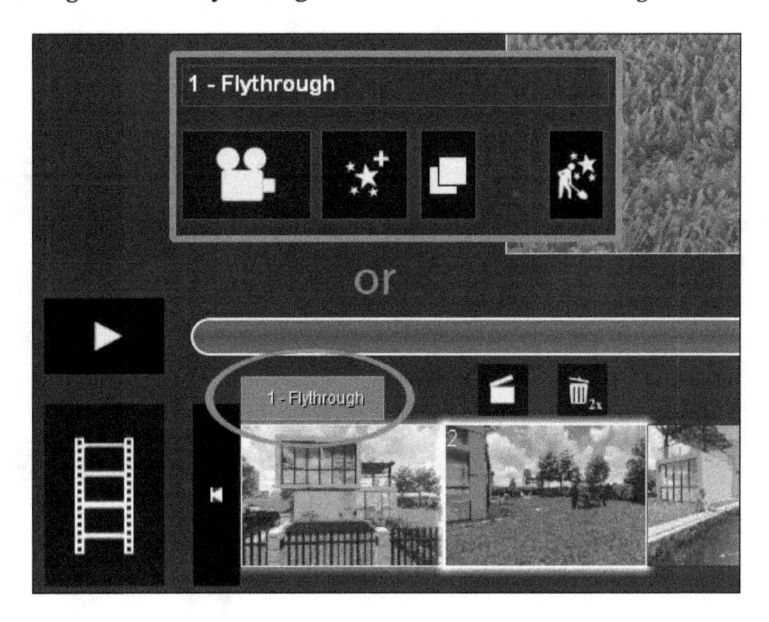

However, this option doesn't give us the opportunity to rename the clip for something more interesting, and this is when we have to turn our attention to the top-left corner, where we will find a small textbox. This feature is really hidden, because it is not so obvious that above the button, there is a textbox where we can type in the new name for the clip, as shown in the following screenshot:

This will certainly help us keep the movie organized, because there is nothing worse than trying to make sense of a complete mess. Good habits like this keep a smooth workflow, but what if we need to change the position or even delete a clip?

Deleting and controlling multiple clips

Deleting a clip is an action that needs to be taken seriously, because contrary to what happens in the **Build** mode, we don't have any **Undo** button. So, if you delete the clip, it would be lost forever. It is best if you have a backup by saving the scene with another name. How can we perform this action? When you select a clip, two options pop up above the clip, as shown in the following screenshot:

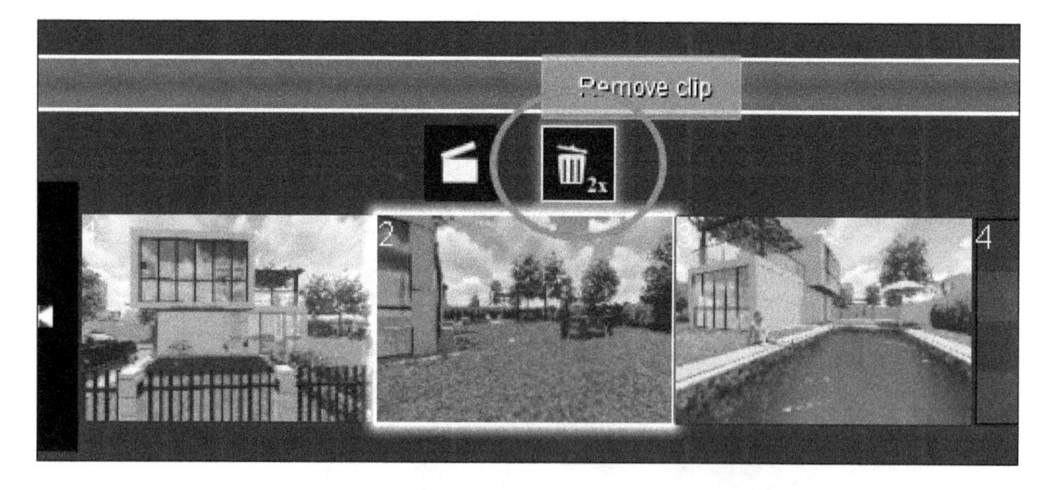

The button that concerns us now is the **Remove clip** button, as highlighted in the previous screenshot. We need to double-click to remove the clip. However, there is a way to avoid deleting the clip, and this is by moving it to the end of the movie. The only catch is that later, we need to specify the frame length of the movie so that it doesn't include this clip. This is something that will be covered in the next chapter.

How can we move and rearrange the clips?

As you might have discovered, Lumion is a very friendly and intuitive tool, so moving and changing clips is not that difficult. We need to press and hold on a clip with the left mouse button and then drag to remove the clip from the current position. Now that we control a small thumbnail that represents the clip, we can move along the clips at the bottom, and an arrow appears showing that we can insert the clip in that location, as shown in the following screenshot:

In the previous screenshot, the clip in the fourth slot is going to be placed between the second and third slots, making this clip the third in the row.

Lumion is still limited in this area, because we cannot copy and paste clips or even divide a clip in different parts. Most of these actions can be achieved if we use the saving and loading camera-position options, but this does not allow the best workflow. However, what Lumion lacks in controlling clips, it makes up for in power-animation techniques that can be used to drastically improve the quality of your movies.

Step 4 – animating objects and effects

Now, we have got to a point where time, patience, and skill can deeply enhance the movie we are creating in Lumion. What is the reason for this? Lumion is shipped with some powerful effects that we had the opportunity to cover in the previous chapters, and we might think that effects are some enhancements related to image and video. However, some of the effects in Lumion are directly related to animation, and they can be found under the **Objects** tab. Let's have a look at how these effects work and how they can be used in a project.

Lumion's animation effects – a quick overview

As mentioned in the beginning of this book, we can truly import animations. These are very limited because we can only import move, rotate, and scale animations using the frame rate of 25 frames per second, and the file format needs to be FBX or Collada. This is when some problems start to appear, because we cannot import vertex, morph, or bone animations, which are needed to animate people.

However, Lumion provides a great solution with these animation effects, which, in turn, can aid us with simple and basic animations or much more complex ones. A word of caution: this is not a very easy topic, but hopefully, with the aid of this book, you will unlock and fully master the potential of Lumion's animation effects. Why don't we start with the simplest animations and leave the hardest effect for later?

Animating layers with the Hide and Show layer effects

Do you remember that time after time, the need for layers was mentioned? The benefits of using layers are that they not only improve the viewport's speed and the workflow by having an organized scene, but we can also use them to animate objects. This is possible thanks to the two effects called **Hide layer** and **Show layer** found under the **Objects** tab.

The Hide layer, as the name suggests, hides 20 layers that can be created in Lumion. This effect is different from all the other effects in Lumion because it is possible to add more than one Hide layer effect to the scene. However, this effect is tricky to work with, because once the effect is applied to the scene, everything in the first layer is hidden, and this effect cannot be animated.

Then, the Show layer does precisely the inverse by showing the layer selected, but in this instance, we can animate or keyframe the values of this effect. The Hide layer hides the layer specified while everything else remains visible, and the reverse happens with the Show layer effect. Keyframe is something we are going to cover with the Near Clip Plane effect, but in simple terms, we can keyframe values during the length of the clip or movie.

These two effects can be used in very specific situations. One possibility is to combine these effects to hide and show sections of the project while doing the render. Why? When working with massive areas, this is a good way to optimize and decrease the render time. If this is not seen, it is not rendered, and it saves time. The workflow for this is complex and requires loads of patience in order to divide the project into different sections, but this is something that can be planned before even starting the project in Lumion.

Sky drop with Lumion

Sky drop is, perhaps, the effect that needs a very good explanation to be used in any project. The **Sky drop** effect does precisely what the name suggests: it lets objects fall from the sky. The setup of this effect is very simple, as shown in the following screenshot:

The **Offset**, **Duration**, and **Spacing** settings control when the object appears, the time it takes to fall, and, finally, the height of the bounce of the object when it hits the ground. A possible application of this effect is, perhaps, a way to introduce a specific building, giving a more dynamic touch to the movie.

Animating a section cut with the Near Clip Plane effect

This next effect is a powerful tool when combined with camera animations. The reason is because we can cut the geometry and 3D models like a plane and look inside the buildings. This effect works in the same way as cutting a plane in front of the camera, and the following screenshot can help us understand how it works:

Near Clip Plane is an effect found in the **Camera** tab, and we only need to tweak one setting, **Near clip plane**. As mentioned earlier, imagine we have a plane parallel to the camera that cuts the geometry, and with the **Near clip plane** setting, we tweak the distance of this plane from the camera. The previous screenshot shows a practical and useful application of this effect where we had a wall that was right in front of the camera. With this effect, we don't need to change the camera position in order to remove the wall; this saves time and gives us the opportunity to create other views that are otherwise impossible. The next screenshot demonstrates how we can show the interior of the building without even entering by using this effect:

However, once the camera starts to move, we will cut everything in front of the camera, and this is something we don't want. One solution is creating a particular clip with the **Near Clip Plane** effect and then continuing the camera path with a different clip. However, the second option is more efficient and also gives us the opportunity to understand what a keyframe is and how we can keyframe the settings found in most of the effects.

Keyframe

The act of creating a keyframe is called keyframing. This is the method of assigning a value to an object at a specific point in time. For example, as in the previous screenshot, where we removed the wall, we need two things for this to work in an animation:

1. Start with a wall removed.
2. After 2 seconds, remove the **Near Clip Plane** effect in order to not cut the other geometry.

For this example, we need to create two keyframes, and to create a keyframe, we need to press the small dot next to setting, as shown in the following screenshot:

We will set the first keyframe and then adjust the value to specify the value for the **Near clip plane** setting, removing the wall in front of the camera. The second step is to move the time bar to where the camera starts to move and create a second key frame. After setting the second keyframe, we need to adjust the setting again to save the new value. Can you see how two white lines were drawn in the time bar? Have a look at the following screenshot, showing a closeup:

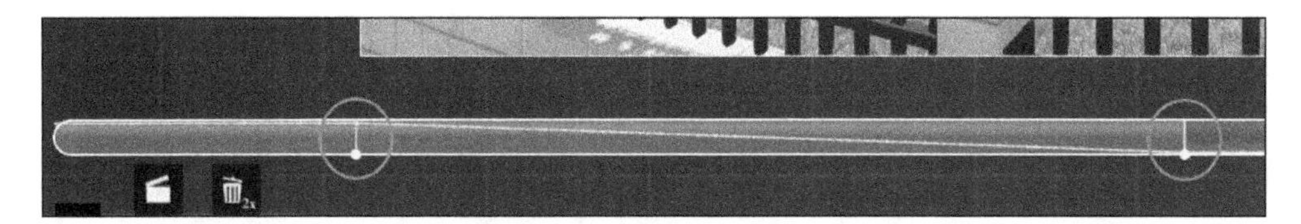

When you set more than one keyframe, Lumion generates the in-between frames, resulting in a smooth change of that parameter over time, and this is called linear interpolation. Animating an effect is easy, and we only need to keep in mind to create the keyframe first and then adjust the value. However, what if we need to delete a keyframe or tweak the ones created? Have a look at the following screenshot that explains how we can perform these tasks:

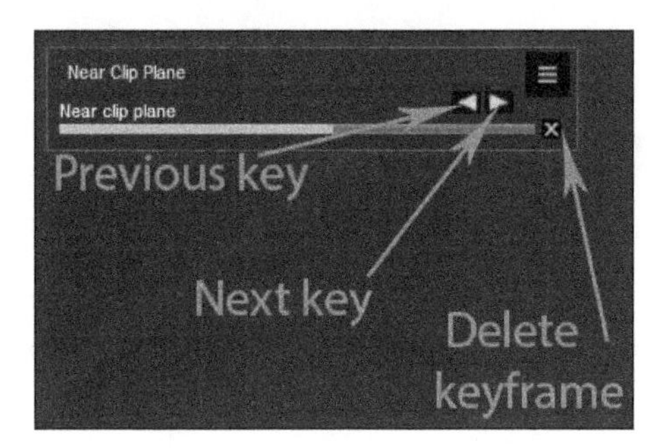

As soon as we create a keyframe, these options become available, and they provide all the control we need.

This overview provides enough information for us to move to more complex ways to animate 3D models in Lumion.

Simple animations with the Move effect

Now, things start to get more serious with animations, and for the next effect, we need to arm ourselves with patience and time. It is only with time and patience that we can create complex animations and bring life to our 3D world. Let's start by creating a simple animation with the Move effect found in the **Objects** tab.

What can we animate with this effect? The answer is everything. Of course, animating a tree might not sound too practical; the truth is we can animate everything with this effect. Lumion has some 3D models that are specially conceived to be animated, such as cars, people, and birds, but this doesn't mean we cannot animate other elements such as fog or even fire.

Let's add this effect to the scene and then click on the icon with a pencil. This action allows us to select an object that needs to be animated, which, in our case, is a man walking down the street, as shown in the following screenshot:

The animation with the Move effect is very easy, because we just need to specify the start and end positions of the 3D model. The steps for this animation to work are as follows:

1. Click on the **Start position** button and select the Move tool from the toolbar.
2. With the Move tool, select and drag the 3D model slightly to set the initial keyframe.

If something goes wrong because the 3D model suddenly changes the rotation, ignore it.

3. Click on the **End position** button and with the Move tool, drag the 3D model to the final location.
4. Click on the **Start position** and **End position** buttons to check whether the keyframes were set correctly. Then, we can continue animating other settings such as the rotation and many more.
5. Click on the Back button to save this animation.

When animating people walking, you need to be sure that the path you trace is big enough for the clip you create. In other words, if you have a clip of 10 seconds but the walking path is small, the person will be walking back and forward in a loop. With transports, it is a different situation, because in this instance, if you have a 10-second clip with an animated car, the car will take seconds to cover the path, even if it is just a few centimeters long.

This means we need to plan ahead what elements will appear in a frame and for how long, and this also proves the importance of using several clips instead of one massive clip. Also, can you think of other practical applications? All the small things together create an impressive movie, and with this effect, we can really animate small things. What about animating the rotation of a door to open when the camera is passing? What if we animate water coming from a fountain by animating the scale of the water sprinkle? These are small touches that, when combined, can create a beautiful movie, making it stand out from the crowd.

However, don't you feel that this effect, although great, doesn't provide the freedom we need to create more complex animations? That is why Lumion has the Advanced move effect, which has a more complex animation system.

Animating curved paths with the Advanced move effect

Although we have mentioned that this effect is more complex and allows more intricate animations, don't feel overwhelmed by this effect. In reality this effect gives us the opportunity to add more keyframes, thus allowing a more complex animation.

For this example, we will animate the same man walking and turning to another street. Let's start by adding the Advanced move effect to the scene and then clicking on the button with the pencil icon to start creating an animation. The tools available are more complex than the ones in the previous effect; this is shown in the following screenshot:

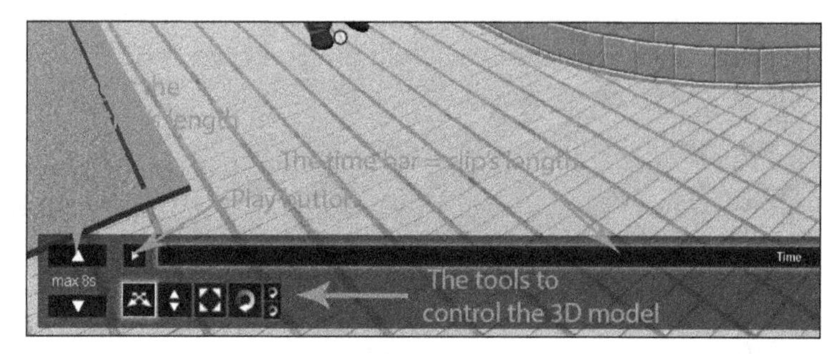

Instead of the **Start position** and **End position** buttons, we have a time bar that is equivalent to the clip's length. In the example shown in the previous screenshot, the length we have for the animation is 8 seconds, and we can scrub along the time bar using the left mouse button to stipulate when the animation starts and ends. The steps for this animation are as follows:

1. Move the time bar to the right time, and using the Move tool, set the first key by slightly moving the 3D model.
2. Move the time bar to the end of the window and use the Move tool to set the end key.
3. Then, between these two frames, create the keyframes needed to create a smooth, curved path.

In the end, we want to create something like this:

In this instance, we used only four keyframes, and the beauty of it is that we only used the Move tool, which, once more, proves just how amazing Lumion is. When we provide enough keyframes, Lumion can adjust the 3D model's rotation, thus creating a smooth curve. This, however, gives us a responsibility. Look at the previous screenshot again and see how easy it was to create only three keyframes, but this would create a path with right angles. With a path like this, Lumion doesn't have enough information to create a curved path, and the result will be the 3D model doing a strange rotation.

Before we finish, we can use the Play button to check the animation, and if needed, we can tweak the animation or delete a keyframe using the **Remove key** button, as shown in the following screenshot:

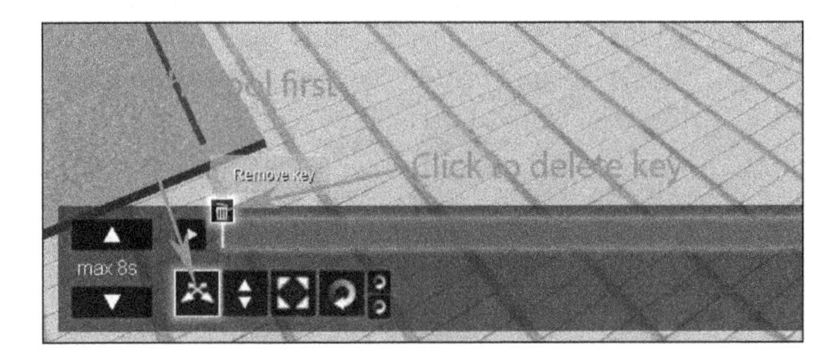

After clicking on the Back button to save the animation, there is an additional setting we need to cover. Below the button you clicked to start the animation, there is a setting called **Time offset**.

This setting is `0` by default, and this means that the animation will start without any offset. However, when we start to increase this value, which is measured in seconds, we start to offset the animation. So, if we use a value of `1`, the animation starts with an offset of 1 second, and this can be really useful when we need to delay or move the animation forward in relation to the clip, without having to change or tweak the entire animation path.

Summary

This was, without doubt, a cornerstone in the process to master Lumion and create professional and efficient animations. As you learned, creating a great movie in Lumion is not just about pointing the camera at an object and start recording. You first learned how to create a camera path, and then, you learned tips to improve these paths. Then, you saw how important the composition and camera filming techniques are for your animation to stand out from the ordinary architectural visualizations. After learning how to edit and organize clips, you learned a very complex stage in this workflow—creating animations with effects.

However, these effects are just the start, because there is so much you can do with the effects we will cover in the next chapter. The next and final chapter will be the climax of all the hard work we went through, so without any delay, let's see how we can create a walk-through visualization.

10
Creating Walk-through Visualizations

Starting from where we left off in the preceding chapter, we will keep developing the architectural walk-through. At this moment, we have covered everything necessary to have a good and solid movie with great animations and composition. We are almost at the end of this project, but then again, we can add an extra touch that is only possible through Lumion's supplementary video effects.

In this chapter, we will cover the following topics:

- Lumion's video effects—a quick overview
- The **Entire Movie** mode
- The Sound and Stereoscopic effects
- Copying effects from the **Photo** mode
- Editing the project in the **Movie** mode
- Animating the focus
- Adding Motion Blur
- Handling a camera
- The Rain and Snow effects
- Playing safe with the Broadcast Safe effect
- Importing a movie and an image
- Exporting an entire movie or sections of the movie
- Using render passes

Some of these effects will enrich the movie's realism and further effects will help to display the project in a creative and professional style. Just before we export the movie in several different formats, we will learn how to use sound to generate a deep and evolving environment and then, in conclusion, we will export the movie as a video file or a sequence of images. Let's start by covering some specific ways to work with effects in the **Movie** mode.

Lumion's video effects – a quick overview

Lumion's effects are not new to us since we have been using them with the **Photo** mode. All the knowledge we built throughout the book while using the effects in the **Photo** mode can now be applied in the **Movie** mode. However, the **Movie** mode has a few more effects and these are commonly related with movement, like the ones we covered in the previous chapter.

Nonetheless, even in the **Movie** mode, some of these effects are only accessible when we use the **Entire Movie** mode.

The Entire Movie mode

In truth, the **Entire Movie** mode is more like a submode of the **Movie** mode. So far, we have learned how to create clips that when combined create an entire movie. The **Entire Movie** mode only comes into play when we start doing animation or using particular effects. Animating using this mode is not practical in most circumstances and some of these reasons were covered in the previous chapter, so what can we do in the **Entire Movie** mode?

The Lumion's effects for video can be applied to clips or to the entire movie. What could help you choose the effects that are useful to the final result we want to achieve? Think of effects that don't need major adjustments. For example, if you want to replace the clouds using the Clouds effect, it doesn't make much sense to use the same effect in 10 clips. This is one of the situations where you can use the **Entire Movie** mode. When you want to affect all the clips with the same effect and few changes, the **Entire Movie** mode is the best option.

Where can we find this mode? On the left-hand side of the window, below the Play button, we have another button called the **Entire Movie** button, as shown in the following screenshot:

When we click on this button, apparently nothing changes, but if we look closely at the interface, some buttons have disappeared, leaving only the New effect button, as shown in the following screenshot:

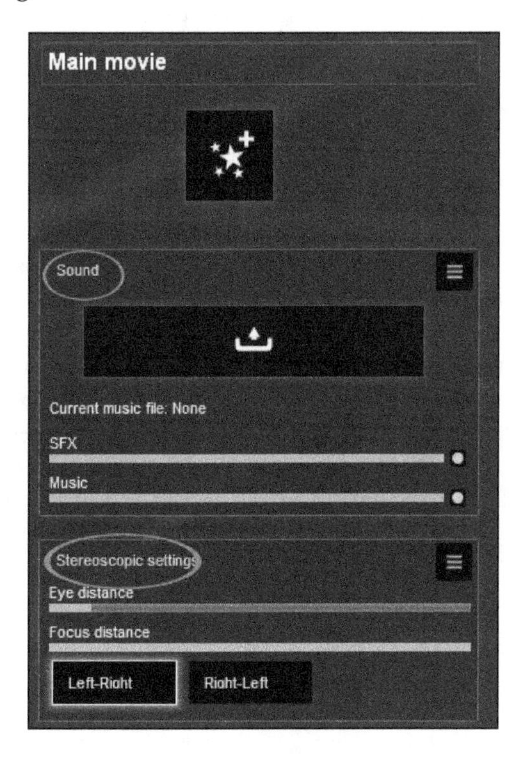

In the previous screenshot, there are two unique effects displayed for this submode—**Sound** and **Stereoscopic**.

Two exclusive effects – Sound and Stereoscopic

The Sound effect is something you would want to use in your scene to eliminate the need of extra software to add sound to the video. This is not the same as adding sound to the project using the sounds available in Lumion. Let's say the client wants to do a voice-over for the movie, explaining what the viewer is seeing in each shot. For this to happen, we have to use the Sound effect that becomes available only once we move to the **Entire Movie** mode.

Have you ever seen a movie with 3D glasses? Actually, it is not 3D, but instead stereoscopic, which is a technique to enhance the illusion of depth in an image or a movie. Lumion can produce a 3D movie or to be precise, a stereoscopic movie. We need special eyeglasses ensuring that our left eye sees only the left image and the right eye sees only the right image.

Before we cover more effects that can bring further realism and a special touch to the movie, let's see two important aspects that can expand the workflow in this mode.

Best practices – copying effects from the Photo mode

Let's look at the best practices to copy effects from the **Photo** mode. That's right! Typically, a project can be a series of still images and small clips that are combined together and provide all the visual aids that are indispensable for the client. Normally, the images come first and all our hard work, including tweaking and adjusting the effect's parameters, can and should be copied from the **Photo** to **Movie** modes. This is also possible the other way around. There are some restrictions while copying effects from the **Movie** to **Photo** mode, but these are related only to the animation effects. Also, this is not a magic formula because we still need to adjust some effects in particular when working with global illumination and depth of field.

Copying the effects from one mode to another is very easy, as you can see in the following screenshot:

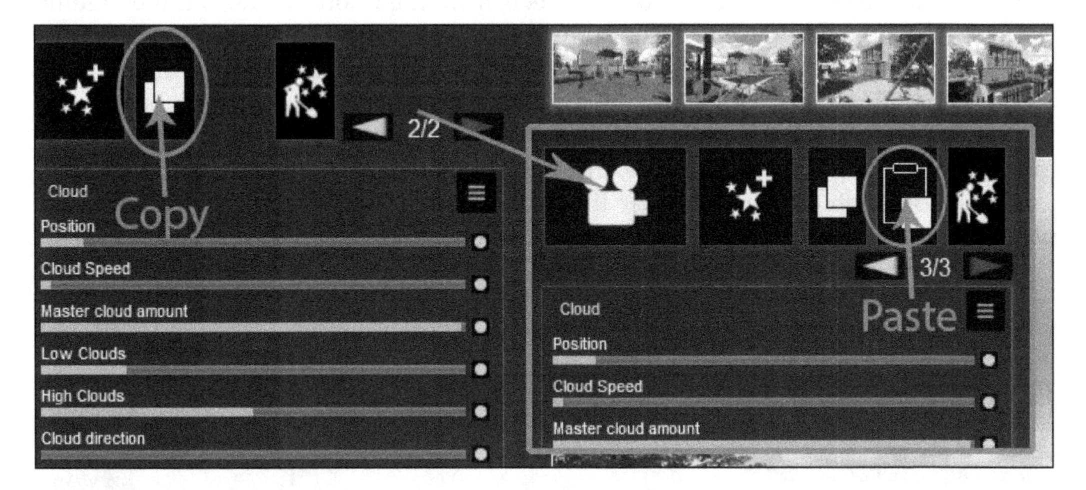

In both the modes, we have a button called **Copy**, and once we click on this button, a new one appears called **Paste**. With the **Paste** button, we can do the following:

- If in the **Movie** mode, copy the effects from one clip to another
- Copy and paste effects from different modes
- Clear the effects from the **Photo** or **Movie** mode

The third option is a technique that can be used when we have a clip or photo with loads of effects that need to be removed. For this trick, you have to select a clip with no effects or at least create one, click on the **Copy** button, and paste the clip on another clip or photo. Because we didn't copy any effect, once we press the **Paste** button, Lumion deletes all the effects instead of having to remove the effects one by one.

Now that we have copied all the effects, there is an extra step we can take to see if the effects are producing the desired outcome. This is particularly useful in the **Movie** mode, where our camera position is already defined and locked.

Editing the scene in the Movie mode

We have most likely copied some of the effects from the **Photo** mode, and they seem to blend perfectly with the clip. With some effects, this can be easily perceived, but with others, it can be challenging to check, like if we have to tweak the Ambient scale in the Global illumination effect. In the **Photo** mode, we can simply move the camera close to the area, check the effect, and using the shortcuts, get back to the saved camera position. In the **Movie** mode, this is slightly difficult since we don't have the same freedom with the camera. Once the clip is created, the camera is locked in this position, restraining any opportunity to move closer and verify the effect.

In both modes, there is a truly magic button called **Built with effects**, and the following screenshot represents what is possible:

Why don't you have a go with this feature? Suddenly, we are back to the **Build** mode, where we can perform any typical task such as adding a new 3D model or relocating an object, but the fantastic thing is that we can actually see the effects applied in the **Photo** or **Movie** mode. The example in the previous screenshot shows that we have the Rain effect, and once we click on the **Built with effects** button, it is possible to see this effect in real time while editing the scene.

Depending on the number of effects, the viewport can start to slow down, making it unpractical to make major changes using this feature.

Even after copying the effects we used in the **Photo** mode, there are a few additional Lumion effects that can be used to increase the level of realism and make the scene more interesting. Let's see how this is possible.

Improving the movie using additional effects

Throughout this book, we have virtually covered every single Lumion effect available in both the **Photo** and **Movie** modes. But we still have a few more great effects that can boost the movie's quality. Some of these effects simulate what happens in the real world when we use real world cameras, and this is one of the reasons why using such effects can add layers of realism. Where should we start?

Using depth of field and animating the camera's focus

Depth of field (**DOF**) is not a strange term for us. In *Chapter 7, Creating Realistic Visualizations*, we covered what DOF is, but just as an introduction.

While using a real camera, we need to use both shutter speed and the aperture to change the amount of light that hits the sensor. This not only controls light, but also controls or changes the depth of field. The depth of field is a measure of how much of your scene is in focus. If you need to have a closer look at this subject, check out the *Depth of field* section found in *Chapter 7, Creating Realistic Visualizations*.

The **Depth of Field** effect can be found under the **Camera** tab, and these are the settings we can find:

- **Focus distance**: This is used to specify where the camera should focus
- **F stop**: This removes some of the blur, but more importantly, creates a gradual transition between sharp and blurred areas
- **Smoothness**: This is used to create sharper edges, but you probably should leave this at `1`
- **Isolate foreground**: This controls the layers of DOF in front of the camera, but doesn't produce a good result the majority of the time
- **Expansion**: This works great for close-ups to get a sharper look at the 3D model in focus

However, this information might not be enough per se, particularly when we have to animate this depth of the field. You understand how animation works and what each setting does, but let's see how to combine them together to create a beautiful and eye-catching movie.

Instead of using a very complex scene, we will use the following scene to help us comprehend how to effectively animate the camera's focus:

No doubt your scene will be by far more complex than the one shown in the previous screenshot. In a deep analysis of this scene, we have four cylinders with an equal distance between them of 3 meters. This means that the last cylinder is more or less 10 meters away from the camera, and this information is very important in understanding how the **Depth of Field** effect works. You can easily create a scene similar to the one shown in the preceding screenshot that will help you to master this fantastic effect.

Firstly, let's try to set the **Focus distance** slider to something around `2` or `3`. Can you see that close to the camera, the ground and objects are sharper in comparison with the elements in the background? This is because in using the focus distance, we are telling the camera the distance in meters that we want to be focused and sharp.

We can effortlessly see why using depth of field is a great technique. Not only can we create a sense of depth, but we can separate the object from any distractions, putting us in control of where the viewer focuses his or her attention. This is also a great way to create transitions between clips.

The first step involves working with the **Focus distance** slider and seeing how it works with the subject, and creating a keyframe for the distance of the different objects that need focus. This may not be easy to set up because the quality of the viewport does not always correspond to the final output. One way to ensure that we have the correct focus distance is by rendering just a frame and seeing if the **Focus distance** slider needs further adjustment. We will learn how to do this later in this chapter.

The subsequent setting that needs some adjustment is the **F Stop**. This setting is directly related with the amount of DOF we have in the image, and if you lower this setting, we get something that is called Bokeh. *Bokeh* comes from a Japanese word that literally means blur, and it refers to the quality of an out-of-focus area in a photograph or movie, as shown in the following screenshot:

Of course, there are more interesting subjects than a basketball, but you can see how this effect can make your movie far more interesting.

The concluding step when working with the **Depth of Field** effect is the use of the **Expansion** setting. This setting controls the size of the area that is in focus and once again, we have to keyframe new values for all these settings. As you may notice, tweaking, adjusting, and animating this effect is not easy for the reason that all the values are extremely sensitive. As a solution, we definitely have to use the *Shift* key to perform small increments.

> As mentioned before, the *The Third & The Seventh* movie is a great example of how this kind of DOF animation is used. This movie is an example of composition, color, lighting, and camera animation.

By now, the movie we are producing is full of effects that add layers of realism, but since we have animation, something essential must be done to remove the artificial look.

Adding realistic motion blur

Something that you probably have experienced while driving a car or traveling by bus is looking out of the window and seeing the world moving so fast that everything outside becomes blurred. The same thing happens when a camera is used to record a movie, and this is because the frame or photograph doesn't represent an instant of time. The time it takes to take a photograph or record a frame is defined by the exposure's setting. In most situations, the exposure is enough to create a sharp image, but there will always be some amount of motion blur. This is an important concept to understand because when we first add the Motion Blur effect to the movie, nothing happens.

Possibly, you are now trying the effect and seeing that nothing in the movie has changed at all. Nevertheless, why don't you try to press the Play button and see this effect in action? The following screenshot shows the difference in this effect being used:

The best way to see how the Motion Blur effect is affecting the clip or movie is by dragging the time bar to the middle of the animation and tweaking the effect. Motion Blur is one of the simplest effects to use, and you can rest your mind because Lumion's team has developed this effect perfectly. The effect can only be perceived when there is an animation, so if the camera doesn't move at all, no motion blur is added. Also, the amount of motion blur is proportional to the camera speed, which means that if the camera moves slowly, there will be a very small amount of blur in comparison with a brusque camera animation.

Motion blur is something that, although not entirely perceived during the animation, our brain can easily recognize when it is being used or not, and it is another element that makes a movie believable.

At this point, we have begun to understand that the world created in Lumion is too perfect, and it is our assignment to add imperfections and natural elements to reduce the artificial feeling. The camera plays an essential role here, and there is yet another effect to control Lumion's cameras.

Walking and handling the camera

In real life, when shooting a movie, the director uses some tools, such as cranes and tracks to stabilize the camera. The first lesson we get from this is that we have to treat cameras in Lumion the same way we would in real life. This is a small detail that has a massive impact on the movie's quality. What about the second lesson? The second lesson is that we can mimic the way a camera would record if using a crane/track or when we hold a camera.

Lumion has a great effect called **Handheld Camera**, found under the **Camera** tab. This effect can mimic the result we get when someone is holding a camera and recording. The first question that may pop up in our head is: why should I be interested in this effect at all? Don't I need a smooth animation for a prefect architectural visualization?

The truth is that we can use this effect to give a subtle effect to the camera that recorded the clip. Just because the effect is designed to mimic someone walking with a camera doesn't mean we cannot use this for a different purpose. And this leads to the second question: how can I use it?

Let's start by adding the **Handheld Camera** effect to the clip and playing with the settings available to reproduce something like this:

We can see that the initial purpose of this effect is to create the look and feel you would get from a very old recording camera. This may be something you want to use for a personal project or for open-minded clients. The feeling we get from this effect is different from what we see in architectural visualization, and initially, our first reaction may be to discard this effect. And here is when we need to think of ways we can use this effect to enrich the movie without creating an amateur look. The settings used to create what you see in the screenshot were the following:

Shake strength is the first setting we have to work with in order to enhance the camera quality. Of course, a value of `3` creates a very clumsy walk, almost giving the feeling that the camera weigh tons, but why don't you have a go with a value between `0.1` and `0.3`? Depending on the camera path, the addition of this effect is almost imperceptible, but this is exactly what we need for a believable animation.

We have the opportunity to control and animate the **Focal Length** setting. The use of this effect can be a better solution for when we have to create a zoom.

The **Tilt** setting gives us the perfect opportunity to introduce a rather interesting camera technique: the **Dutch tilt**. What is the Dutch tilt? Have a look at the following screenshot:

A Dutch tilt is a camera shot in which the camera angle is tilted off to one side so that the shot is composed with vertical lines at an angle to the side of the frame, giving a dramatic effect. This also has the effect of putting the viewer off balance by creating a feeling of disorientation, and your movie will hardly go unnoticed if you use a Dutch tilt, but when using a slight tilt, this can be enough to give a different artistic perspective in contrast to the straight shots. Using the camera's slight tilt also allows you to show more of the subject in the frame, and this proves to be useful when we have buildings with different heights that need to be placed on the same frame.

These features can help us to improve the clip's quality substantially, and consequently, the movie is created. Let's have a closer look at some visual effects that can be used for very specific situations.

Visual effects – Rain, Snow, and much more

In most situations, the effects mentioned in the topic might seem inadequate, but we have to keep in mind that every project is different, and even the most initially unsuitable effect can later become very useful. Even if you are not planning to use these effects in your current project, it is always good to have in mind where they are and what can be accomplished with them.

Winter time with the Snow and Rain effects

The Snow and Rain effects can be found under the **Weather** tab, and when we compare the settings side by side, there are a few common adjustments to be made, such as controlling the density, wind, and speed. There are two essential settings, **Drop Distortion** in the Rain effect and **Snow layer** in the Snow effect, that make these effects more believable. However, when we apply these effects, can you see something that needs correction? Have a look at the following screenshot:

The arrows help by pointing to the fact that on a rainy or snowy day, we don't have such sharp, harsh shadows. How can we solve this problem in both situations?

The following screenshot shows the effects we need to tackle this issue:

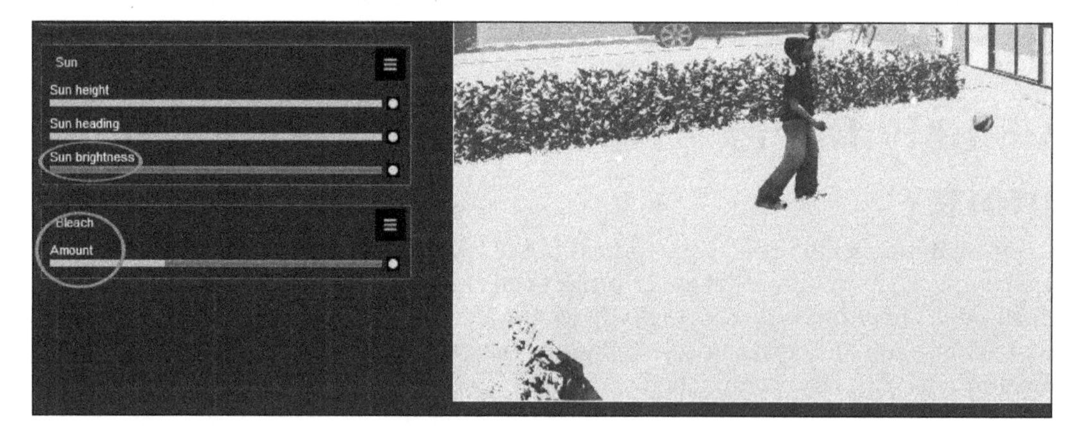

The effects we need are as follows:

- **Sun**: Using this effect, we can only tweak the **Sun brightness** setting to remove the shadows completely. However, this removes some light from the scene and to compensate for that, we have to use the **Bleach** effect.
- **Bleach**: This is an effect that makes the light areas brighter and the dark areas darker.

By now, you may ask whether there are additional ways to improve the movie by extending a still image using additional Lumion resources. The answer is yes and we will have a quick overview of some of these effects.

Best practices – attending to small details with Lumion effects

One of the cornerstones for a great movie or still image is the various small details we add to the scene, and this has a massive impact on creating something believable. Again, there is a need to have balance while using the available Lumion effects; we don't have to use every single effect just because they are there.

For example, under the **World** tab, there is an effect called **Underwater**. This effect completely submerges the project, creating a beautiful play between caustics, reflections, and volumetric light. This effect has a narrow application, but can be perfect when we create aquariums and marine scenes.

The next detail or effect we can use has a wider application, as shown in the following screenshot:

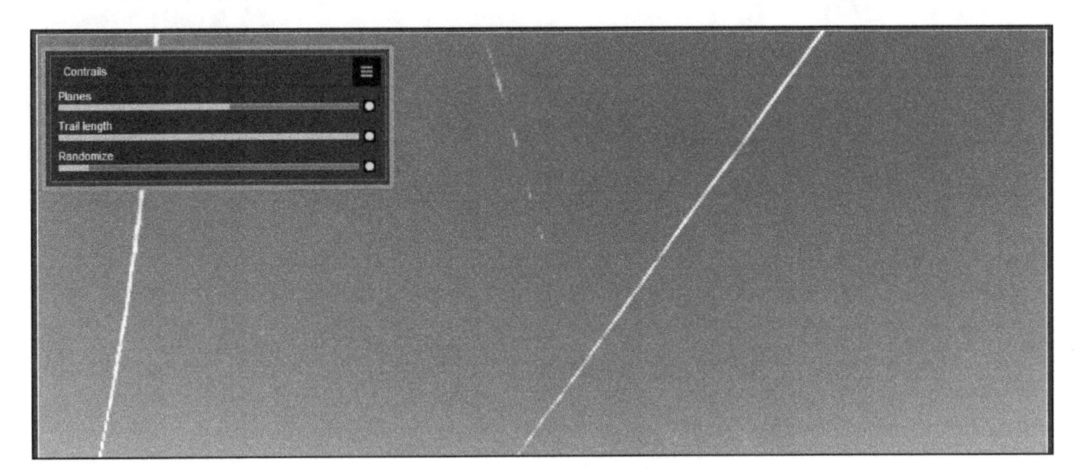

The **Contrails** effect adds planes to the sky and also the trail they leave behind. This is the kind of effect that needs to be added with balance in mind, unless we are working on an airport scene.

> To see the trails with good quality, press and hold the *U* key.

Moving to the **Weather** tab, we can find another effect called Foliage wind. By default, there is wind inside Lumion's world and we can see this effect by adding a tree and looking closely at the leaves. The default value of `0.1` works perfectly and there isn't a need to change this except when working on a particular project.

A special touch with falling leaves

From the name of this topic, it is easy to guess what we are covering next. Falling leaves is something we don't have in either of the **Photo** or **Movie** modes, and for this, we need to get back to the **Build** mode. In the **Build** mode, open the **Objects** menu and click on the **Effects** button, as shown in the following screenshot:

Inside the **Effects Library**, select the fifth tab, where we can find three options of leaves. Like a 3D model, we need to select and place one of these options in the scene and immediately, we can see some happy leaves moving inside an imaginary box. This is nothing special, until we open **Falling leaves Properties** and start tweaking not only the color, but specially the **Wind X** and **Wind Z** options. These two settings are crucial to add some life to the leaves and make them behave like they would in the real world.

Let's stay in the **Build** mode and see something further that is unique in Lumion.

Enriching the movie using sound

While working on a project, you probably would have noticed a button in the **Objects** toolbar called **Sounds**, as shown in the following screenshot:

What we have here is almost like a hidden treasure, and once you open the Sound library, you will understand why. Place the button over any thumbnail and appreciate the hard work of Lumion's team for producing these accurate and balanced sounds.

The process is very simple like almost everything else in Lumion. We select a sound and then place the sound close to the area where it is needed. You can see in the previous screenshot that the sound was placed near an area with people. After this, we have an icon representing the sound, but to control it, open **Sound Properties**. With any sound, we always have two circles:

- The yellow circle: This represents an area where the sound can be heard loud and clear, and it is controlled using the **Min distance** setting.
- The green circle: This represents the maximum distance till where we can hear the sound, but the sound will start to fade once we leave the yellow circle. This circle is controlled using the **Max distance** setting.

Then, it is up to your imagination and it's time to populate the entire project with specific and well-designed sounds. When everything is assembled together, the result is outstanding.

Can we export the movie now? Well, there is something we can have a look at before exporting the movie and it doesn't hurt to know.

Playing safe with the Broadcast Safe effect

Firstly, this is something that will only be useful if your movie will be broadcast on TV. For television, there are two main video formats:

- **National Television Standards Committee** (**NTSC**)
- **Phase Alternating Line** (**PAL**)

The countries that use the PAL system are North America, Japan, and South Korea, and the NTSC is used in most of Europe, Australia, and large parts of Asia and Africa. This is the reason why some DVDs from Europe may not play in North America.

Did you notice that Lumion has everything? Yes, Lumion has an effect that can safeguard you in case you need to export the movie in the NTSC or PAL format.

The **Broadcast Safe** effect for some reason is found under the **Artistic** tab, and once we apply this effect, there are two options:

- **NTSC**: Here, you need to use 30 frames per second
- **PAL**: Here, you need to use 25 frames per second

At this stage, if you are happy with the entire movie and eager to render the clips for different countries, move to the *Render the final movie* section because next, you will cover some final touches to create a professional movie presentation.

Final touches using the Titles and In/Out effects

Aren't we done yet? In the 3D world, there is always room for improvement, but in most cases, we don't have time. The next few things can be considered in the final stages before exporting the movie, and then you will realize that it took longer to create the project than to render the final movie.

Just a reminder: while creating a clip, we can select an external video that needs to be incorporated into the movie. The same happens if we need to use an image, but there is a small detail that needs to be taken into account, as shown in the following screenshot:

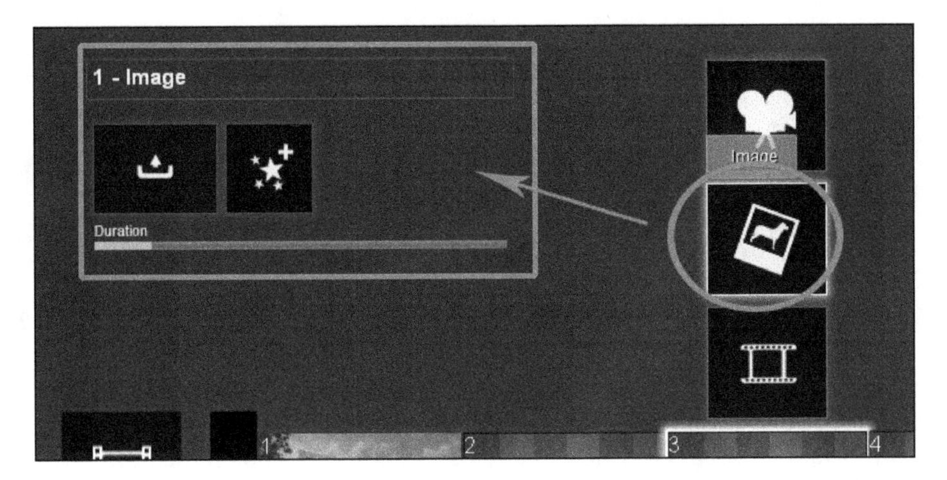

With a video, Lumion knows the length of the clip, but with an image, we have to specify the duration of the clip as exemplified in the previous screenshot.

Did you know that even with imported videos and images we can use some of Lumion's effects?

Let's look at two more effects before we start exporting the movie. We'll start by exploring the **In/out** effect and why it is so important.

Fading in/out – transitions between clips

Fading in/out is based on a film technique called *Dissolve*, where a gradual transition is created from one scene to another. The same technique can be used in Lumion, which allows us to create smooth transitions between clips.

Firstly, we have to select a clip where we can control the fade in and out technique. The effect we need is called **In/out** and can be found under the **Style** tab. This effect has four variations, as shown in the following screenshot:

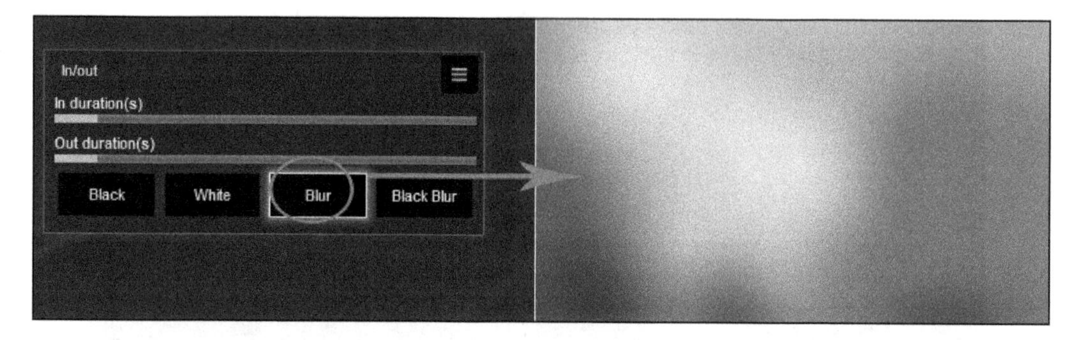

Usually, each fade has a duration of 1 second, and the previous screenshot shows that time can be controlled using **In duration(s)** and **Out duration(s)**. How long a transition should be between different clips or scenes depends on the mood the client wants to set. The client may need more time in the beginning of the movie to show the logo and some additional text, but then eventually the fades between scenes should be fairly quick, giving the sense of a dynamic environment.

Adding text and logos with the Titles effect

The Titles effect, such as the **In/out** effect, is found on the **Style** tab, and this effect is so rich that it would take another chapter to cover entirely what is possible with this effect. After applying this effect, it is possible to add text directly to a movie and control when it starts and how it blends with the scene.

The **Start At (%)** setting works with percentage. This means that if your clip is 20 seconds long, the text will appear after 2 seconds if you have a value of `10%`.

This doesn't seem special, but that is because we haven't yet clicked on the magic button. This button is the one with the pencil icon and when pressed, opens a window full of possibilities, as shown in the following screenshot:

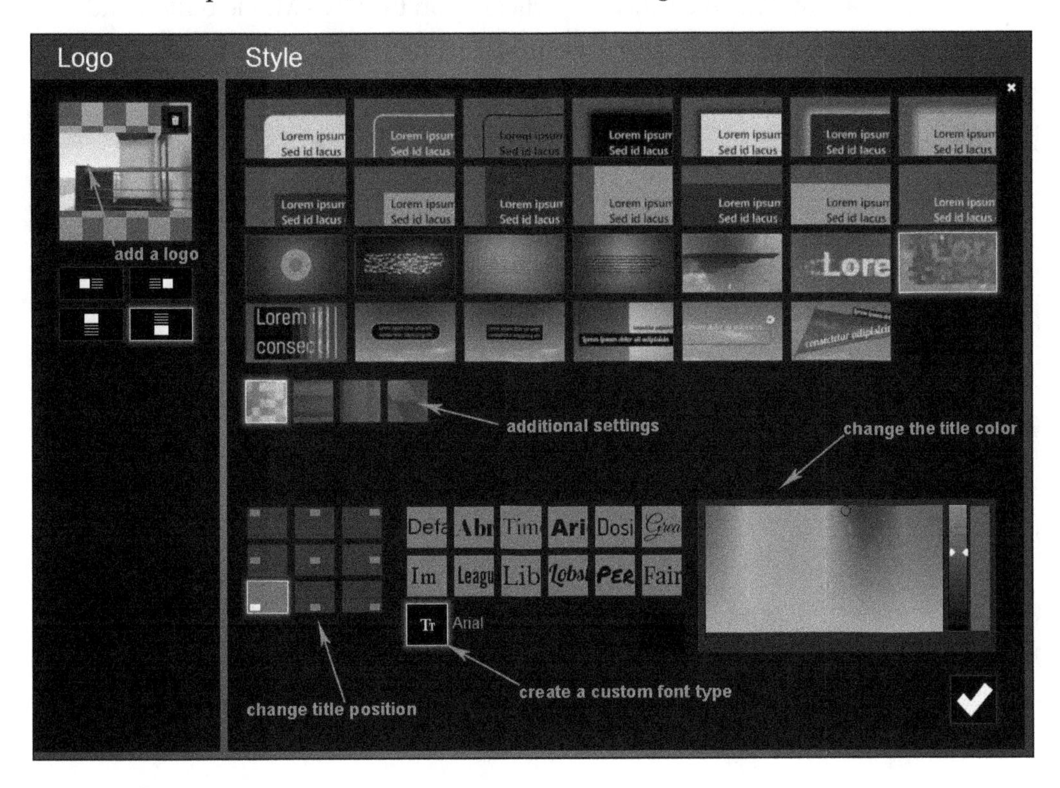

Where should we start? It is hard to tell because we have at least 27 styles, and as you can see in the previous screenshot, it is possible to change the title's color and create a different transition using additional styles when available. Now, finally, let's export the movie.

Rendering the final movie

Rendering the final movie is the climax to all our hard work. The hours of modeling, tweaking materials, adding 3D models, and adjusting dozens of effects will pay off once we see the rendered movie. Even in this stage, Lumion presents us with several options that will prove useful for different situations.

Exporting an entire movie with two clicks

One of the first and most logical options is to export the entire movie as a single video file. The fastest way to do this is by clicking on the Save Movie button and then the **OK** button, as shown in the following screenshot:

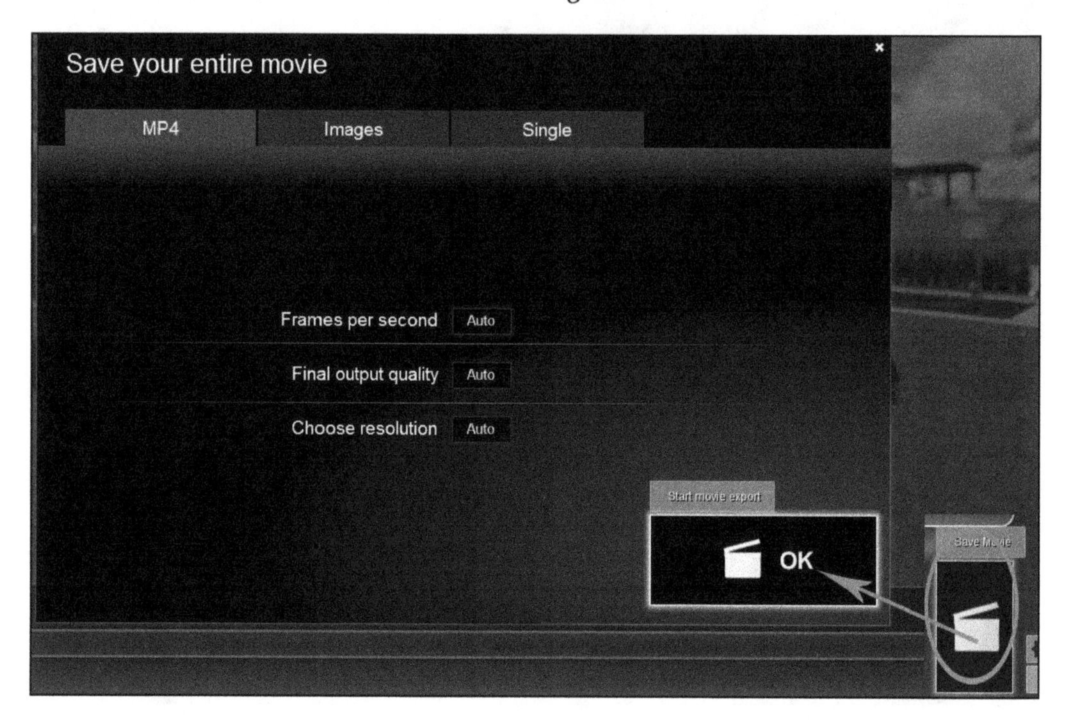

The Save Movie button opens a window that allows us to export the movie in one click without the need for any additional configurations. The settings used by default are: 30 frames per second, the best quality, and a resolution of 720 p. Technically, we need three clicks to indicate where we want to save the movie.

However, this doesn't mean we have to rely on the default settings because if we click on the **Auto** button, these actions give access to additional settings, as shown in the following screenshot:

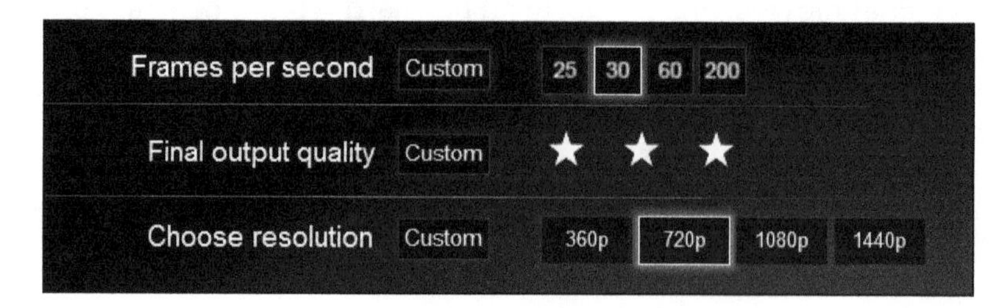

Not only is it possible to change the frames per second, but we can also change the quality and resolution of the movie. These last two settings are very important, in particular when we need to send an initial draft to a client. If the client only wants to see the camera animation and how the scene is composed, the best option we have is exporting a movie with low quality and a lower resolution.

[Restart Lumion before beginning the rendering process because this action when rendering complex scenes can improve the render time.]

We mentioned that there are other possibilities for exporting a movie. Do we really need them? And why should we consider using these additional exporting options?

Best practices – exporting individual clips and a sequence of images

Firstly, why would we even want to export a clip one by one? The quick answer is because of the flexibility we get while using this technique. Exporting single clips can be quite useful, particularly when we wish to manipulate these different clips later with video editing applications like Adobe Premier. How can we do this? Instead of clicking on the Save Movie button, select an individual clip and two small icons appear, as shown in the following screenshot:

The button we want is the one called **Create movie from clip**, and once we click on this button, the **Save your entire movie** window appears with the same options we have when saving the entire movie. If your movie is composed of several clips, this means you have to perform this action for each one, but in the end, it pays to have some freedom to tweak and edit the videos that compose the movie.

When saving the movie, did you notice the two additional tabs next to the **MP4** tab? This is where we can find some additional and useful features to export a movie.

Best practices – rendering a sequence of images

The expression "frames per second" is not something new to us. A movie can have 25 fps or 30 fps, as we saw in the *Playing safe with the Broadcast Safe effect* section. A movie is made up of a sequence of frames that when played at high speed, give the sensation of motion and instead of exporting a video or even a small clip, we can export these frames, which when combined, create the movie.

Is there any particular reason to render all these frames? If we had the flexibility of using individual clips, then we will find more flexibility and control by exporting the individual frames. With colored frames, we also can export specific render passes that can be used to tweak lighting, add color grading, and perform post-production activities to achieve a better result. How can we export the movie in such a way?

When we click on the Save Movie button, the window that appears goes straight to the **MP4** tab, but what we need is the **Images** tab, as shown in the following screenshot:

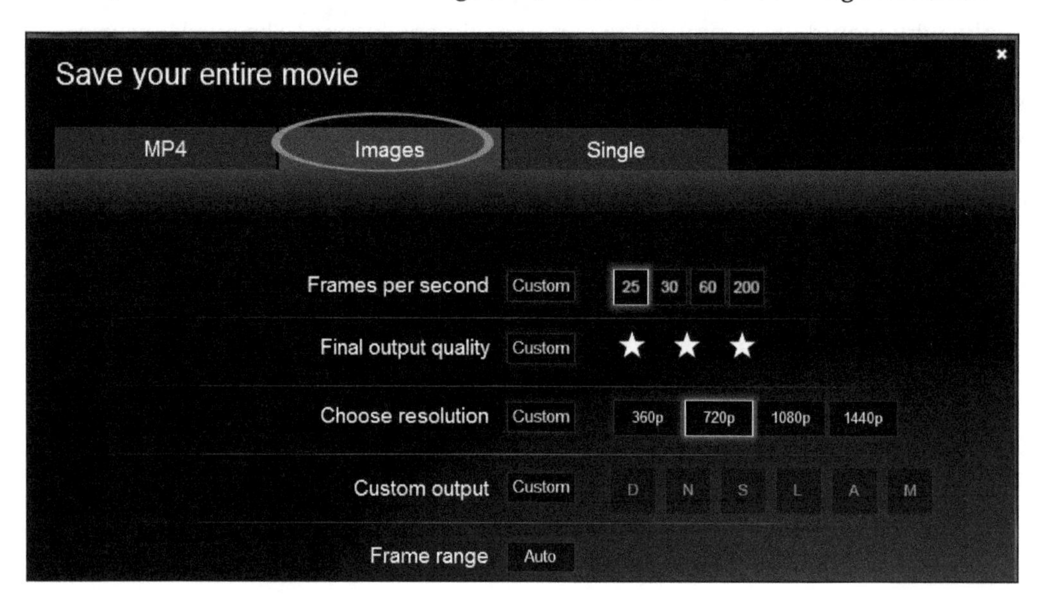

The initial three settings are the same as we saw in the **MP4** tab, so that should be very straightforward. However, when we move to the **Custom output** option, we start to feel the true power of using a sequence of images.

As the **Custom output** option is mentioned, let's export specific render passes such as lighting, reflections, and other formats that can later be combined with our original image, providing far more than the final output. This is something we are going to see in a few paragraphs.

> If you use the additional custom outputs, Lumion initially renders the colored image first and then renders the additional formats, and this happens for every single frame.

The final option, the **Frame range** setting, is divided into two categories: **Shots** and **Range**. The best way to explain what each setting does is by having a look at the following screenshot:

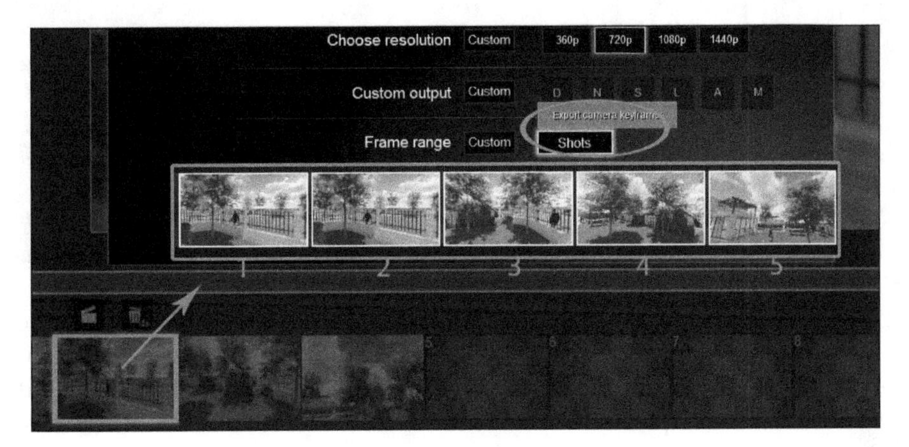

The **Shots** option is fairly easy to understand: if you use five camera keyframes or snapshots to create a clip, Lumion picks this information and exports each snapshot used for each clip. There is a practical application for this feature. Let's say we have five or more camera positions that we want to export as still images. Instead of exporting one by one, we can easily create a clip containing the camera positions and in one go, export all the images while you enjoy a nice cup of coffee or tea.

For the **Range** option, things work in a different and more complex way. When we click on this option, two text fields appear with some numbers inside. These values depend on the size of our movie, and by default, the values will be the first and last frame of the movie, giving you the full extent of the movie.

> It is important that you select the correct frames per second or FPS because this will influence the amount of images exported. Then, when importing the images on another application, you need to specify what FPS you used.

If you want to export the entire movie, just click on the **OK** button and the movie is exported as individual frames. However, if we only need a small section, how do we know which range of frames to use? If you put the mouse over one of these fields, a small preview will appear, as shown in the following screenshot:

In the previous screenshot, we divided the image to show that when we put the mouse over the `0`, the image on the left appears and when we put the mouse over the `550`, the image on the right appears, and this is used to determine how we are doing on time. Finally, the last question we may have is: what are these render passes we mentioned previously?

Render passes

The **Custom output** menu gives us the opportunity to export different render passes or render elements. These are the raw elements produced by the rendering engine and when combined, create the final image. The benefit of using render passes is that we can combine them, having much greater control over the look of the final image.

Let's have a quick overview to understand what information we can get and a brief explanation of what we can do with render passes. In the **Custom output** menu, each letter represents one of the render passes and we will use that as a reference:

- **Material ID**: This is represented by **M**. A color or ID is assigned to each material used in the scene. This render pass is used to isolate areas and tweak the colors in the image.

- **Sky alpha map**: This is represented by **A**. This is a black-and-white image that works as a mask and can be used to replace the sky with a different one or control the sky without affecting the rest of the image.
- **Depthmap**: This is represented by **D**. This is a grayscale map with information regarding the distance of the 3D models from the camera. The most practical application for this render pass is to simulate fog and DOF.
- **Normalmap**: This is represented by **N**. This is similar to the one used to create bumps in the materials. This can also be used to change the light direction, although doing so is not necessary with Lumion.
- **SpecularReflection map**: This is represented by **S**. This image stores information regarding the surface's highlights and reflections. This is useful to improve the reflections and also tint the image.
- **Lighting map**: This is represented by **L**. This is an image with the light and brightness information for each surface in your project. This gives great information to improve the contrast and shadows and allows us to control the light.

This is the final render result of each of the render passes:

Summary

The last chapter of this book closes with the remaining details you need to know to be able to say: I completely mastered Lumion. We pick up from where we left off from the previous chapter and went through a few more movie effects. You learned how to use depth of field and motion blur to make the movie more believable and added some visual effects, such as Snow, Rain, Contrails, and Falling leaves. You saw how important Lumion's sounds are and how they can make all the difference. Finally, after all the hard work, you learned how to export the movie as a video file, a sequence of images, and taking advantage of the render passes. What is the next step?

The truth is that we always have room to improve our skills. Lumion is a tool that can be compared to a pencil. Just because we know how to use one doesn't mean we have the skill to draw perfectly. So, what can you do to improve your skills? Start by creating a library with images from other artists that inspire you and then study them carefully.

Learn more about composition and photography because that will help you when composing still images and movies. Then, you can learn more about color correction and color grading to improve upon the final look of the images and movies exported from Lumion. And after this?

Practice, practice, and practice!

Index

Symbols

A

M

N

T

U

V

W

Z

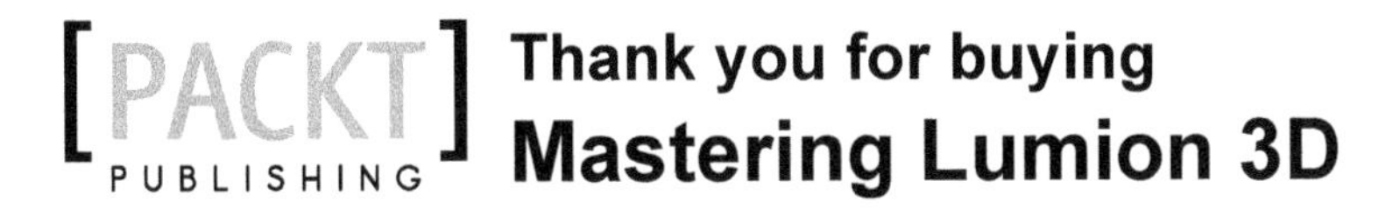

About Packt Publishing

Packt, pronounced 'packed', published its first book "*Mastering phpMyAdmin for Effective MySQL Management*" in April 2004 and subsequently continued to specialize in publishing highly focused books on specific technologies and solutions.

Our books and publications share the experiences of your fellow IT professionals in adapting and customizing today's systems, applications, and frameworks. Our solution based books give you the knowledge and power to customize the software and technologies you're using to get the job done. Packt books are more specific and less general than the IT books you have seen in the past. Our unique business model allows us to bring you more focused information, giving you more of what you need to know, and less of what you don't.

Packt is a modern, yet unique publishing company, which focuses on producing quality, cutting-edge books for communities of developers, administrators, and newbies alike. For more information, please visit our website: `www.packtpub.com`.

Writing for Packt

We welcome all inquiries from people who are interested in authoring. Book proposals should be sent to `author@packtpub.com`. If your book idea is still at an early stage and you would like to discuss it first before writing a formal book proposal, contact us; one of our commissioning editors will get in touch with you.

We're not just looking for published authors; if you have strong technical skills but no writing experience, our experienced editors can help you develop a writing career, or simply get some additional reward for your expertise.

Lumion 3D Cookbook

ISBN: 978-1-78355-093-7 Paperback: 258 pages

Revolutionize your Lumion skills with over 100 recipes to create stunning architectural visualizations

1. Build spectacular architectural perceptions in seconds using real-time technology.
2. Learn how to apply the inbuilt effects in Lumion to enhance your project to a whole new level.
3. Bursting with practical examples, and simple, clear instructions to help you produce advanced visualizations with an expert level.

Getting Started with Lumion 3D

ISBN: 978-1-84969-949-5 Paperback: 134 pages

Create a professional architectural visualization in minutes using Lumion 3D

1. A beginner's guide to architectural visualization.
2. Tips and tricks for modelling, texturing, and rendering using Lumion 3D.
3. Add a special touch to your images with Photoshop.

CPSIA information can be obtained
at www.ICGtesting.com
Printed in the USA
LVHW061138240723
753289LV00006B/349